For
Broncos Fans
Only!!!

By Rich Wolfe

Published by Rich Wolfe and Lone Wolfe Press with Sams Technical Publishing, LLC, under the Life Press imprint, 9850 E.30th St., Indianapolis IN 46229.

Copies of this book can be ordered directly from the publisher at 1-800-428-7267 or at www.samswebsite.com.

The author, Rich Wolfe, can be reached at 602-738-5889.

International Standard Book Number: 0-7906-1342-5

Photos provided by, and used with permission of Rich Wolfe, *Sports Illustrated,* Newsradio 850 KOA, Rich Clarkson and Associates, and the individuals whose stories appear in this book.

Interior design from The Printed Page, Phoenix AZ.
Cover design from Mike Walsh, Phoenix AZ.
Editorial Assistance provided by Rich McArdle, Andy Lindahl, Lynn Rosen, Joe Palladino, Dale Ratermann, Ellen Brewer, and Dana Eaton.
Author's Agent: T. Roy Gaul

This book was published with help from Newsradio 850 KOA and the Denver Broncos Football Club.

Printed in Canada.

> **Page Two. In 1941, the news director at a small radio station in Kalamazoo, Michigan hired Harry Caray who had been employed at a station in Joliet, Illinois. The news director's name was Paul Harvey. Yes, that <u>Paul Harvey</u>! "And now, you have the rest of the story......** ➡

DEDICATION

To

Each of the Great Broncos Fans

and to

My parents, Melvin and Frances Wolfe
who had the foresight to nurture my love for sports
and the thoughtfulness not to name me after my father.

ACKNOWLEDGMENTS

What a blast it has been doing this book. Wonderful people helped make it a reality starting with Ellen Brewer, my indispensable side-kick of many years in Edmond, Oklahoma; ditto to Barbara Jane Bookman in Falmouth, Massachusetts; and the good guys at Sams Technical Publishing—Dale Ratermann, and Dana Eaton. Let's not forget Wonder Woman, Lisa Liddy, at The Printed Page in Phoenix and the prettiest Broncos fan in Arizona, Carol Reddy, also in Phoenix.

How about a big thank you to Steve Harbula at the Denver Broncos, the Denver Broncos Marketing Department, Ted Smith at King Soopers, and all the great people at Newsradio 850 KOA, especially Andy Lindahl, Lynn Rosen, and Joe Palladino. A tip of the hat to all those interviewed who missed the cut—we just ran out of time. Three chapters were cut indiscriminately due to space limitations. We'll do it again next year. But the biggest thank you, the deepest bow and grandest salute to 850 KOA's own Rich McArdle, a hard-workin', great guy.

PREFACE

"God love 'em, God bless their hearts." When those words are spoken in certain parts of West Texas, many people believe that the speaker—at that point—has carte blanche to say whatever nasty things he chooses about those people…as if God will forgive slander if the proper preface is spoken first.

So, too, with Broncos fans. In this book they'll share their memories, their thoughts and their dreams. They'll even talk about the Kansas City Chiefs and the Oakland Raiders. In regard to the latter, God love 'em, God bless their hearts.

Several years ago I tried to interest publishers in a series of books involving fans of certain teams. They laughed; said no one would be interested in other fans' stories.

When I became my own publisher five years ago, I knew I would test this idea. The first book, *For Yankee Fans Only*, sold tens of thousands of copies. The second, *For Red Sox Fans Only*, sold out immediately as did its rather substantial reprint. *For Cubs Fans Only* not only became the best selling book in the history of the Cubs, it sold over four times the previous record. It is my feeling that the football fans books will do even better and there was never a question that one of the first books on NFL fans would be the Denver Broncos. The list goes on but it became apparent that Broncos fans are special. The pride they exhibit for their hometown and their team is truly remarkable.

Now is a good time to answer a few questions that always arise. The most often asked is, "Why isn't your name on the book cover, like other authors?" The answer is simple: I'm not Stephen King. No one knows who I am, no one cares. My name on the cover will not sell an additional book. On the other hand, it allows for "cleaner" and more dramatic covers that the readers appreciate, and the books are more visible at the point of sale.

The second most frequent query is, "You sell tons of books. Why don't they show up on the best seller list?" Here's how the book business works: Of the next 170 completed manuscripts, 16 will eventually be published, and only one will ever return a profit. To make the *New York Times Bestseller List*, you need to sell at least 30,000 copies nationally. Sales are monitored at certain stores, at big book chains, a few selected independent book stores, etc. My last nine books have averaged well over 60,000 units sold, but less than 15,000 were sold in bookstores. Most are sold regionally, another deterrent to national rankings. While I'm very grateful to have sold so many books to the "Big Boys," I'm a minority of one in feeling that a bookstore is the worst place to sell a book. Publishers cringe when they hear that statement. A large bookstore will stock over 150,000 different titles. That means the odds of someone buying my book are 150,000-1. Those aren't good odds; I'm not that good of a writer. For the most part, people who like Mike Ditka or Pat Tillman—previous book subjects of mine—don't hang around bookstores. I would rather be the only book at a hardware chain than in hundreds of bookstores.

Example: My *Remembering Dale Earnhardt* hardcover sold several hundred thousand copies, mostly at Walgreens and grocery chains; places not monitored for the "best selling" lists. The paperback rights were sold to Triumph Books, Chicago. They printed 97,000 paperbacks—all sold through traditional channels. My hardcover did not appear on any bestseller list. Meanwhile, Triumph had a paperback on Earnhardt that made number one on the *New York Times* non-fiction trade list. Go figure. Also, I never offer my books directly to Amazon.com because I can't type, I've never turned on a computer and I keep thinking that Amazon is going out of business soon. For years, the more customers they recruited, the more money they lost…so sooner or later, when the venture capital is gone, the bookkeeping shenanigans are recognized, and the stock plummets, look out. Meanwhile, maybe I should call them.

Since the age of ten, I've been a serious collector of sports books. During that time—for the sake of argument, let's call it 30 years—my favorite book style is the eavesdropping type where the subject talks in his or her own words—without the "then he said" or "the air was so thick you could cut it with a butter knife" waste of verbiage that makes it so hard to get to the meat of the matter. Books such as

Lawrence Ritter's *Glory of Their Times* and Donald Honig's *Baseball When the Grass Was Real.* Thus, I adopted that style when I started compiling oral histories of the Bobby Knights and Harry Carays of the world. I'm a sports fan first and foremost—I don't even pretend to be an author. This book is designed solely for other sports fans. I really don't care what the publisher, editors or critics think. I'm only interested in Broncos fans having an enjoyable read and getting their money's worth. Sometimes a person being interviewed will drift off the subject but if the feeling is that Denver fans would enjoy the digression, it stays in the book.

In an effort to get more material into the book, the editor decided to merge some paragraphs and omit some of the commas, which will allow for the reader to receive an additional 20,000 words, the equivalent of 50 pages. More bang for your buck...more fodder for English teachers...fewer dead trees.

All that Broncos fans need these days is a patient spouse, a loyal dog and a good quarterback. As for the Chargers and Ravens: God love 'em, God bless their hearts.

Go now.

Rich Wolfe

CHAT ROOMS

Chapter 1

Growin' Up
With the Broncos

Broncos Memories—Like Broncos
Heroes—Never Grow Old

IT WAS LIKE PLAYIN' HOOKY FROM LIFE

RICHARD AGREN

Richard Agren is 59 years old. He has been a Broncos fan for 47 years. Agren was a track and field athlete at Clark College in Portland, Oregon.

We were real wide-eyed kids who went to the games. My buddy and I had to catch the bus and make a transfer and go to the stadium. We went through all the eras with the striped socks, and it was a terrific time in our life. It was one of those periods that, as a kid, was really memorable. Because of our friendship with an owner's son, we got to spend some time on the field and in the locker room. That was really a kick, too.

We were just in awe of professional athletes, and we didn't have much else in the way of professional athletics then. We didn't have much football in the city because the University of Denver gave it up. If you wanted to see football, you either went to Boulder or you went to CSU, if you could call CSU football at the time.

The chance to see professional football was pretty compelling. When we got to walk down on the sidelines and in the locker room, our eyes were the size of fifty-cent pieces. I'd walk in and see Bud McFadin, and he'd have a big cigar in his mouth. Jacky Lee would be smoking a cigarette. It just shot holes in my perception of what these guys were—athletes. I know these guys don't do it anymore, but back in those days, their attitude was "I can smoke and play football." They also showed up for training camp to get into shape. If you show up in training camp today, thinking that's where you're going to get in shape, you're going to be dead. You've got to show up and be ready to go from day one. The whole thing has changed.

The locker room was always in disarray. This was a team drawing plays in the dirt. How organized could they be? You didn't get the sense that this was a really well-oiled machine that just had everything down to the nub, as far as the way they were operating. That's the way the AFL was—it was an upstart league. I can remember their first game was on a Friday night, and the Broncos played the Boston Patriots, and they beat them—the final score was 13-10. Gene Mingo kicked the winning field goal. It was played in Boston, and we were listening to it on the radio. Gene Mingo was the **PAUL HORNUNG** of the AFL. He was a halfback and a place kicker, too.

We had a real passion for the Broncos, and I don't think any of the other kids in our elementary school felt like we did. I don't remember anybody except us getting on the bus. Some days we'd be doing that, and it would be snowing outside and the weather would be lousy. I got a number of footballs there because they didn't have the nets at the time. Back in those days, they couldn't afford to lose footballs. Now they use nets just for the safety point of view because if they kicked balls up into the stands, the people would be crawling all over each other to get a football. I got these balls in various ways. I got one just walking along the outside of the fence, parallel to the field. Somebody threw a pass, which was overthrown and bounced over the fence, and I caught it. There were various ways you could get a ball. It wasn't that difficult because the attendance at the games in those days might be 13,000 or 14,000 people at the stadium. These were usually high-scoring games, so there were lots of chances for a ball.

> **At Notre Dame, 1956 Heisman Trophy winner PAUL HORNUNG played halfback, fullback, and quarterback; punted, kicked-off, kicked field goals; ran back punts and kickoffs; and was a starting safety. Against Iowa that year, he ran a quarterback sneak 80 yards.**

A COACH IS A TEACHER WITH A DEATH WISH

KENNETH CRAWFORD

Kenneth Crawford, 50, was born and raised in Denver. He coaches football at Regis Jesuit High School in Denver.

I must have been eight when I went to my first Broncos game. I had a neighbor who worked at the post office, and he was a Broncos season ticket holder. I was a bat boy for the post office. I had a good year working for them, so they gave me a ticket to a Broncos game at Bears Stadium. I was just amazed. It was a small stadium to a lot of people, but it was gigantic to me. My mom didn't have a lot of money, but I knew I had to find a way to get to more games. I'd go out and sell soda and hot dogs. I'd catch the bus on Sunday mornings to Bears Stadium and stand in line with a bunch of other kids to get to sell hot dogs. First couple of games, I didn't make it in. I learned the system as to how to get in. I also figured out that if you sold all your drinks for three quarters, and turned your stuff in by the end of the third quarter, you could manage to watch the fourth quarter. My cousin and I had it down. We would go every Sunday. We'd get up at 5 a.m. and catch the bus. We'd wait around all day to get in, and we'd be there until the sun went down. Eventually, we got in trouble waiting for the players to come out of the locker room after the game. My mom threatened to not let me go again. I had to make her understand that was the only way I could see the players. I had just about every autograph then. I did that for three years. I sold either hot dogs or sodas. I moved up to be able to sell both at once. The season ticket holders in my section knew me by name.

I'd save my money from that and buy my mom and sisters birthday and Christmas presents. One year my mom told me to spend the money on myself. I saved enough to buy a season ticket for one year, but I didn't renew it the next year. It was the first year that the West Stands were up at Bears Stadium. Instead of selling hot dogs and sodas, I sat and watched the game like the big-time guys. I was able to go down on the field and shake Floyd Little's hand once. I didn't open my hand for two days! I can remember fans throwing a loaf of bread at Lou Saban. I didn't know why, but I was there. I was there when Saban fired Floyd Little for fumbling the ball. Those are great memories. I remember Marlin Briscoe beating the Miami Dolphins. I would take so much grief at school for being a Broncos fan.

The old Bears Stadium had old green wooden bleachers. If you squirmed too much you'd take some splinters home in your hind side. It was an L-shaped stadium. North and West stands only. They built the South Stands later. They'd bring in portable bleachers for the early Broncos games to make it into a U. When they voted for a new stadium, they voted it down. I was a kid and really wanted a new stadium for the Broncos. I was so upset with the adults for not voting for it. Later, it broke my heart to see them tear down Mile High Stadium. INVESCO Field is lovely, but the Broncos and Mile High really go together. Bears Stadium was an ugly sight, but was the home of the Broncos.

To me, being with other Broncos fans is like being with family. Me, being a little black kid with a season ticket, it was neat. Everyone asked how I got my ticket. I'd always tell them about selling hot dogs, soda and my paper route to save the money. The fans around me would always buy me hot dogs and sodas at the game. It's always been like a family to me.

Mondays are blue when the Broncos lose. I try to guard it off. The last thing I want to do is answer the telephone. I recently remarried, and one of the first things she learned about me is that Sundays belong to the Broncos. We love each other, and she understands. I'm 50-years-old, you wouldn't think it would hurt so much when the Broncos lose. When my high school kids lose, I have something at stake and should hurt. I don't know why it still hurts so much when the Broncos lose.

WE'RE NUMBER ONE!!

CRAIG WRIGHT

Craig Wright, 50, lives in Glendale, Arizona. His family has Broncos ticket priority number 0001.

My grandfather got the ticket priority number 0001 and left the account in a living trust. The tickets have been in the family's hands since '59. My grandfather knew the Phipps brothers, and perhaps, that's one of the reasons that we have Priority 0001.

The Broncos honored the top 10 priority ticket holders with game balls. Our family was honored at a game last year and my wife and I got to go out onto the field for a presentation. My wife had never been to a professional sporting event of any kind. We were ushered through the tunnel and went to the sidelines. Prior to the Star Spangled Banner, I was told to go out on the 50-yard line at the center of the field, and the woman riding Thunder started off from the south end zone and trotted by and tossed a ball to me. The announcer said what the presentation was for. It was quite an extraordinary experience, having my wife there, on the sidelines, her first sporting event ever.

I have never been anything other than a Broncos fan. I never "became" a Broncos fan—I was always a Broncos fan. In '59, when my grandfather obtained the tickets, I was three-years-old, so it was completely natural for me to expect that every season I would be at several games. Sometimes I would sit with my grandfather and his wife, Pat. I never knew anything about Priority 0001 until I was well into adolescence. My grandfather never made a big deal out of it. It was just something that he loved. He was a sporting freak. He loved baseball and football and hockey. We went to Air Force Academy games and University of Colorado games and University of Denver hockey games. Football was just another experience—a tremendous experience. I don't remember exactly the first game I went to. I must have been five- or six-years-old, but sitting in those seats was part of my upbringing. It was part of my family's enthusiasm and part of my blood. So several Sundays a year we would be at the stadium watching the Broncos lose more often than not, but my grandfather never let any of us leave a game before it was over. Many times during those early years, the Broncos would be losing, and people would start leaving the game during the fourth quarter, but we never did that. We would always stay in our seats and watch the game until the end—and many times it was well worth it. For example, several times I remember Floyd Little would make some daring run or someone would make a kickoff return or a punt return or something.

I was on the old Mile High field three times. I was a Little League player for the Wolfpack Park Rangers at Congress Park in Denver and we got to go out onto the field. Years later, in '72 and '73, I was on the field as a member of my high school marching band. Those were tremendous experiences—marching on the field that I had seen from my grandfather's seats so many times before. And the seats that he chose way back when, and had never changed, were right between the 45- and the 50-yard lines, on the west side, 30 rows up.

It was a different era then. The people dressed nicely all the time. My grandfather always wore a tie. Probably the first game I remember vividly was in '64 against the Boston Patriots. Many times my grandfather would use his seats with some business partners or friends. If we decided to go to that game, we had to find our own tickets. And way back then, it wasn't that big of a deal. You would go to the box office and say pretty much where you wanted to sit. And my father said to us that Sunday, "Let's go to the game today, and let's catch a ball. We'll sit in the end zone and catch a ball." That was before the nets kept the ball from going into the end zone, and before they had wider hash marks, as well. Gino Cappelletti was the field goal kicker for the Patriots at that time. They got stalled and stopped inside the 10-yard line. Gino and his holder set up right, and I could see it was a straight line right to my father, who's about 6-foot-4. They snapped the ball and Gino kicked it right at my father. My father stood up, caught it and handed it to me. I still have that ball with the AFL logo on it. That was probably my most vivid memory. Interestingly enough, we weren't sitting in my grandfather's seats.

Every time we went to Mile High, I would enter at the south end zone, so I could be on the field level. I don't think you're able to do that now. Of course, the fans and the field were separated by a chain-link fence, but I always loved being close to the field.

In '03, I had the opportunity to re-establish contact with my father. We had fallen out of touch. I went to a game with him for the first time in about 30 years. And it was almost exactly 40 years since that game in '64 with the Patriots. It was quite fun to be in the stadium with my father again after almost 40 years. That's the kind of legacy that my family shares regarding the Denver Broncos.

When they built the new stadium, we kind of demanded, and the Broncos kind of resented, giving us the first choice of seats in the new stadium. We chose seats as close as possible to the exact same seats my grandfather chose all those years ago. At my grandfather's passing in '87, Pat Bowlen called my grandmother. I don't know how many team owners do that. It was something quite special.

Mile High and INVESCO Field are like home. Of course, I was sad when they decided to build a new stadium. As elegant and well-outfitted as INVESCO is—quite a superior building—I'll never forget the particular smell and the particular feel of walking through the entry and up to the concessions stands and sitting in the seats at Mile High. It was home. It started out as Bears Stadium, and it went through its changes. When I moved recently, I was looking at some old pictures and saw the old Holiday Inn that used to be there. You could see from the top of the Holiday Inn into the stadium. I think it is sad, because they were tearing down part of what I felt was my home. It became so familiar. Every time I walked on that field as an adult, I remembered the times there with various family members. It was very emotional. I would always get excited. It took awhile for my friends or family who were with me to understand how deep this ran for me. I would be quiet for a long time and I would just look and I would just smell and I would just absorb a feeling of being on that field again sitting in my grandfather's seats. But that is part of the joy about the experience now, that if my grandfather were alive, he would have said, "Way to go guys. I would pick those same seats again if I could."

I've gone through many phases of being a Broncos fan, from rabid to casual. Now that I'm 50-years-old, I don't jump up and holler as much as I used to years ago. But the first time the Broncos won the Super Bowl, I was living in New Mexico, and I was at a party with some friends and my former wife. And people would ask her, "What's wrong with Craig? What's going on with Craig?" And she would say, "Nothing. Nothing is wrong with him. He's a Broncos fan and this means more than you know to him to have this team finally win and do well and to see Denver recognized as a truly great sports town."

To this day, I'll watch a baseball game in its entirety, which is a rare thing for me, but I do that because that is what my grandfather did. Always. I always think of my grandfather. Sadly, my grandpa never got to see the Broncos win a Super Bowl. I still wish I could see him. I still wish I could sit and watch a game with him, but 20 years after his death, he's still with me.

The formula for the NFL Quarterback Rating System is actually a recipe for chili

YA CAN'T GO TO HEAVEN
UNLESS YOU'RE A BRONCOS FAN

ANDY LINDAHL

Andy Lindahl is a 32-year-old Denver native. He works at Newsradio 850 KOA, covering the Broncos.

I grew up a Broncos fan in a Broncos household. Both of my parents were big football fans. It was known that we would be home Sunday afternoons to watch the games. I'm the oldest of four boys and football was in our blood here. You set your watch by when the Broncos were playing. We went to church early to be sure and get home in time to see kickoff. It meant that 9:30 a.m. Mass was standing room only if the Broncos played at 11 a.m. Often times, the priest would comment about the Broncos on game day, sending up a special prayer for them. There were a number of priests who were big fans. Father John Wind would come to our house and watch the games with us. Father Wind would sometimes have a beer or two and take a nap after the game. We didn't get to go to many games and didn't have season tickets. We watched the Broncos on TV. You really couldn't get a ticket then, as there was a 10-year waiting list for season tickets.

We were a loud family—lots of yelling at the TV. Mom called Elway by his first name—John. My dad's name was John, and with Father John Wind there, it was always pretty funny when she was yelling at the TV. My friends knew not to come over when the Broncos were on. None of us had any interest in playing until the game was over. We never missed a game. I can remember watching Monday Night Football games, looking for Denver Broncos highlights during the halftime show. It really upset me when they didn't show a Broncos highlight! Growing up, everyone was a Broncos fan. We'd decorate our school rooms in Broncos colors. We could pay to wear our

Broncos clothes on Fridays. I can remember my principal wearing an "I Threw the Denver Snowball" T-shirt and being so proud of it. Everybody was walking around sporting the look. It was Broncos, Broncos, Broncos. We had the Nuggets, too, but that wasn't the same....

I lived in North Denver, and I used to throw the football to myself and pretend to be the players. We had a nice-sized side yard that hit the sidewalk. The grass between the sidewalk and the road served as my end zone. I'd catch the ball and pretend to be Steve Watson. It's how I entertained myself until my brothers got a little older....

I can remember having a crush on a blonde girl named Shylynn. I went over to her house on a Sunday and she had on her Broncos shirt and Broncos earrings. That was top of the mountain for me back then. We hung out for awhile, but I went home to watch the game with my family—I wasn't going to miss watching the game with my family. That was the game with "The Drive." The ball was on the 2-yard line. Elway escaped the rush a number of times. It was a bullet pass to Mark Jackson that made the difference. That drive was just to tie the game. Right into the Dawg Pound. A field goal won the game and it sent us to the Super Bowl. The two weeks leading up to that Super Bowl—everything was Broncos. Broncos songs, mostly cheesy parody songs, were playing. Highlights were shown over and over. When I was about 12, my brothers and I were such Broncos fans that we'd move all the furniture in the living room to the walls and we'd play football in the living room with a rubber football. We'd go out in the snow and do that, too. We'd pretend we were the Broncos players. Lots of times in the snow, we were all bundled up to where we could barely move. It was the same during recess at school. We'd be our favorite player and take a Nerf football out and go at it. I was always Steve Watson.

I remember being real disappointed after that Super Bowl. The Broncos couldn't find the end zone from the 2-yard line and just couldn't overcome it. The Giants seemed to catch every break that game. We went back 10 years later and started out strong. Next thing we knew, the Redskins had scored 35 points—by halftime. Heart wrenching—especially in the second half when you knew there was no shot.

I didn't like hearing the negative press on the national sports shows. It made me mad, and I took it personally. It used to drive me crazy....

We'd play a lot of football in the street in our neighborhood. We'd get together right after the Broncos game was over. We could play for at least 90 minutes early in the season. When it was just my brothers and me, we'd play "John Elway Comeback." The premise was that my brother, Greg, would be my receiver, and we'd have 10 plays to get to the intersection at the end of the block and score a touchdown. Nick would be the rusher on defense. Kevin was the youngest, and later he'd be a receiver, too. Nick would chase me around just like in the game. We'd play that a couple, three times a week. My friends would play sometimes, too.

As I got into high school, my parents divorced, and my dad went back to Texas. My mom would often be at church on Sundays working the bingo games. My best friend would come over and watch the games. We'd save our money to order a pizza and then play football after the game. Mom would watch the games with us sometimes. I became super loud during the game—always coaching the TV from the couch. I remember in '89, Steve Atwater's rookie year, I was lucky enough to go to a game. I'll never forget it. It was the first game I got to go to as a kid. We sat at the top of the fifth level—all the way to the top of the stadium. I remember it being so high that you couldn't see anything. We woke up that morning and it was snowing cats and dogs. Mom said we couldn't go to the game. I was hell-bent on going to the game. Tickets were in the lower part of the South Stands. I wasn't worried about what I'd see in the South Stands. My neighbor across the street, named Johnny Walker, who had been hit by lightning, he knew how much I wanted to go to the game. He and I took the bus to the game. We marched 10 blocks to catch the bus to the stadium. We made our way into the stands and had to sweep snow off the seats. It was not a full stadium. They lost that day. I can remember Bobby Humphrey having a great 80-yard run for a touchdown that got called back on a holding call. I can remember my fingers and toes hurting as they thawed out after all of the walking through the snow and sitting at the game.

I can remember reading Dick Conner's articles in the Sunday paper. He always found the positive in everything. He was blunt, but still found the positive. I used to read every article I could find on the Broncos. I'd wish my summer away waiting for training camp to start. I knew everything about the Broncos.

My mom's friend took me to a game against the **CHICAGO BEARS**. I'd watched so much Broncos football that their formations would tip me off to their plays. I turned to the gentleman next to me and told him Elway would run the ball in on this play. Sure enough, he did. Right up the middle. The gentleman who took me to the game took me to a tailgate party that day, too. They invited us into the RV and I walked inside to find Sammy Winder, starting running back for the Broncos! He was eating and talking like he was a regular guy.

I didn't go to another game for a long time. I went to a Monday Night game—Chiefs versus the Broncos—Joe Montana versus John Elway. I took my girlfriend, Janeane. We sat in the South Stands. I wanted to take one of my friends I had always watched games with, but he couldn't go. Janeane wasn't a "real" football fan, but she wanted to go. The Broncos started making a comeback against the Chiefs. I remember the crowd being at a fevered pitch. It was the coolest thing ever—a quarterback sneak right into the end zone. Elway spiked the football. It was great! He was only 20 yards from me. During the drive, my girlfriend let out a cheer—"Go Mecklen-burg!"—a defensive player. She was trying so hard to be a part of the game, and just missed by a bit. The stadium was dead silent after Montana led the game-winning drive.

For the '97 Super Bowl, we were in my basement, jerseys on, flags out. We were really optimistic. I was worried for awhile, but it turned out to be what I believe is the best Super Bowl game ever played. It had Hall of Fame quarterbacks and superstars at all the positions. It was amazing. I'll never forget Dave Logan's call on the radio at the end of the game. Watching John—I call him John because he was in

The **CHICAGO BEARS** wear blue and orange because those are the colors that team founder George Halas wore when he played for the University of Illinois.

my house, on the TV every Sunday. It was like the team was family. I can remember working at Newsradio 850 KOA and fielding calls from crying fans, so excited about winning the Super Bowl.

My wife, Andrea, bought tickets to a playoff game the next year for me. I wore my Terrell Davis jersey. The players were incredible. I just knew that this was Elway's last season. The lap around Mile High is what really signified it. It was an incredible feeling. They won the Super Bowl versus Atlanta that year. I had a Super Bowl party and we're all very superstitious. My friend Jay went to the restroom. The TV broadcast came back from commercial late, and we wouldn't let Jay out of the bathroom until the game was over. We took him a TV so he could watch the game in there. It was like he was bad luck watching the game with us! He spent at least 15 minutes in the bathroom watching the game. He didn't want to jinx the Broncos. I'll never forget the feeling in the city after those two Super Bowls. It really was "we" and not just the team. It's amazing what the team does for this community.

I can also remember producing a game on the radio—the "Goodbye Game" from Mile High. It was a flag football game with Elway versus Montana and some other all-stars. It was the Broncos versus the NFL. It was a great event. It brought back so many memories from my youth. It was a sandlot-type game, like playing in the street with your friends. It was the perfect way to finish out the stadium.

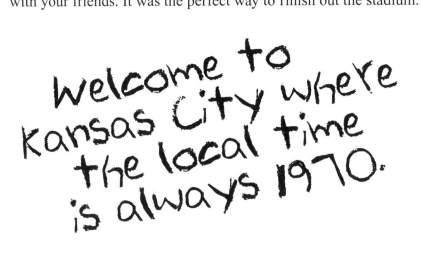

Welcome to Kansas City where the local time is always 1970.

YADA, YADA, YADA

Going to Broncos games is one of the things I look forward to every year. My grandpa has been a season ticket holder since the '60s. His priority number is under 1,000. We've really built a relationship going to the games with him. We've been going for 23 seasons. It was the best thing I did growing up. I can remember getting a call from my grandpa on Thursday or Friday telling me I'd be going to the game on Sunday. That was always special. My first Monday Night game was against the Oakland Raiders. The Broncos lost in the fourth quarter. It was hard to wake up for school the next day. Growing up, I didn't get to go to all the games, but I went to most of them. I always cheered harder at the Monday Night games knowing that the whole country was watching. Monday mornings are tough when we lose. They are not good! It's almost like waking up with a hangover. Physically you are OK, but emotionally you are drained. When the Broncos win, you are excited to get up and read the paper and about the game. When they lose, you just want to forget about it and move on. The loss sticks with you for a couple of days.…Elway was the greatest quarterback to ever play the game. He helped build Denver. I don't think we'd have the Rockies or the Avalanche if he hadn't been successful with the Broncos. He means more to the city of Denver than most people will ever realize. The Orange Crush has taken on a whole new persona. It described the defense, but now I think it is about the loyalty and support of the Broncos fans. We have had sell-outs for 30 years. The support is unmatched by any other city. The Mile High Salute was special, too. Terrell Davis and the Super Bowl wins—that era was great, with the Broncos getting that first Super Bowl. That salute showed respect for the city. They used to put "Rocky Mountain Thunder" on the scoreboard to get us stomping in Mile High Stadium. It was so loud you couldn't hear yourself think. To walk into Mile High on a Sunday afternoon was special. There were some games I watched in that stadium that I will always remember. I can remember as a kid crying for two days after losing to the Giants. When the team finally got back with Elway and Davis, we knew they had a chance and could do it. You aren't a true Broncos fan if you didn't shed a tear of joy after that Super Bowl win. Elway came back and dominated the next season, and was the Super Bowl MVP—that's the way a legend should retire.

——BRANDON IDEKER, 27, Financial Advisor, Denver, Colorado

I was raised by my godparents and they instilled football in me from as early as I can remember. They were from Chicago and were huge Bears fans. They rooted for the Broncos, too. I liked **WALTER PAYTON**, but couldn't get into the Bears. I remember watching the Broncos games instead of going and playing with my friends when I was four or five. I went to my first game when I was in eighth grade. My step-dad had season tickets in the South Stands through his work. If the weather was bad, my step-dad would take us to the 404 Bar to catch the double-decker bus to Mile High Stadium. We would even go without my step-dad sometimes. I can remember going to a Houston game with my brother in '84. It was so cold and there was a blizzard. My mom bundled us up in our Broncos garb until we could barely walk. Last year, or the year before, against the Raiders may have been colder. My wife's family had season tickets. I went with three of my friends to that game. You could see the swirling snow. By the end of the game, I had six inches of snow piled on my head and shoulders. We knew a lot of the people around us. We were young, so it was a bit intimidating. I was such a fan that nothing was going to keep me away from the game. It was crazy in those stands, but I was young and focused on the game, so I don't remember much of the craziness around me. I'm still very focused when I'm at a game. I don't go to party, but to watch the game. I'm pretty intense. My wife even questions whether I have a good time. I'm just intense about it. I preferred Mile High to the new stadium. The atmosphere was exciting. The new stadium is nice, and my family's season tickets are on the Club

> In the last 30 years, the record for the most touchdown passes thrown by a non-quarterback is held by <u>WALTER PAYTON</u>, with eight. In football pileups, Walter Payton would lie at the bottom and untie his opponents' shoelaces. That's why many defenders put tape over their laces.

Level on the 50-yard line, so they are very comfortable. The new stadium may have driven out some of the "real fans." New stadiums lose some of the emotion of the older stadiums. I don't have access to season tickets for the upcoming season. My wife's family gave up their season tickets after 30+ years due to the rising cost. I'll have to work to get seats this year.

————JOSH PERKINS, 34, served in Afghanistan and Iraq with the Marines

I can remember when I was studying at the Archdiocese of Denver, we could get special leave, and I was able to leave to go to a Broncos game with my father and my fellow seminarians. We sat in the East Stands. They felt rickety and temporary. It was a bare stadium at the time. The Broncos lost badly, but it was great to see them play. We always had our hopes up. When they first started, they had this silly horse on  their helmets. It looked like a cartoon. It didn't look professional. They also had single facemasks, which were new. When we won the AFC Championship Game in 1977, there was a good 30 seconds of total silence in the stadium while the win soaked in, then everyone went nuts. I just sat there looking at the 00:00 on the scoreboard, showing time had expired. Everyone was 100 percent behind the team. We knew playing the Cowboys in the Super Bowl would be tough. Coach Landry had a very well-rounded team. I have to admit that my interest has waned in later years. My family isn't as into it as they used to be, and as I've gotten older, I'm not quite as interested. We've seen a lot of changes lately with the team. It's tough to replace Elway. It seems like now it's more about what shoes they're wearing, the money, etc.

————JOHN POLLICE, retired from a 27-year teaching career

At a very early age, maybe eight-years-old, I remember watching Mark Jackson and the Broncos winning the AFC Championship game. I jumped on my couch celebrating. You don't really understand at that age what it means. It's almost more exciting now to look back at it. My dad was able to get us tickets to the Super Bowl versus the Giants, and we stayed at the same hotel as the team. The access we had to the team was unprecedented. We got autographs and

pictures and got to talk with players—things you cannot do now in most cases. You could approach the players. When you are an eight-year-old kid, they'll do almost anything for you. Even with all their focus on the game, they still took the time to sign autographs and do pictures. I really wanted to meet Mark Jackson, because my dad's name is also Mark Jackson. I wrote him a letter as part of a class assignment that year. I told him that he was my favorite player and that I'd like to meet him someday. I found him at the hotel and he said he remembered getting the letter. He picked me up and talked to me. And we took a picture of him, me and my dad. That made my entire year. A guy who took the Broncos to the Super Bowl knew who I was! I met John Elway and took a picture with him, too. The one thing about football for me is that it's been more than just something to watch. It's amazing to me how emotionally attached you can get to the game. It is just a game, yet we're emotionally attached. We build it up to more than it is. I've been extremely fortunate to have season tickets through my family that my grandfather has had since 1963. They're right on the 50-yard line, 30 rows up from the field. They're great seats. No place is quite like Mile High Stadium was. It was as loud as you can get—75,000 fans strong.

——**ALAN JACKSON**, production director at 630 KHOW

As an Alamosa High School student in the late '70s I was a rabid fan, living and dying Broncos. I loved football, despite playing on a not very good team. My junior year, 1976, I saw an ad for the Ray May football camp in Grand Junction and decided to go. I couldn't wait to meet a real pro football player, let alone the Broncos' middle linebacker. So I dug out some of my 4-H steer money and asked my dad if I could go. Despite the fact I knew no one in Grand Junction, and the only way to get there was on the bus, he said yes. Without pre-registering, I was on my Great Broncos Football Camp Adventure for the summer. I arrived in Grand Junction with the flyer in hand, and made my way to the high school to find out details on the camp. I was lost and the place was deserted. I finally found someone who told me the camp had been cancelled due to poor attendance, but Ray May would be there the next day for a one-day camp. No problem. I asked around for a cheap place to stay, headed downtown, dug out my 4-H steer money and got a room at a "hotel" for $10. I didn't consider myself a country hick, but I was naive, so one can only imagine the kind of place I was staying at. I settled in and went out to explore. I came across the movie theater and went in late. It happened to be Martin Scorsese's *Taxi Driver.* I was so upset the rest of the night I didn't sleep. I don't know if the music from the bar on the first floor, the neon lights from Main Street, or the paper thin walls separating the rooms contributed or not. It was like a B-movie.

The next morning I collected my things, had a bowl of hot cereal and a banana at the closest cafe and made my way back to the high school. I was in awe of both Ray and his assistant. He was an amazing human being, from biceps that seemed too large, to shorts that seemed too small. I figured they didn't make shorts any bigger. And his assistant! I remember her being "big boned" and the most beautiful face I had ever seen in my rather limited experiences. They were both really nice to me—and to each other. We ended up calling my dad and Ray promised my dad that he would make sure I got home okay. I spent the rest of the day at camp, which turned out to be a complete waste of time. Ray then fed me and we spent a little time together. Then he asked me where I was staying. I told him the first thing that popped into my mind—the rectory of the Catholic Church. We found it, and I asked the priest for a place to stay. He gave me a room for the night. By this time I was so exhausted I was not feeling well. After a comatose night, I awoke not feeling well at all. The next day, the priest took me to meet Ray. I expected to get back on the bus, but we got in his van, or whatever it was, and we headed out of town. I fully expected him to head south and take me home, but we went to Denver, where he said he would buy me a plane ticket to Alamosa. I remember telling him it would be cheaper if he just took me back, but he said no. By this time I had a fever and barely remember the trip. I do remember spending a lot of time noticing Ray's assistant, and we chatted awhile, but most of the awe was gone. After an amazingly long day we ended up at Stapleton Airport. Ray bought me a ticket, waited for me to board, and I was on my first plane ride. I must have been a sight, because the stewardess noticed me right away and asked me what was wrong. I think my fever was 102 degrees by this time. She took good care of me with 7-Ups and snacks. I think I was in love by the time we landed. My folks were there to meet me with my dad beside himself for letting me go in the first place and my mom tearful from worry. About 45-minutes later, I was back home, thus ended my great Broncos Football Camp Adventure. Ray May flunked his physical the next year and was cut from the team. I blamed the assistant.

———ANTHONY LOBATO, Central City, Colorado

 When I was in middle school, I can remember going on vacation to Washington, D.C., in July and being flabbergasted that the Redskins weren't on the front page of the sports section. In Denver, the Broncos are always in the forefront. I'd never experienced a TV blackout until I left Denver. I couldn't understand why they occurred. I moved to Minnesota and couldn't watch the Vikings, because they couldn't sell enough tickets.…The Orange Crush defense was made up of my favorite players. They got me excited about football and about the Broncos. The Albino Rhino was great, too. Steve Atwater, as well. The Three Amigos were great. Football can be so much about identifying players and a series of events that make you feel like you are a part of the team, even if you're watching on TV. You get so emotionally invested in the team. Watching all the heartache made watching John Elway go out on top very gratifying. He stayed here his entire career and is so associated with this town. It's almost like his name is "John Denver," he's so associated with Denver. It's that strong. He's tough to replace. Watching his retirement speech was sad.

———STEVE THORESON, 36, an attorney who lives in Austin, Texas, with his wife and his dog, Denver

Chapter 2

Foaling

1960-61

1962-66

1960-61

1962-67

There Was a Win Chill Factor
Back In the Rockin' '60s

WHEN DENVER CALLS, YA GOTTA ACCEPT THE CHARGES

FRANK TRIPUCKA

Frank Tripucka is a 78-year-old World War II veteran. He played professionally for the Detroit Lions, Chicago Cardinals and Dallas Cowboys. He played for the Broncos from 1960-63.

In 1959, I had coached a couple of games with the Saskatchewan Roughriders. They made me the head coach even though I was the quarterback. They had fired the head coach with three games left in the season. I was 34 at the time. I didn't take the job for the next year. I got a call the next year to go to Denver and help out with training camp for four or five weeks. I went out and the next thing I know, we're playing an exhibition game, and I'm playing in the second half. Four years later, I'm still there. Those were the first four years of the Denver Broncos franchise.

We had second-hand uniforms. The general manager was a very frugal man—cheap as hell. Dean Griffing was his name. They brought these uniforms in from the minor leagues. He'd been the general manager of a minor league football team. Brown pants, striped socks—the stripes went up and down. White jerseys. They didn't fit anyone, either. The guys were all good sized, and the uniforms were all too small. Griffing was only there two years. Jack Faulkner came in next and had been an assistant coach with the San Diego Chargers. New uniforms—major league ones, too. That was the third year.

I was the starting quarterback in the very first Broncos game, in Fenway Park against Boston. We won our first two games. The other team owners had a ton of money, so I knew the league would last. There might have been 8,000 fans at that first game. The second game was against the New York Titans. We stayed back east between the games. The first home game was at Bears Stadium. There were maybe 10,000 fans there. We won our first five, then lost the next five games. Bob Howsam owned the Broncos along with Gerry Phipps. The team needed more money, so they brought Phipps in. He was the general contractor for many of the buildings in downtown Denver.

Prior to the games, we'd have pregame meals at the bar up the street from the stadium. After our meal, we'd watch the films from the last game. I always came home after the season was over—back to New Jersey. I had a liquor store and a bar there.

I remember at the early games, there was a big push for season ticket sales. That third season with new uniforms—the fans went nuts. We didn't have the nets behind the goal posts then. The fans wouldn't give the balls back. It made the GM nuts. He'd go up into the stands to get the ball back! They'd boo him and still not give him the ball back. Most of the players were guys who hadn't been drafted by the NFL. We had a couple of guys who had left the NFL. Al Carmichael had played at Green Bay. We had John Wozniak and Stan Williams from the **DALLAS TEXANS**, too.

I'm still a Broncos fan. My kids are New York Giants fans, and we have season tickets. The kids have Jets tickets, too. One of my sons, Kelly, played in the NBA and has wonderful memories of playing the Nuggets.

Even in the early days, we traveled by plane. We'd stay for a couple weeks, though, if there were games near each other.

It was tough to imagine what the Broncos would turn into. The people were just beautiful. The fans in Denver were great. The players are bigger and faster today. They keep getting bigger every year. I can remember the tackles weighing maybe 260. Now they're over 300 pounds. I think the fans are much as they were then—they haven't changed much.

> **In 1952, the New York Yankees—an NFL team—moved to Dallas and were called the <u>TEXANS</u>. They scored their first touchdown as the Texans when New York Giant punt returner, Tom Landry, fumbled on the Giants 22-yard line. Do not confuse them with Lamar Hunt's Dallas Texans of the AFL, later the Kansas City Chiefs.**

WE WERE BONA FIDE.
WE HAD PROSPECTS.

BOB SCARPITTO

Bob Scarpitto was an outstanding wide receiver for the Broncos from 1962-67. The Rahway, N.J., native was a standout at the University of Notre Dame and currently resides in central California.

I was drafted by the New York Giants, but played my first year in San Diego. Then I played six years in Denver. When I was with San Diego, Al Davis was my end coach. Sid Gillman was the head coach. Chuck Noll was on the staff, too. Sid used to have someone in every city who would sneak out and watch practices. Denver would play touch football instead of practicing part of the time. The scout called Sid and said they were playing touch football. He told the scout to get out of the bar and get to the practice. He didn't believe him. The linemen were the running backs, the receivers were big linemen. They did it to have a bit of fun.

When I got to Denver, they had the vertical striped socks. Then they went to the orange and blue uniforms. They had a ceremony at the beginning of the season in '62 to burn the socks. Our first training camp was in Ft. Collins at Colorado State University. Jack kept bringing in new players, trying to find a good team. We probably had 150 players go through training camp. We only carried 35 players on the roster. Over half the roster was new from the previous year. We played at Bears Stadium that held maybe 35,000 people. We started 6-2 that year and then ended up .500. The fans were crazy then, too. Enthusiastic. They had a good time, especially in the South Stands.

The head coach went from Faulkner to Mac Speedie, then Ray Malavasi. Lou Saban came in after that, in 1967, for my last year. Saban was a good friend of George Steinbrenner and later became president of the New York Yankees. Wahoo McDaniel was crazy in training camp. Wahoo couldn't drink very much. He got mad at someone in camp, and we heard a big gun go off. Someone made him mad, and he was shooting down the hallway at a garbage can. Coach took the gun away from him, and then he was fine.

I go back each year for the Broncos reunion. They put us up at the Adam's Mark. There are usually about 120 players each year. A lot of them are from the 1960s. I see that the old players are either in really good shape still, or they've let themselves go. The majority of the linemen and running backs have either had knee or hip replacements. I've not had to do that, yet. We have a big dinner on Friday night with all the retired players, along with the corporate sponsors. Saturday we have a golf tournament. Saturday night the Broncos Alumni Association put on a dinner with a band. On Sunday we have a brunch and then go to the game.

I grew up in New Jersey, so it was neat to also be drafted by the New York Giants, but they had only one rookie make the team in the previous year. When I signed with the Chargers, they were in L.A., but said they were moving to San Diego. They said they'd have a bunch of rookies make the team, so it was attractive to go there.

I had heard that the New York Titans—now the **JETS**—had some problems in the early years of the AFL. The league had to come in and help them financially. I can remember in 1963, there was an issue with the Broncos ownership and there was talk of moving the team to Arizona. Gerry Phipps, who owned part of the team, bought out the other owners, including Cal Kunz, for like a million dollars and kept the team in Denver. Had Phipps not completed the deal, the team likely would have moved within a couple of years.

I get autograph requests from all over the country—one or so a month. Considering how long ago I played, that's amazing. Mostly, they send me the bubble gum cards. I enjoyed playing in Denver. It was a very small town then. The fans were great. The fans would comp us meals and such. We all worked in the off-season. The

During a 1979 game against the New York Jets at Shea Stadium, a remote control model airplane crashed into the stands at half-time, hit a Patriots fan and killed him.

minimum salary was $6,000 a season. I worked at the Colorado National Bank for four years. I lived in Denver year-round as most of the players did. I ended up out near Golden. There were no branch banks then. Some other players were teachers, some worked for car dealerships, insurance companies. We almost always had to work in a sales-type job, since it was only part of the year.

If you met Al Davis once, he remembered your name. I worked for him as a part-time scout in 1969. During the week I was working for an insurance company doing recruiting and training. I worked college games on Saturday and NFL games on Sunday. There was no interleague trading until 1970, so I was scouting NFL players for him. We were looking for who was playing on special teams, who was on the bench, etc. He put a whole book together, and when the leagues merged, he knew who was who and made a bunch of trades.

I moved to the Denver area in 1962, and then to California in 1970 when I got a Coors distributorship. When I first went to the Broncos in 1962, there were six exhibition games, and 12 regular season games. We got paid $50 per exhibition game. We had six exhibition games preceded by three weeks of training camp…so we were paid $300 total for nine weeks. The general manager in 1960 and '61, was Dean Griffing. We went to Atlanta to play an exhibition game, and we got our checks on the plane. Griffing came in the locker room and offered to cash all our checks for us. A bunch of players endorsed them and gave them to Griffing. We never saw him again, and didn't see the money either. I didn't give him my check. He was to meet everyone by the bus after the game was over. He lived in Atlanta, and we never made it back there. He never went back to Denver.

Ed Cook came from the Titans to the Broncos. The Titans hadn't paid the players in two weeks, and they went to the coaches and refused to play. They gave them checks before practice, and while the players were on the practice field, the coaches were at the bank cashing their own checks. The money was gone before all the players could get their checks cashed.

A GRUNTLED BRONCOS FAN

NORMAN SILVA

Norman, better known as "Stormin' Norman," played halfback at St. Francis de Sales High School. Norman claims to be the original "dress up" Broncos fan and appeared in the March 1979 edition of National Geographic. *He is also featured in the Hall of Life at the Denver Museum. Stormin' Norman uses his super fan status to raise funds for charity as well.*

In 1960, I was working at the post office and heard about this new team coming to town, a new league they were starting. So after work, I would jog over to the stadium. I was into long-distance running. I did a lot of running, and it wasn't all that far from where I worked in downtown Denver. I'd jog over to the stadium and take a peek at them and saw those awful brown and gold uniforms that they had. They looked like a bunch of college guys who couldn't make it in the pros, but they were having fun. I didn't think it could last. I played **VARSITY** football four years in high school, so I was into football. When it came to town, I thought, I got to check this out. Well, I was working on Sundays, and I would jog over to the stadium when I got off of work, usually around 3:30. If we weren't working overtime, I could catch the last half of the game. For the most part, I stood outside of the stadium, looking in, because I didn't want to pay to see just the last part of the game. There was a place on the southwest corner of the stadium—the old Mile High Stadium—when it was first built, you could look from the outside and see most of the field. There were probably a dozen, up to 20 people who would stand out there and watch for free. Well, the guys at the gate would open the gates and

> **The word "VARSITY" is the British short form of the word "university."**

holler at us, "Come on in, we need bodies." There weren't a whole lot of people inside. So I did that off and on for a long time. And whenever I would get over there a little bit early I would slip the guy at the gate 50 cents, and he would let me in. So I would get to go in and watch the game and sit around the 20-yard line. It wasn't a full stadium at all.

I didn't think the Broncos were going to make it. They were drawing plays in the dirt. It wasn't a good grass field, and you would see them scratching in the dirt. It just didn't look like it was a professional kind of thing. They put up some temporary stands on the east side, and they looked like if they got too many people, they might fall over. That's the way it went for awhile, and it didn't look like it was going to fly. In 1966, when we got season tickets, it looked like maybe this thing was going to catch on after all. They switched to blue and orange by then, but I thought blue and orange was kind of a clownish looking outfit at the time. But we hung in and kept going and as the atmosphere got better and better, I picked up a couple more tickets. Eventually, they started expanding the stadium.

I started dressing crazy, having fun. My friend had a big, long, blue and orange tie that I would wear and little by little, I got into different outfits. I was working as a volunteer clown at one of the church bazaars, and I had an orange wig that I bought because of the Broncos. I decided that someday I would wear my clown outfit to the stadium, so I wore my orange Afro wig, and I put white makeup on my face and I put the Broncos D emblem on my cheeks, and around my mouth I turned the D on the side where it makes a smile, kind of. I got my picture in one of the papers for that. I made up a sign, a big No. 1 sign that I put on a stick. That picture was published in *National Geographic* with an article on the Rocky Mountain area. My parents were proud. Over the years, I got my picture in a lot of different publications.

I was walking around to the stadium one time and a kid came running up to me and asked for an autograph. I didn't have a name to sign and didn't know what to do. It stumped me for a second. I thought, "I can't put my own name down. This kid later on would look at that and think, 'Who's this, what's his name?'" You know, anyone who is named Norman at one time or another gets called Stormin' Norman. So I wrote, "Stormin' Norman, Number One Broncos Maniac." After that, I was locked into that name. I used it from then on. So that's how Stormin' came about.

The Broncos have meant the world to Denver and to me, too. Out west, in the mountain towns, nobody knew of any sports. So the Broncos put us on the map, even though we were the rug of the league, everybody wiping their feet on us. Back in 1967, the Broncos played an NFL team for the first time, in preseason. We played Detroit and Alex Karras made the remark, "I'll walk back to Detroit if Denver beats us." Well, Denver beat them. Come 1978, when we finally got to the Super Bowl, a neighbor of mine told me he could get tickets, so I told him that I would drive my van. We drove through Texas and it was covered with ice. We finally got to New Orleans and pulled up to the stadium. We saw a bus pulling away, and thought it might be the Broncos team bus. Then out of the stadium door ran Haven Moses and a couple of guys after him, hollering for the bus. They missed the bus. My neighbor was driving the van at the time, and he hollered out the window, "You guys need a ride?" They said yes, and in popped—let me see if I get them all right—Rick Upchurch, Haven Moses, Riley Odoms, Paul Smith and Rubin Carter. We had five studs in our van. I had pulled the back seats out for the trip, and we had a big foam mattress on the floor so we could all sleep. The players were spread out on the mattress and sitting wherever they could. We drove about 10 miles outside New Orleans to the airport where their hotel was. I got some movies of that, so I did document it. We also got autographs from all of them. They started talking and it was crazy.

Just getting around Mile High was so much easier compared to the new stadium. I used to carry a megaphone around with me, so I could holler at the defense. They don't let me carry a megaphone anymore. The Barrel Man, they allow. He's got all kinds of privileges the rest of us never get. He's The Man.

PARKING: $5, EXIT FEE: $10

LOUISE DAVIDSON SCHWARTZ

A Denver native, Louise and her family parked cars during both Denver Bears and Denver Broncos games for decades. Their parking lot monies helped pay her and her siblings college tuition.

My parents lived on 20th and Federal, so when we were growing up, we saw Mile High being built. My parents decided it would be a good idea to acquire some property. They really didn't have extra funds; they were really hard working. They went to the city and county. Much of the property around where the Stadium was being built was on tax liens, so my parents were able to acquire a lot of that property.

Over about 10 years, they acquired probably 30 or 40 lots surrounding the stadium on Bryant St., etc. My sisters and I would work in the parking lots every single night there was a Bears game. I was 10 at the time, and I would stand out there with flashlights and my money apron and charge a quarter a car.

As we became older and became teenagers, we would have to have our boyfriends work in the lot to make sure they got our family's approval. That was just how our family operated—we had a lot of together time. My parents would gather the money after we worked and they would stay up late at night rolling the change. That's what my teenage years were—taking it to the bank. Through all this, my dad retained his day job and worked full-time.

We were all spread out all over the place. My sisters and I would be at all these other lots and we didn't necessarily get any help because ours were much smaller. We would park two rows and an aisle, two rows and an aisle, two rows and an aisle. And we would charge what started out as $2.50, and then it went to $5 and then $10 in the more recent times. When there was going to be a huge crowd—the police would tell us when they were expecting a huge crowd, and we would have multiple signs for pricing. When we first got there, we would charge $5 a car, and the lot would be maybe half full, and then a huge amount of traffic would come and we would raise it to $10. On the exact same day, we would pull out a different sign. The cars that were right there when we switched the signs saw it. We would let them in for the lower price, it was called "doing business by the bootstrap." We didn't have a business plan or anything.

When it got really crowded and people were begging for spaces because they were late to the game or something, we would start filling in the space we had left and then the lot would be totally jammed. You couldn't get out of it unless you waited until the cars in the aisles moved. We would go home before the end of the game because the people would be so irate. You couldn't get away with that today!

These lots were not paved—they were dirt lots. When my dad died in '67, my mom was in great fear the city was going to make her pave the lots, which would have cost a fortune. We were still just getting Sunday money. We would make a lot of money when there was a game, but there were only about 10 games a year. The city never actually made her pave the lots.

Nobody stole any money that we know of. Life was really nice in Denver in the '50s and '60s. When we were called a "cow town," things were easy. We didn't have to worry and we never feared for our lives. We would be out there with these flashlights and orange aprons and people would drive by and they would honk and wave. And we started when we were little. We were out there when we were six- and seven-years-old.

Most nights, there were only eight or 10 cars in the parking lots for the Denver Bears. That area on 20th and Clay and 19th and Clay was a landfill, and that is where they built the stadium. As little kids, my sisters and I watched it going up. It was only a block away from our house.

My mother took the business very seriously. There she was in her 60s and 70s with her sister, who was 10 years older, running the lot. It was pretty amazing to see that at the time. My mother remained a huge fan of the Broncos. She got four season tickets and she even went to Super Bowl XXIII. Mom watched every game, and insisted on buying her car from John Elway's dealership. She was a real character and she was totally identified with the Broncos. My siblings and I really admired her for her business sense and her hard work ethic to go out there in all kinds of weather and all hours to make sure that she could pay the girls' way through college.

I was sad when they tore down Mile High. We never envisioned it being torn down when we saw it being built. It was so exciting to have it built there over a landfill. The Denver downtown was low rise. This was before I-25. The Stadium must have been one of the biggest structures in Denver at that time. It must have been about 1955 when it opened. We had a double car garage, we lived on the corner. We only had one car, so my parents were able to rent out the garage to someone. And they rented to someone by the name of Andy Cohen who was the manager of the Denver Bears at the time. So that was our closest brush with fame. He was the manager and he was very nice and we got a big kick out of it.

Al Davis's ego applied for statehood today. If approved it would be the third largest.

I LIKE IT, I LOVE IT, I WANT SOME MORE OF IT

I've been a Broncos fan since the Fall of '62. That was the year that, as an 11-year-old boy, I almost lost my dad. He was in a very serious automobile accident and sustained permanent brain damage and other physical injuries. He spent several months in the hospital recovering. Shortly after the accident, the Moose Lodge in Longmont hosted a kids' boxing tournament. Back then, Longmont had a population of about 11,000, but that didn't keep a couple of Denver Broncos players from attending. One of my friends, Eddie Garcia, and I decided to box against each other. We were probably the smallest guys who boxed that night. We pummeled each other pretty good and must have put on a pretty good show because we were awarded prizes for the 'Best Fight of the Night.' We had our pictures taken with the Broncos football players, and were awarded tickets to a Denver Broncos football game. I had never been to a football game in my life. Heck, I had hardly ever been outside of Longmont. My mom didn't drive, so I didn't know how I was going to get to the game. As it turned out, my best friend and neighbor, Kyle Rubik, told his dad, and Mr. Rubik took us to the game. My first Broncos football game was at the old Denver Bears Stadium. The Broncos were playing against the 'Boston' Patriots. This game is one my fondest memories because it came at a time when I needed to take my mind off of my dad. It was still during this time that we didn't know if he was going to survive. Thank God he did, and he is now an 85-year-old great grandpa! Well, back to my first game. The Broncos trailed the Patriots most of the game, and what made it worse was that there was a very obnoxious woman who was cheering for the Patriots. Every time they scored or did something good she would say "Stick with the winner" while she was looking at us. As the game went on, there was a Denver running back named Billy Joe. I remember cheering on Billy Joe and eventually the Broncos came back and won the game. I still remember as we left the stadium, I looked at that lady and said "Stick with the winner." I was hooked as a Broncos fan from that day forward.

——RON ROMERO, Longmont, Colorado

 I was a baton twirler and took lessons from a lady named Mary Anne Matherly. We were probably some of the best twirlers in the state. We became a group of several girls who performed at different functions in Denver. When the Broncos started, they wanted to have some cheerleaders and all of us became **CHEERLEADERS**. We were on the sidelines during games wearing little Western costumes. I thought that was neat, but I wasn't into football in the least. I knew so little about football that I really didn't know when to cheer or when not to. One of my girlfriends ended up dating one of the Broncos, Goose Gonsoulin. Besides that, the only perks we ever got were the tickets. A lot of games, it would snow and be so cold that I would just be freezing to death. Those were the longest three hours of the week for me. I had to be out there three hours! Now I think, what a great thing, because I'm such a fan, but then it didn't seem that way. I was freezing in my costume, so somebody gave me a blanket. I huddled under it on the sidelines and someone took my picture. It ended up in the local paper showing me as the coldest person at the game. My mother saved the picture and once in awhile, I have to "prove" to someone I truly was an original Broncos cheerleader. The ironic thing about football is that after I married and had two sons, my husband wanted the boys to enjoy football, so I started watching it and wanting to understand it. I get into it so much! I've learned more and more, and I've been a fan for so long. I never miss Broncos games. In fact, I branched out to where I watch a lot of the other teams, too. Now I think, oh, wouldn't it be great if I could be a cheerleader again, knowing how much I enjoy football now, compared to back then. I really wasn't scared

> **When the Dallas Cowboys CHEERLEADERS started in 1972, each earned $15 per game—the same amount they receive today.**

performing, because my mom had started me in ballet and baton from the time I was about three- or four-years-old, and I had performed all over. I had done USO shows, and I was with a band. The only thing I remember being scared of on the sidelines was that the players might hit me. I don't have my uniform any more. I finally got rid of all that a number of years ago. The Broncos put Denver on the map. I can remember people thinking Denver was such a cow town. People probably thought that cattle were herded through town.

——**BEVERLY BARELA**, Lakewood, Colorado

There were no Nuggets, no Avalanche, no Rockies. The Broncos were Denver's first big-time, big-league athletic team. When the AFL and NFL merged, Denver was in the NFL, and that was an enormous deal. Denver was a lot smaller, and to be in the NFL was a big deal! Football is the outdoors, cold-weather, battle-the-elements kind of a deal to me. Football is not a gentle sport, and I think it's better played outdoors. Never a domed stadium for Denver!

——**DAN GREEN**, 59

We were in a group of neighbors who bought season tickets in '70, and our 16 seats were in the top row of the South Stands by the AA sign. In those early years, we took turns bringing peanuts, popcorn, hot dogs and Hamm's pony kegs of beer (which was allowed in those days). No "beer man" ever made it up to the top of the South Stands. Instead of tailgate parties at the stadium, we took turns having brunch in our homes before we headed to Mile High Stadium. At one of these brunches, we decided to make a sign to take to the game. This was during the Lou Saban era, and we were disgruntled with "half-a-loaf" games and the losing seasons. Our sign, "LYNCH LOU," was hung at the top of the South Stands. The next morning, there was a photo in the *Rocky Mountain News* taken with a telephoto lens of our sign and, of course, there were all of our smiling faces! Shortly after that, Saban was fired—I am sure it had nothing to do with our sign! During the Saban era, we did not have much to cheer about. A first down now and then was about all. Steve Tensi was the quarterback. He could throw the ball a mile, but no one could catch it. No wonder we took a pony keg of beer, which didn't go far with 16 people!

After 36 years of Broncos football, the most memorable game was the AFC Championship game when the Broncos beat the Raiders to go to their first Super Bowl. I will never forget the electric feeling in Mile High that day. It made all those losing seasons we had sat through worth it. Our group of 16 is now down to only three originals, but now our kids have joined the group with their kids. I have lots of fun and great memories of our beloved Broncos.

——TOM GUETZ

In 1960, I lived on East Sixth Avenue, just a little bit west of Lowry. My buddy and I would get in for $1.50 in student seating in the North Stands. In those days, they had the original ugly uniforms. Nobody had ever heard of any of the players. I don't know if Bob Scarpitto was on the team then, but he was the only player I had heard of, because I had followed him at **NOTRE DAME**. We'd go down every week, but one week I had been sick and my parents wouldn't let me go in the snow. The Broncos were playing the Chargers. My older brother convinced them to just let me ride with him in a heated car, so he drove me down to the stadium. We parked in a lot on the field which overlooked the right-field corner, so I could see the game there. They hadn't yet put up the material to block people from watching the game from there. People used to sit up there all the time instead of paying to get in. So we watched the game from there in the blizzard. In the midst of that blizzard, you could see one Chargers player, Ernie Ladd, who stood out like a sore thumb, because he was so big. It was exciting for us, because my best friend and I were both in eighth grade when the Broncos started. Then, through our high school years, we were there almost every game. My dad had a store nearby, and he used to bring booze to the trainer—things were loose in those days—and the trainer would give my dad massages and then the trainer would get me sideline passes. We could just stand around there on the sideline.

——STU ZISMAN, 58, Greeley

> **Johnny Lattner, the 1953 Heisman Trophy winner from NOTRE DAME, didn't even lead the Irish in rushing or receiving that season.**

Chapter 3

The Old Man and the Wee...

And Mom Makes Three

HIS GRANDFATHER LIKED WORKING WITH PEOPLE. HE WAS A MORTICIAN.

ANDY FOX

Andy Fox is 46-years old and lives in Kerr-ville, Texas, and as a child always dressed up to go to Broncos games as was the tradition in his family. His grandfather played football at Denver University, having worn the Broncos uniform before it was a Broncos uniform.

You may remember Howard Mortuaries. I believe it's Olinger Moore Howard mortuaries now. Well, the "Howard" of that is my grandmother—her maiden name. We called my grandfather "Daddy Guinn" when he was alive. He worked in the mortuary. And he had a unique talent that he could remember your name and face and then remember you years later. You could talk to him for 10 minutes and then see him on a train years later and he would say, "Andy, how are you doing, and how's your wife?" So he was a natural in the funeral business. Howard Mortuaries was where he worked forever. And the story goes that he just took off one day and went down to sign up for season tickets. He knew the Broncos were coming to town and went down and got in line for season tickets.

I knew he was always involved with the Denver Bears, and he knew everybody that there was to know in Denver at that time. He and my grandmother were regulars at Taylor's Supper Club, which was way out in the middle of the sticks in Lakewood. They knew all the entertainers and Taylor's Supper Club was where everybody went. I imagine Daddy Guinn was more than just a casual bystander in helping the Phipps brothers bring this franchise to Denver in '59. He knew the Phipps brothers and they were regulars at Ma and Daddy Guinn's cocktail parties. There had to be some other connections. Daddy Guinn went to Denver University; the original Broncos equipment came from DU. Daddy Guinn played football at DU. Denver University donated all the original equipment—that's where the clown socks came from. At one point, we had a pair of those original clown socks that Daddy Guinn was given. So all of the equipment the first year they played was donated from DU and it wasn't until '61 that they actually got their own uniforms and were really truly a professional team. So there is a lot of background there that really has never been fully explained. The Broncos have said that the season tickets were just first come, first served. So a good conspiracy beats the truth anytime almost, so it has always been thought that there might have been more to it than that. There might have been a "Why don't you put Guinn high on the list—he's helped us a bunch" type of philosophy. So I don't know, and it is entirely possible that there wasn't that much action. I mean, the Broncos season tickets now are a big deal, but in '59 when they first signed up for them, it might not have been a big deal. Maybe the people were sitting down at the ticket windows with nothing to do and no one to buy tickets and Daddy Guinn happened to be one of the first few people in line. But he bought four season tickets on the 50-yard line. There is a little question as to how far back they were. They were probably somewhere between 12 and 15 rows up off the field in the original stadium. As Bears Stadium became Mile High Stadium, they built additional seats closer to the field. Then when they did the big remodel of Mile High Stadium, they moved the field 10 yards, so the seats ended up being right on the 40-yard line, closer to the horseshoe part. So when we moved to the new stadium, we were trying to get back as close as we could to the 50-yard line, just to have Daddy Guinn's seats close to where they originally were. It is really just fun to carry on that kind of sports tradition—the second-longest streak of sellouts in the NFL.

As a kid, my dad had four seats—he had his own priority number and they were different from these seats. We would go to the games and we had to get dressed up. You had nice turtlenecks and a nice coat and your black shoes. And you froze to death because you had these nice nylon dress pants on in the late '60s that were fashionable, and you're at the game and you are freezing to death. And, by tradition, you don't leave the game early. You don't leave a Broncos game until it is over. And that is one of the things we have a little fun with.

Whoever sits in the seats, they have to cheer for the Broncos, and you don't leave the game until it is over. If we find out you leave the game before it is over, you don't get tickets next year....

I remember one game when I was a kid. It was the fourth quarter and the Broncos kicked a field goal. And I remember just absolutely going wild. The stands were just going crazy. People were cheering, yelling, screaming and giving a standing ovation. It seemed like we cheered forever. You would have thought we won the Super Bowl on that field goal. And we were playing against the Kansas City Chiefs. The final score was something like 66-10. But when we kicked that field goal you would have thought we won the world championship. And they just beat us silly, like usual....

I had flown to Denver to watch John Elway retire and christen the new INVESCO Field. It was the first regular season game—a Monday Night game when we played the New York Giants. The game was on September 10, and that next morning, 9/11 happened. So I was stuck in Denver for a week while that all went down. That was kind of an auspicious start to the new stadium. What was very ironic about the whole thing is that we had played the New York Giants and they were stuck in Denver as well. Everybody remembers where they were and what they were doing, and my memory of that was football....

What it really is is a memory of my grandfather. It's a memory of him and his love for sports. It's all about the family. That's what it is and that's what it brings us back to. Yes, it's a sport, it's an event and it has become almost not a sport anymore. I'm not telling you anything you don't already see. Back when you were a kid, even though they were horrible, you just thought, that's the deal, that's it. And that's one of the reasons we have such a fun time. It's family—that's the connection. Everybody knows when the schedule comes out, and family members get the first pick of the tickets. My sister started to go to games again last year. It's all about family, tradition and longevity.

When I first moved back to Denver in '84, we got a couple of end zone tickets to the Monday Night Packers game. Well, it was snowing like crazy, and we weren't even sure we could get to the stadium.

So we sat in the end zone seats in our sleeping bags. We crawled in them and zipped them up to stay warm. On one of the first plays of the game, the Broncos intercepted a pass and ran it back for what we later found out was a touchdown. It was snowing so hard that we couldn't see the guy. We could tell by the cheers at the other end that it was either a good play or we had scored a touchdown. And we turned around and there was six points on the board. We saw the interception, but we never saw the score. That was one of the fun memories.

When Mike Shanahan was hired, I knew Pat Bowlen was serious about being a competitor. You take every major sport now and you can't say that about every team. There are maybe 12 or 15 owners in all of those together who really want to win. And I said, "Man, this is it!" So when they won the Super Bowl, we were very excited. It was really gratifying to see that come to Elway and to see that come to Denver. They said, "This is for the fans," and that is really, truly what it was. It was for those 66-10 drubbings, for the people who come out and sit in the snow, and for all those sellout games. It's quite a story for the people of Denver. It says, "This is who we are and this is what we want to be known for."

Pat Bowlen has put together what I would call a first class, respectable organization in an industry that is known for not having that as its moniker. There are a lot of guys that are just looking for the big bucks. The Broncos organization, on the other hand, makes sure their players are citizens, and not just out there running around with the big dollars. They want everybody in their organization to be somebody that you would like to have as your next door neighbor, and I think that is quite a tribute to Pat Bowlen and the way he does things.

MOM WAS THE KANSAS DISTRIBUTOR OF BRONCOS LOVE

MEREDITH SLOAN

Colorado native, Meredith Sloan, 45, currently lives in Wichita, Kansas. Every Broncos game brings back fond memories of her mother.

I'm a Colorado native, and my parents got their season tickets in 1961. I was born in April. Had I been born in October, I'd have been born in the stadium, because I know my mom wouldn't have missed a game

In 1997 when the Broncos had won 12 straight, my husband and I were living in Wichita, Kansas. My mom was there as she had been diagnosed with lung cancer. The Broncos looked to be on the road to the Super Bowl. We had been to all the previous Super Bowls, and we were talking about going that year, too. My mom was against us going—she was sure that the Broncos had lost because we had gone to all those Super Bowls. She was really a die-hard fan. It was never about winning or losing for her. She just loved the Broncos. As it got closer to the Super Bowl, she was against going. My son, Austin, was eight-years-old at the time, a Broncos fan in Chiefs territory. He got so much grief when the Chiefs beat the Broncos that year. As we approached Christmas, my son's letter to Santa talked about the Broncos, and the letter back from Santa told him to "hang in there and keep believing in his Broncos." The Broncos ended up in the Super Bowl in San Diego against Green Bay. Our friends, who were Chiefs fans, started rooting for the Broncos to be supportive of my mom. One of Austin's teachers even called to congratulate him after the Broncos won the Super Bowl. He told her he knew they would win, because Santa had told him if he just believed, it would come true. That is indicative of the whole spiritual thing about rooting for the Broncos. It's all about rooting for the team, regardless of wins and losses.

When my mom was in the last days of her life, and we were talking about her final arrangements, she told me she either wanted her ashes to be sprinkled on Longs Peak or at Mile High Stadium. She didn't want the new stadium. She was very traditional. She called Gail Stuckey, the ticket manager, and found out about sprinkling ashes at Mile High. My mom died on July 4, 1998. She ended up with her ashes in an old popcorn tin with the old Broncos logo on it. My son made a collage of Broncos players. My husband took the popcorn tin to the mortuary and told them the ashes needed to be put in it, and that the collage my son made needed to go in there, too. And a Beanie Baby, born on January 25, the day the Broncos had won the Super Bowl. The mortician thought he was nuts. Austin wanted his grandmother to have a well-decorated place in heaven. We went to the next Super Bowl in **MIAMI**, too. We bought four tickets from a ticket broker. My husband, son, and I went, and the fourth seat was for my mom. We didn't take the popcorn tin, but instead left the seat empty in her honor. We had lots of opportunities to sell the ticket, but didn't. For us, it's a family love. It had the emotional attachment of a high school championship to us.

Mr. Bowlen has done a tremendous job of keeping the spirit of the old Broncos alive, even with all of the corporate pressures of pro sports today. It's a spirit that the Phipps brothers brought to the team in the original days. The first Super Bowl in New Orleans had that high school spirit. Everyone on Bourbon Street was either a Cowboys or Broncos fan. We ran into Floyd Little there. It wasn't quite so corporate then. The fans then were really fans of the teams. Now it's more corporate and the people there got tickets from their boss and aren't often fans of the teams playing.

My best friend growing up was Lisa Hardy. Her dad was director of player personnel. She rode the horse that has now become Thunder for a couple of seasons. I was her assistant down on the field. It was an incredible experience. We got there early before the game. It was different then. Security was much different. We could talk to the

> **Do you confuse Miami (Ohio) with MIAMI (Florida)?**
> **Miami of Ohio was a school before Florida was a state.**

players. Two of the nicest people we met were Joe Montana and Dwight Clark. They were playing for the 49ers. We were waiting for everyone to leave after the game so we could load up the horse. Joe and his wife love horses. They came over and talked to us about horses. They were such nice, regular people. Because of Lisa, I was afforded a lot of opportunities to meet the players, go to parties and more.

A lot of people don't know that before the Broncos worked with the city to have a season parking pass area, we had to wait in line to get parking passes. We spent three nights in line once to get parking passes. Later, the Broncos took over the parking pass situation. It was like waiting for concert tickets. The parking passes were more about location, and supply and demand. Everyone wanted their spot. We have an RV pass now, to park our RV in the tailgate area. It was one of those things where you saw all the same season ticket holders. It was still such a family thing then. Everyone knew everyone who sat around you. You knew everyone in line for the parking pass, too. We camped in line, cooked out, played Frisbee. We slept in our lawn chairs in line. It really was the beginning of tailgating. A few people in that group had campers they'd bring. It was a really neat family type activity. This was before we had been to the playoffs. Those were the golden days of the team. It was a golden time, a simpler time. We used to be lucky to win a game.

The night we won the Super Bowl against Green Bay, my mom and I sat up and drank three bottles of champagne watching the post-game coverage. Because of that, I love the team and love it when we win. I feel bad for the players when they lose—makes me want to bake cookies and take them to the players to make them feel better.

IN 2001, VANDALS DID $400 DAMAGE TO MILE HIGH STADIUM... THEY IMPLODED IT.

STAN SCHWARZ

Stan Schwarz has lived in Colorado since 1955. His father was an iron worker and he used that to his advantage at a Pittsburgh Steelers game. He went to college in Michigan and now operates an electronics company. Schwarz believes that in time, INVESCO will develop good memories for fans as Mile High Stadium has.

You didn't have a choice about being a Broncos fan in Denver. In the '60s, when the team came here with the AFL, you were just so happy to have a team that you rooted for them. I was five-years-old when my dad first took me to a game. I can remember going with my dad or grandpa, and we would take the bus down to Bears Stadium before they changed it to Mile High. They had ugly brown and orange uniforms. I can remember thinking how cool it was to be sitting in the stands at a "real" football game. We used to listen on the radio, but it was cool to sit there with my dad and watch them lose.

The Broncos were such perennial losers in the early days that you rooted for your favorite players. We watched other teams' all-star players come to town. The Broncos didn't win at all for a number of years. When they started winning, we wrapped our arms around them and kept rooting. We jumped on the bandwagon and started riding with them. I never saw any place support a team like Denver did. Businesses painted their buildings orange. They decorated and tailgated. People endeared themselves to the team, because they had always been the underdog.

You think about all the memories. My favorite uniform is the bucking Bronco from the '60s. We had season tickets in the South Stands, usually in the top row under the scoreboard. They were a bunch of lunatics in the South Stands. One year there was a Raiders fan who was being extremely obnoxious. He really got the Broncos fans cranked up. They grabbed this Raiders fan, picked him up, and held him over the edge of the stadium. They were going to drop him until he apologized. The cops came and arrested them all. If an opposing fan came into the South Stands and could behave, it was fun. When they would get out of control, the South Standers tossed beer on them.

My dad helped build the East Stands at Mile High Stadium. He was an iron worker. It was neat going to the games and hearing my dad tell me what still needed to be done. It was neat to be there knowing my dad helped build that stadium. When they first built those stands, putting them on water to move them around, it was state-of-the-art at the time. They used to have car shows at Mile High. They'd have Broncos players there with the cars. Great memories.

The "whirlybird" may be the most memorable play. Elway spinning into the end zone made people go crazy. I had 50-60 people at my house for that game. As soon as the game was over, my dad said, "Let's go to the airport." We didn't even think twice about it. We went to meet the plane. People were waiting along the fence for the plane to arrive. It was bitter cold. Everyone went nuts when the plane landed.

My dad has a Super Bowl football that is signed. He displays it proudly. I have two Mile High Stadium seats that I bought. They are sitting in my basement. I've never figured out just what to do with them. I can remember them trying to get Red McCombs to change his name to Orange during the Orange Crush years! New fans need to know that you have to live and breathe orange, and you embrace the team. Once a Broncos fan, always a Broncos fan.

My son, Ryan, experienced the same thing I did with my dad. To walk into the stadium holding your dad's hand is special. I remember doing it with my dad, and to do that with my son brings tears to my eyes. It chokes me up. It's not so much about the game, but about the people you're with. You develop a bond. That's what's really cool. I can remember my son watching Elway. That was when he developed a fire for the game, and he now plays back-up tight end on his college team. Those are the memories you hold on to.

THE WRITE STUFF

JAMES MERILATT

James Merilatt, 31, is the publisher of Mile High Sports Magazine *and has been a Broncos fan "since birth."*

My grandma knitted an orange and blue stocking cap for me. I was wearing it in my first picture. My son Ben was wearing his own Broncos stocking cap in his first picture, too. My first memory is when I was 4-years-old, in '77. My parents and grandparents went to the Super Bowl. I was in our basement and my parents were making signs to take to the Super Bowl. They were using sheets and making signs late into the night. I remember having to stay home. We had orange balloons to pop when the Broncos scored, and unfortunately, we still had plenty of balloons left. I can remember my parents getting back the next day, but I don't remember much of the game. I mainly remember the stuff surrounding the game.

Rooting for the Broncos is a family thing. Both of my grandfathers had tickets. My dad used to go with my mom's dad even before they were married. We'd go tailgate and have homemade rigatoni. We tailgated with my dad's parents and sat at the game with my mom's parents. It was a pretty cool experience. A lot of my family memories are Broncos related. We'd go to San Diego or L.A. to games, too. Every Sunday for road games, we'd go to my grandparents' house. I learned most of my cuss words from my grandfather yelling at the TV!

We used to go to training camp in my grandparents' RV. We'd go watch the scrimmages. They were meaningless games, but it was a huge deal for us. Camp was in Greeley, Colorado, and was six weeks long. You could get physically close to the players. You could walk right down to the ropes and see the players. I got high-fives from the players and autographs, too. It made them seem like real people. It was that way, too, during the season.

We'd go to a restaurant across from their training camp, on 58th and I-25. Burgers and Italian food. It might have been more of a bar than a restaurant. It always smelled of beer and cigarettes. The players would watch game films in the banquet room there on the old film machines. The waitress there really liked my grandfather and would take my brother and me back there to meet the players. No coaches, just players. It was a Thursday night thing. They used an old school projector. The players seemed like mountain men. They were huge, at least to me as a kid. They were always accommodating to my brother and me. We used to take orange pieces of construction paper back there for autographs. We've framed them and have them in our Broncos billiards room.

In '83, I was 10. We were at a Broncos versus Colts game in Mile High. It was Elway's rookie year. Elway had been drafted by the Colts, but refused to play for them. We were down, 19-0, with seven minutes left. Elway led the Broncos on three touchdown drives to win the game. The last score was in the north end of the stadium. The Yellow Pages confetti came raining down from the box seats. My dad always used to give fans a hard time, in a fun way. Many of them had left when it was 19-0, and he was giving the fans leaving a hard time about how they would miss the comeback. He probably did that many weeks, but he was right that time. Elway's first comeback came against the team he shunned.

At Mile High, we used to sit in Section 326, Row 8, Seats 1-6. When my dad didn't go, I'd get to sit on the aisle. On the metal steps to the right of us, there was a hole in the stairs the size of a soda can. They didn't fix it for like four years. People would catch their toe or heel in it every game. It was part of the charm. We placed bets on who would trip on it. It gave the stadium character and charm. I miss Mile High. The Mile High Quarterback Club was in the second level of the North Stands. You could go down there on a Wednesday night to see the Club. We'd meet players and coaches. The stadium was empty, so it was eerie. The Club is in the basement of INVESCO Field now. We don't have that kind of access to players and coaches now. There used to be 25 people or so at those events. There would be questions and answers and some one-on-one time with them. It was pretty cool.

The South Standers ripped up the stands after the final game at Mile High Stadium. The Broncos didn't make the playoffs that year. The South Standers tore the place apart, even though there was a chance of a Wildcard Game the next week. I'm not sure where they would have sat. That stadium had a lot of history to it. My dad would tell me stories about the field being lowered six feet to help visibility, about the levels being added, and the East Stands being added. The East Stands floated on water so they could be moved for baseball games. The stadium had little peculiar things about it that gave it charm. The boxes, or sky boxes, were on the cutting edge when they were built. They were very '80s, though. They were on top of the fifth level, all the way at the top of the stadium.

We sat in the same seats forever. Two rows in front of us, a guy had a big long plastic horn. Fans named Chuck and Chuck, Jr., sat in front of us. I don't know anything about them except that they sat in front of us for 20 years. They were part of our Broncos family. The guy in Seat 7 next to us was Herman Yost. He was the old football coach from Thomas Jefferson High School. My grandpa always sat next to him and told old football stories. When we moved to INVESCO Field, the questionnaire had 19 questions. We are still in Section 326, pretty close to the same location. Chuck and Chuck, Jr., are right behind us now, instead of in front of us. Chuck is probably 70 now. I think he's a grandfather. As a kid I was the one who knew who all the players were at the preseason games. While other 6-year-olds were watching cartoons, I was memorizing the Broncos roster.

We used to have an "announcer" behind us at Mile High. He did play-by-play during the entire game. He's not near us at INVESCO Field, though. He'd try to predict the play and was almost always wrong. It was quite a collection of characters in our section. It was really cool when Barrel Man would come into our section and start the Wave. We felt responsible, and some pressure, to start the Wave. You didn't want to screw that up.

BITS AND BITES...BEGGED, BORROWED AND STOLEN

We loved taking our kids to the Broncos' training camp. My daughter was eight and she would say, "God Bless You" to the players after she got their autographs. The players really seemed to appreciate that. The players now are obsessed with being superstars and making money. I don't think they appreciate the fans and the game.

—KATHY POLLICE, 58, retired teacher

When I was in the second grade, I was a bit of a rowdy child and was placed into a behavioral disorder class. Our teacher, Mrs. Pope, was a great soul. She had all the kids write down what they liked to do more than anything, with the promise of being able to take part in our favorite activity at the end of the year if our behavior was up to her standards. Understandably, most kids wrote down things like eating ice cream, roller skating and riding bikes. My favorite thing, however, was watching the Denver Broncos. Up to then, as a 7-year-old, I'd never been to a game, but enjoyed watching them on TV. The end of the year came and went, and I was upset that I didn't get to take part in my "favorite thing." Mrs. Pope, however, did not disappoint. The following fall, she came to my classroom and announced that she would be taking me to a Denver Broncos versus Cleveland Browns game. My first game, and in the South Stands, no less! The game itself was a blur, but the memory remains!

My best memories of the Denver Broncos, however, always revolve around my father. Being hooked on attending games live because of Mrs. Pope, my dad was all but forced to pony up and start taking me to games. The very next season just happened to be John Elway's rookie season. His very first game at Mile High was a preseason game versus the Seattle Seahawks. Other than it being the first game the "Duke of Denver" graced the storied Mile High turf, what stuck out was that the Broncos wore white uniforms at home due to the late summer heat—something they haven't done since, and I'm not sure they ever did before. Years passed, and my dad and I attended other games, including a Raiders game where a scuffle broke out right in front of us, the '97 home opener against the Kansas City

Chiefs when they broke out their new blue uniforms, and their playoff victory over the Jacksonville Jaguars, also in '97, when we got to go into the locker room after the game and shake Elway's hand. But during my last year of college in another state, and after my Dad had moved to Texas, he and I both flew back to Denver to go to John Elway's last regular season home game in 1998 versus... the Seattle Seahawks. Talk about coming full circle! Not only had we attended Elway's first game at Mile High, but now his last regular season game against the same team. What also made that game special was Elway threw his 300th career TD pass and Terrell Davis surpassed the 2,000-yard mark.

I've attended many games and have seen many teams—college and pro—all across the country, and there are some great fans all over. But the passion and loyalty shown by Broncos fans equals—and in many cases—surpasses any I have witnessed! Not only do the Denver Broncos unite the state of Colorado, but the ENTIRE Rocky Mountain Region, as well. We bleed orange and blue. We believe in Mile High Magic. And we're proud citizens of Broncos Country! I will continue to go to as many Broncos games as I can afford, but they will never come close to the memories I made with my father!

———CHRIS FALLETTA, 30, Denver

It would tear up my dad, because the Broncos used to lose a lot. The way he used to compensate for that is he'd always bet against them. Every week, people would come in and say to my dad, "Stanley, I know the Broncos are going to win this week." He'd say, "Okay, I'll bet you." I knew it still tore him up when they lost, but he could always say, "Well, I won my bet." He hedged his feelings that way....There was something called a "Cub Pass" for the Bears baseball games. During the baseball season, there was this pass—you would pay $1, and if an adult accompanied you, you would get in free. One of my friends and I got in to 40 games that year for that $1. We would just walk up to grown people and ask them to walk in with us, and nobody ever turned us down.

———STU ZISMAN, Denver native

I was 6-years-old when I went into the Quarterback Club with my dad. I'd been attending Broncos games for two years by then. In those days, they had pictures all around the Club. There was one prominent spot on the wall that said, "Reserved for Broncos Super Bowl Pictures." I looked at my dad and said, "Dad, why are they saving that spot? The Broncos will never be in the Super Bowl." For my 21st birthday, I had the option of going to Las Vegas with my dad or going to the Broncos Super Bowl in Pasadena against the New York Giants. I picked the Broncos. When Denver finally won the big game, I was in Manchester, England. I was sent there to open the European operations for a big U.S. franchise. While I was there, I coached and played **LACROSSE**. Needless to say, I had a Super Bowl party at my apartment in Manchester. There were 18 English friends who showed up to watch the game, which started around 11 p.m. in the U.K. I served American tacos and lots of beer. We watched every play. Most of my friends had never watched an American football game, but they learned the game very quickly. By the end of the game, all of them were cheering and the partying went through the entire night. I think I converted all of them to being Broncos fans.

————*GREG BUTLER*, Coldwell Banker realtor

There I was, sitting in Seat 6, Row 30, Section 537, at INVESCO Field. It was my first NFL playoff experience. I went prepared. I had on my orange Jake Plummer jersey, my Broncos beanie cap, my Broncos coat and my son's Broncos backpack stuffed with munchies, hand warmers and football cards. The temperature was about 45 degrees and the sky was clear and full of bright stars. The fans around me were very energetic. To the right of me in Seat 5 was A-Train, a 4-foot-9, 100-pound, growing 10-year-old boy. A-Train was in his best Broncos gear. He had on his personalized, blue and orange, No. 81, Broncos jersey with the name A-Train in white block letters printed on the back. He was wearing Levi blue jeans and an orange and blue beanie cap. I asked A-Train, "Why did you choose number 81 to have on your jersey?" He replied, "Because it represents my birthday, August 1." I was impressed with his creativity. When the Broncos scored a touchdown or had a big play, A-Train

LACROSSE is the national sport of Canada...not hockey.

handed out high-fives with people all around him. A-Train acted like he was a friend with everyone. He told me that he once was voted "Fan of the Section" at a previous game when he dressed up in his football pads and had on his **JOHN LYNCH** jersey. The smell of nachos, pizza and hotdogs filled the air as vendors walked up and down the aisles selling their products. A-Train purchased a beverage in a souvenir cup and a personal pizza. I told A-Train about a vendor at Sun Devil Stadium in Tempe, Arizona, at an Arizona Cardinals game who would walk up and down the stadium selling red licorice. The vendor was at every game I attended, screaming, "Reeeeed licorice!" I would buy a licorice as long as he was selling it. I also shared with A-Train that I had been following Jake Plummer's career. I watched Jake when he played for Arizona State University and how he broke records at ASU in his senior year. He had an undefeated season and helped the Sun Devils to the **ROSE BOWL**. When Jake became a free agent and signed with the Broncos, I told A-train that I was really excited, because I believe Jake will take the Broncos back to the Super Bowl. The Broncos have been back in the playoffs three years in a row since Plummer has been the quarterback. In the last 30 seconds of the game, time stood still. Everything went into slow motion. I found myself hugging and jumping up and down with a complete stranger. I saw full cups of liquid refreshment and personalized pizzas thrown high into the mile high air. I heard fans screaming, cheering and crying. The smell of gunpowder filled the air from the launching of the fireworks. If I could measure the energy level from 1-to-10, it would have been a 12. During that last 30 seconds of the game a thought crossed my mind—playoff tickets $212.49, gas, food and lodging, $70, experiencing a playoff game with your first born son, A-Train, priceless.

——RICHARD GRAY, Colorado Christian University

JOHN LYNCH threw out the first pitch in the history of the Florida Marlins organization. The cap that Lynch wore that day is in the Baseball Hall of Fame in Cooperstown.

The Rose Bowl Parade originally had nothing to do with the **ROSE BOWL** football game. It was a celebration in Pasadena for the ripening of the oranges.

Jake Snakenberg

My 14-year-old son, Jake Snakenberg, died September 19, 2004, from a head injury he sustained in a freshman football game at Grandview High School in Aurora, Colorado. Our family was quite touched when at the visitation we noted a flower arrangement sent by Mike Shanahan, Pat Bowlen and the Broncos organization. At the visitation, a local artist, Jay Mason, who had done a number of portraits of professional athletes, approached us. He told us he had been commissioned by some of the Broncos players to do a portrait of Jake. Though I am not sure exactly which players were involved, Jay mentioned Nick Ferguson, Kelly Herndon and Dwayne Carswell—as well as Carmelo Anthony from the Denver Nuggets. Jay Mason made sure to have the beautiful portrait of Jake done by the next day so it could be displayed at Jake's funeral. The portrait is five-feet by about three-and-a-half-feet! Jake was an avid sports fan and would have been so incredibly proud that these professionals took the time and found it in their hearts to think of him and our family.

———KELLI JANTZ, Centennial, Colorado

My mother, a huge Broncos fan, had come to live with my husband and me in Southern California when she became very ill. The Thursday before her death in '91, she went into the hospital. Saturday night, the day before a Broncos-Raiders game, she told me she wanted to have something to wear so that people would know she was a Broncos fan. I offered her my Broncos earrings, but she turned them down. She said she wanted an orange hair ribbon so that there would be NO chance that anyone would think that she was a Raiders fan. Sunday morning, I went to the store to buy her hair ribbon. When I returned home, I was told that she had just passed away. So, to her dying day, she was a true Broncos fan.

———LESLEY BRADLEY, Payson, Arizona

every day. He was admitted to Hutchinson Hospital on October 19, 1997. He was still in the hospital when the Broncos went to the Super Bowl in 1998. They had given him Demerol during the third quarter, but I taped the game so he got to see the win later. He passed away March 11, 1998 at almost 38-years-old. I will always cherish these years and the joy that the Broncos brought to him. The Broncos won the Super Bowl in 1999 on my birthday.

——DOLORES KREHBIEL, Kingman, Kansas

When my brother and I were in grade school in the '70s, we both played **LITTLE LEAGUE** football. Our mother was the team mother. She wanted to make helmet lamps for the team to give away at our end of year banquet, along with the trophies and team coats. Back then, finding turf to line the bases of the helmet lamps wasn't that easy to get. So, late one night or early one morning, I remember being in our mom's car wondering what we were doing at the Broncos' training camp at that time of night. Well, I soon found out, because I was put to work soon after our arrival. She needed turf to line the helmet lamps, and the Broncos had plenty of it. We didn't break into anything, though. Outside the fenced area, surrounding the trees and edge of the sidewalk, was plenty of turf.

——STEVEN RAVER

My folks have had season tickets to the Broncos since 1990 when we moved to Colorado. I was 11, my brother was six. We had four tickets. We'd go as a family. One week, my mom couldn't go, so I took a friend. My dad got up to go to the restroom. In the time my dad was gone, my friend and I convinced my brother that he was adopted, and we'd brought him to the Broncos game to introduce him to his real family. They'd be taking him to his real house. He was traumatized for many years afterwards. He was crying his eyes out. He was crying so hard we had to leave the game early. Dad said he wouldn't take me to any more games, but he still took me. Everyone in our section was booing and screaming at me for acting that way. We still talk about it when we're together.

——LUKE STAHMER, Colorado Crush executive

> **More U.S. kids today play soccer than any other organized sport, including youth football. Perhaps, the reason so many kids play soccer is so they don't have to watch it.**

An empty cab pulled up
in front of Texas
Stadium and Terrell
Owens got out.

Flush twice—
it's a long way to
Oakland!

Chapter 4

Sweet Home Mile High

The Land of Ahs

WHAT'S THE DIFFERENCE BETWEEN GRASS AND ASTROTURF? I DON'T KNOW. I'VE NEVER SMOKED ASTROTURF.

MIKE FABIAN

With apologies to Tug McGraw...

Mike Fabian, was born five miles from Mile High Stadium. He is currently working on a Masters Degree in Counseling Psychology and is self-employed running an outpatient mental-health agency with his wife, a licensed therapist.

After obsessing over the pending destruction of the great Mile High Stadium, I convinced my wife that I desperately wanted a pair of stadium seats from Mile High for my birthday. For $200, she thought I was crazy. But, I stood my ground, and after waiting way too long in line, I had my orange pair of seats. Then, after 9/11, I heard that firefighters were going to be selling pieces of the turf from Mile High, with funds going to benefit local service providers. I knew I had to jump at this opportunity to have my living piece of NFL and Denver history. So, I hopped in my car and drove down to the soon-to-be-scrap East Stands and waited in line—again too long—to buy my rolls of green love.

I had recently built a wonderful raised vegetable bed in our backyard for my wife's veggies and flowers. She's a psycho gardener. I wasn't sure what to do with a living substance that somewhere carried Elway's and Morton's DNA from sweat inside itself, but I knew the chain of custody had to be maintained—it was not to be cross-contaminated by any other lesser turf. So, I plopped my 10-square feet right in my wife's new veggie garden, which was recently tilled and ready for the next growing season. Gosh, I built the bed, so I should get a say on its use! Anyway, she wasn't too happy, but again, I "held my turf." I have wonderful photos of the freshly cut pieces of history being watered, taken through my kitchen window, with my dated certificate of authenticity in the foreground. That was 2001.

I developed a ritual of maintenance of the green love that evolved into a personal requirement that the holy green carpet was to be mowed and watered no later than 24 hours prior to an upcoming game. This was sometimes an arduous task, as it required removal of protective fencing and lifting the mower up about 18 inches to get up into the raised bed. Sometime I would get home from work later in the evening and have to mow in the dark. My wife, who is a therapist, thought I had finally snapped. This, combined with my desire to keep the stadium chairs in the kitchen, left her sort of numb. Additionally, the neighbors would come over to prove to each other that they weren't making up stories about ol' Mike down the street, who mows his "Broncos Grass" in the dark.

This year, our family decided that we needed to move. Our kids were getting bigger and the house seemed smaller. The real estate market being what it is, when we got a good offer, we needed to move fast. There was seven years of crap that needed to be put in storage until we found our new home. We were living in an apartment at the time. There was a great deal of stress in my marriage at the time, and I needed to focus on calm, rational behavior and a smooth transition. So, the morning of closing had come, and my precious living history still sat in the veggie bed, alone and cold under a blanket of snow and leaves. I knew that if I was the true fan I thought I was, I had to act. I could not visualize myself, in the years to come, saying, "Yeah, I use to have that. Yep, it was real. Wanna see a picture?" I had to act, now. Closing was at noon. At 10 a.m., armed with my trusty sod knife from college landscaping jobs, I skulked into my now-empty backyard with a whole bunch of plastic bags and surgically removed about two square feet of the green love. I have before and after pictures of the surgery on that sad day, somehow hoping the green Mile High turf would bleed orange when I cut into it. After closing, I spirited the last remaining piece of my loving care back to the apartment to an awaiting orange metal tub I found at a local store. With the best potting soil installed, I placed my traumatized bit of history in its new home. It thrived, and so did my Broncos. If it were not for the lack of focus that day against Pittsburgh, we would have been celebrating a third Super Bowl victory over the lame **SEATTLE** Seabirds in 2006. I might have even splashed a bit of bubbly on my little green friend that day, had we won.

Now, we're in our new home. The stadium chairs are safe and warm in the landing of the stairs, awaiting a framed photo montage I have of Mile High's last days. I have about 50 pictures of the last days and a bunch of newspaper clippings. Anyway, the bit of living history is still alive and well on my new deck, in its orange tub. It struggled a bit, but it decided to come back for this new season. Early on, the turf got a bit long and partially went to seed, and I collected those seed stalks. I still have them in a sealed bag, as a permanent genetic record. I have some friends, special friends, who I let come over and touch the turf and sit in the chairs. I haven't been by my old house so see if the new owners left the turf intact or not. I'm too afraid to look over that fence. I did, however, leave my hand-painted sign identifying the date and place of origin of this grand living testament to the best football town in the country. If some transplanted Raiders fan moved into the house, at least they would know they were ripping up a small piece of NFL history—a price they would have to pay for upon their arrival at the pearly gates. Just like a seashell on the beach, if you put your ear to the grass, you can still hear the roar of the crowd from old Mile High, and if you sit in those chairs, you can still feel the rumble of those old metal plates thundering with the stomps of 76,000 fans.

> During the **SEATTLE** Mariners first year in 1977, they measured the distance to the fences in fathoms. A fathom is 6 feet. For instance, where a park may have a sign that denotes 360 feet, the Kingdome would have the number 60.

BRONCOS FEVER? NO CURE

JAY HOCKING

Jay "Hatman" Hocking, 52, lives in Pueblo, Colorado, and has had season tickets to the Broncos games for 20 years.

They call me "Hatman Jay." That goes back many, many years when my wife and I started going to games in the South Stands and met some of the best people in the world. The South Stands had a bad reputation. The South Stands were the heart and soul of the stadium and of the team. The cheers started there. The reaction to the plays started there. Some people thought we went overboard. I've been going to games since the tickets were less than $15. The reputation of the South Stands was so bad, and I think undeserved. I worked for the local newspaper then, delivering to carriers out of town. The wife of one of my co-workers knitted top hats. She knitted an orange top hat for me and it was a big hit. People would try to grab my hat and someone would grab it and give it back to me. It was a big family in the South Stands. The South Stands did not deserve the reputation they had. In an attempt to clean up the South Stands, I worked to obtain a tuxedo to wear to the games. I live 100 miles south of Denver, so finding a tux was hard. I went to every tux rental place I could looking for an orange tux. I ended up with a white one, threw it in the bathtub with orange dye. To this day, we have little orange dots in our bathtub, but the orange dye did not take to the tux! It was blotchy. I had to have a tux made. To this day, Vivian Hall, my seamstress, has made many, many tuxes. One is in the **HALL OF FAME IN CANTON**. The NFL is the only

> **Marion Motley, Alan Page and Dan Dierdorf are all CANTON natives and are enshrined in the Pro Football HALL OF FAME in their hometown. Page worked on a construction crew that built the Hall while Dierdorf and his father attended the groundbreaking ceremony.**

sports organization that recognizes its fans in their Hall of Fame. One of my tuxes is in the Hall of Fans there. I was in Barrel Man's wedding in my tux. The tux has not missed a game in 20 plus years.

I helped build the reputation of the South Stands. Anything that was close, we let the refs know what was going on. Another vivid memory is the last game at Mile High Stadium. It was on national TV how the South Stands had gotten wild and crazy and demolished the place. What we were doing was taking a piece of history with us. It was going to the trash anyhow. It was just the covers off the bleachers! I have an eight-foot piece of the South Stands. It was like home for 15 years. I had my eight-foot piece of the South Stands and the usher, William—"Don't call me Bill"—just winked at me as I headed out the gate. I'm at the gate and I'm stuck. I turn around and a policeman had hold of the other end of my bench.

I've gone to games for so long, and I have worn a tux to the games for so long, that I am very recognizable. It's like it's my job to get cheers going in the stands. I'm always trying to get the fans fired up and get them going. The magnitude of the game determines what the fans bring to the game and how excited they get. For the big games, they come fired up and ready. One of the biggest things we do is tailgate. It's gotten out of hand even. We had 300 people tailgating with us at the end of last year. I've gone to two Super Bowls—XXXII and XXXIII. My wife Valerie and I, it was like we were out of our minds. We packed up a little trailer that I had built with a mounted grill and a stereo mounted in it. We left at nine at night and drove all night. We got in to San Diego at noon. We went to the stadium and drove through the parking lot. It was on a Wednesday. People were already there. We had our car all decorated for the Broncos and our orange and blue trailer. "Good Morning America" was there with Emeril Lagasse. They asked us to park there and to participate in Emeril's Super Bowl party on "Good Morning America." They had gone out and bought tables, grills, meat, everything. Emeril was doing a Green Bay dish, and Colorado Beef for the Broncos. It must have been 12-inches square. BAM! He was throwing spices all over. When they were done, they gave us the food! We fed a bunch of people with the food from the show. On the way back from the Super Bowl, the trailer crashed! The axle spun around underneath.

We start every season with Tailgating Training Camp. We go up to Greeley. After that Super Bowl, I had to build a new trailer. Stereo, amplifiers, four batteries. It's a little bigger than what you would pull behind a motorcycle. I have a $1,000 grill on it. We built the shell and put the grill on the back. Throughout the season I added more and more stuff. By the end of the season, it was ready to go to Miami for Super Bowl XXXIII.

I have a small pickup with a solid camper shell with a large Broncos logo on the side. I pull the trailer with it. I put a container on top of the truck with two 25-foot telescoping flagpoles. We fly the American Flag, the POW flag, and the Hall of Fame and Broncos flags.

We go to Canton every year for the Hall of Fame festivities. It's the first game of the year. We get together with all the Hall of Fame Freak Fans. I call it the Freak Club. We usually open the trailer, fire up the grill, and they all show up. We all stay in the same hotel in Akron. They even gave us a hospitality room last year so we wouldn't be outside making too much noise. The Green Bay fan wanted to take the trailer into the hospitality room. We tried, and we saw the police and fire department. They had evacuated the entire hotel after the fire alarms went off. The fire department asked why we were still in there. Our gas-powered blender had set off the fire alarms. Lady Titan was there, and when the firemen walked in, she yelled, "The strippers are here!"

I've met a few players, because of the tux. I met Bill Romanowski after a game, and he signed the first tux that I ever had. It had a logo of the horse on the back. That tux ended up in Canton in the Hall of Fame. Unfortunately, Romanowski is now a retired Raider! Whenever I come across a player, I ask him to autograph the bottom half of the tux. All of the tuxes, except the newest one, are covered with autographs. The night John Elway retired, we had a banner that read, "What do you think of that? Thanks John." That was reflective of what the stadium used to put up on the message board after some of the plays—"South Stands, what do you think of that?" The whole preseason we had the banner in the parking lot and hundreds of people signed it. We rolled it up and gave it to Elway. He signed my tux, the first and only time I wore it.

BINGO, I MUST BE IN THE FRONT ROW

STEVE KELLEY

Steve Kelley is anchor of "Good Morning Colorado" on FOX 31. Prior to joining the FOX station, he was the morning DJ at Newsradio 850 KOA. During his 19 years at KOA, Kelley won numerous awards, including the Marconi in 1999. He also worked at KIMN Radio. He is originally from Flint, Michigan, but has called Colorado home for the past 26 years.

Each region of the country had its popular rock station—KRFC in 'Frisco, WLS in Chicago—you pick the city, and there was one big station. In Denver, KIMN was the big station everyone listened to.

Back in the '50s, there was a guy, Pogo Pogue, who did some unusual stunts. He lived in a store-front full of snakes for a 24-hour period. He sat on a pole out at a drive-in theater and lived up on the pole. He also pogo-sticked from Boulder to Denver on an air-powered pogo stick. I didn't realize it was powered, because I recreated the same stunt 50 years later, except I did it on a real pogo stick. There were only a few listeners at the time who said, "You know, his was a gas-powered pogo stick." All of this history with KIMN basically required me to live up to some standards of disc jockeys from the past. I wanted to do something in a very competitive business—very competitive market—to set myself apart.

We were trying to come up with something that might be fun, marathon-like and unique. We just couldn't come up with anything. We thought about roller skating around the state, walking across the state, just something weird where we could raise money for charity.

I was talking to the general manager, Steve Keeney, who is very inventive and creative, and loves to go outside the box. He said he'd gotten a letter from somebody who wrote, "Wouldn't it be interesting to take a skateboard and roll on the bleachers at Mile High Stadium to see what that would be like." All of a sudden, a light went off, and I said, "Hey, I could sit in every seat at Mile High Stadium. That would be fun." But there were items to discuss…one, I had no clue as to how many seats there were at the time; two, how long it would take; and three, logistically, how difficult it would be to pull off, getting through that gauntlet of bureaucracy. Despite those questions, we pursued it.

I thought we could tie it in with a charity, and around the same time in '81, one of my very favorite uncles, Uncle Roy, had just passed away from lung cancer. I wanted to do something for my Uncle Roy. We approached the city, which owned the venue at the time. We had to get the OK from the city. A guy named Joe Choncho, for some reason, took a liking to me. He thought it was just bizarre enough that it would be cute, so he allowed me to do it.

There were 75,123 seats. It looked like it was going to be an easy task, but it wasn't. Far from it. I started in the South Stands, and by the time I had completed 15,000 seats, I could not sit up without extreme pain. I was sitting up and down in each seat. I was dead. My knees were swollen. I looked out at this vast horseshoe before me, knowing I still had some 60,000 seats to go, and I just wanted to give up. I had only finished the South Stands and looked up seeing the rest of this mammoth stadium staring at me when I thought, what have I gotten myself into? It was really fascinating when it happened. People started calling and pledging money for seats and for hours and that type of thing. I started focusing not on myself, but on Uncle Roy, and that carried me on.

We did it in October '81. October in Colorado can give you a little bit of everything. You can have almost 90 degrees and then two blinding snowstorms. I got sleet, rain, snow and sun. It was just amazing. I didn't realize that to do it at night would cost the city a ton of money just to turn on a bank of lights. Initially, they refused to turn on the lights.

At the station, they'd play records and take a break to see "how Steve is doing" out there at Mile High. I'd say, "I'm in section whatever. Blah, blah, blah." I had no idea how difficult it was going to be. All of a sudden, here we were, raising about $8,000, which was a lot of money. Then, a snowstorm hit, and people really started feeling sorry for me, because I was not going to give up. My wife says I have a big heart and a little brain. And, I'm stubborn. I thought, I'm doing this darn thing for my uncle, and I don't care what it takes. I'm going to sit in every one of these seats if it kills me. I think I slept for 11 hours out of four days. I was fairly young—21-years-old—at the time. I literally slept where I stopped. I'd get an hour rest and then I'd keep going along. I put on any number of different things to try to cover up the skin that was being exposed. I went through a pair of jeans in about an hour. We took Ace bandages, and we had Vaseline, and my crotch was raw. Finally, the thing that worked—somebody called in and said I should wear a real tight pair of nylon pantyhose. I don't know how pantyhose work, but darned if they didn't work. You know, after you go through surgery, they give you these things to help you.

I got a lot of suggestions trying to help, and it was really neat how the community came together. People hooked into this combination of Mile High Stadium, this landmark that is so identifiable with the Rocky Mountains, and this guy who was trying to do something for his uncle. We had one telephone line. Subsequent to this, by the way, I had done a number of marathon stunts, and it really developed into something almost like a telethon where we had a bank of phones—10 or 15, and had various charities manning the phones while I would do something weird, like crawling. I started crawling at the stadium on a Monday morning after a Sunday night game at the stadium. The change people lose at a football game is fascinating. I made about $37 just from change that had spilled out of people's pockets, getting beer or whatever. I crawled 17 miles, pogo-sticked from Boulder to Denver, washed 10,000 windows, swam 100 miles at Sloans Lake and did these various things, but it all started with the Mile High Stadium seats. I'd intended to do only that, but, when that was over, a guy named Ed Sardella, the TV anchor at Channel 9, said in an interview after I had finished, "So, what are you going to do next?" It was really amazing to raise $30,000 for the American Cancer Society using just one phone line!

They brought different people—cheerleaders and bands and enter-tainers—just to keep me awake. At 3 a.m., in pitch dark, it gets pretty lonely. Until the very last night, the city wouldn't light it up because it was just too expensive. Then, people started saying "Hey, we want to come by and watch the guy. They were peering through the fence as best they could. They actually then turned the bank of lights on, and the whole parking lot was full of people cheering me on. It was really cool. At the end, they had this "hot tub" in the Broncos locker room. Players, after a game, would go in there and soak in the tub. I didn't realize it, but they had filled it with ice water. That's by design because the doctor said we had to keep swelling down. My thighs and butt were awful—black, blue and green. Imagine 76,000 repetitions of anything. It's very difficult for people to understand how much that is. It was pretty daunting, actually, and, looking back on it, I was real proud to have accomplished it.

That first time, shortly after I had completed the South Stands, I thought, This is insane—nobody should do this. I just kept going. Out of embarrassment, I just couldn't quit. At night it was particularly lonely and difficult because it's pitch black. You're sitting there with no or very few people. You're just going along these seats, and you can't cheat because people have made pledges by seat or by hours. You just have to do it.

I cannot remember the number of the first seat I sat in. I do know it was in the South Stands and it had to be the first bleacher on the east side of the South Stands. The last seat I will never forget, but I can't remember the number of it. In fact, a few years ago, they gave me that seat I finished in, and then they gave me one of the new seats from INVESCO Field as a souvenir.

The city had a "Steve Kelley Day" in October a few years ago. The mayor did a proclamation for me. In recognition, they gave me one of the old seats, which was cool, and they gave me one of the new one, but I never picked them up. There at the recognition ceremony, we couldn't fit them in the car, so I said "I'll get them at some point," and they're keeping them for me. They're setting somewhere.

The best seat in the house truly was the Governor's seat, which is on the east side on the second deck. I remember looking from there and saying to myself, "This is the best seat in the house right here."

Because of that original stunt, I thought it only appropriate that, when they built this new one, I should repeat the feat. I did that in September '01. Interestingly enough, the new stadium only had two more seats than the old, 76,125. They have more in terms of the sky boxes, suites, etc.

The original time took four days with 11 hours total sleep. Keep in mind that I was young. This last one took me five days, and I probably slept a total of 20 hours. You just have to keep going. You have to pace yourself and you have to complete so many if you're going to do it. The irony of the second one, when I did it at INVESCO Field is I didn't know if I could do it at the age of 44; but I was able to pull it off, even though it was a lot more work because I was much older.

I started on September 4, 2001, and finished on September 9, 2001, which was a Sunday. I finished on a Sunday night and **MONDAY NIGHT FOOTBALL** was the very next night at the new INVESCO Field in Mile High, the game where Ed McCaffrey broke his leg. It was a big deal. The very next morning that would have been the big news of the morning while I was recovering. We raised almost $250,000 the second time around, again for the American Cancer Society.

The age factor was really difficult, but the stubbornness factor was still there! I finished effectively on September 9, and then September 10 was the football game, and then there was September 11, 2001—**9/11**.

> **John Lennon's death was first reported to the nation by Howard Cosell on MONDAY NIGHT FOOTBALL...In 1999, Monday Night Football became the longest-running prime-time entertainment series ever, breaking a tie with Walt Disney at 29 years...Even when Monday Night Football ratings hit an all-time low, it still ranks in the top five during prime time for the entire year.**

> **When former Olympic gold medal figure skater Peggy Fleming was stranded in New York following the SEPTEMBER 11TH attacks, she hitched a ride to her San Francisco home with John Madden on the Madden Cruiser, the custom bus that Madden uses because of his fear of flying. They are neighbors in the Bay area.**

It was an emotional picture that people could see through the radio. They caught a glimpse of it, and they really were captivated by it. It really launched my career. I've been here in Denver now for 30 years and have subsequently moved to television. Over the next few years, I did a number of other fundraising stunts, but Mile High Stadium was the one people always remember, saying, "You're the guy who sat in every seat in Mile High!"

I did the 17,000 seats in the old McNichols Arena, which they have torn down, as well. I did that a year or two later, just for fun. That wasn't difficult at all; in fact, it was kind of a joke. They had padded seats, but they had arms on them, which made it a little more diffi-cult....It was almost like I was the emcee of Mile High Stadium. I started doing player introductions and on-field check presentations and kicking contests all throughout the entire John Elway era. There was a time when the old stadium was sitting right next to the new stadium, side-by-side, as it was being built. It was very interest-ing—this old icon of Denver, this jewel, Mile High Stadium, that emotionally people were tied to, and then, this big new flying saucer looking thing which was INVESCO Field at Mile High, this new cor-porate thing.

I've had calls from other cities asking about what I had done, but I'm almost positive it hasn't happened elsewhere. It had gotten a lot of press and brought me a lot of publicity. Selfishly, that was the origi-nal intent. It was like "What can I do to really set myself apart and gain recognition and promotion for the radio station?" But, it turned into something much bigger than I had ever dreamed of. It revealed in me my human weakness and overcoming that for the sake of some-body who had suffered from cancer. It was an epiphany for me, almost at a spiritual level. Once you take your eyes off yourself and your own pain and you start focusing on somebody other than your-self, and you have a greater purpose or a greater cause, even though it's crazy, you can do anything. It was a unique, almost like marathoners get a runner's high, overcoming something like that. Every time I would drive by Mile High Stadium, or go in and look around, I'd think "I accomplished this."

Disc jockeys from around the country would call me. It was almost like a flip type of a thing, like "Hey man, how'd you do that? Give me the secrets? What did you do there? What did it take you—10 hours or something?" I would say "You don't have a clue what you're in for. You don't have any idea what you're trying to do. You're trying to do this for the wrong reason, and you won't be able to do it."

At the time I did it, there was no CNN, no cable, nothing. There was just ABC, **NBC** and CBS, and that was it. It got some national attention—I think ABC covered it through their local affiliate at the time. In a way, it was nothing, but for me, it was a launching pad to almost have a unique identity in this city….

I once punted a football around the entire perimeter of the city—85 miles. Mike Horan, a punter for the Broncos, actually trained me—taught me how to punt. He came out to help me as I would go around the city punting this football. Mike Horan had a charity called "Punt for the Purpose," which helps homeless families gain independence and self sufficiency so I did that for him. It started at halftime at Mile High Stadium. I punted out of Mile High and started the whole 85-mile trek. That was unique because I had sons, aged 4 and 5, and they were out there with me as I started this trek. I nailed that first punt. It was great. It went about 55 yards. Mike had really taught me how to kick. I have a lot of lower body strength, and I guess I kicked with that. This was strenuous—kicking and walking the 85 miles.

I always tried to make these things unique, just on the edge of craziness, but always fun for people. Like, "What's he doing now?" What's he up to now?" Like George Plimpton. I actually got to meet him. He did a similar thing in a large-scale, more sophisticated way, when he did *The Paper Lion* and he played quarterback for the Detroit Lions. He did various things, and I thought it was really unique in what he did. He played goalie for the New York Rangers,

> **NBC** Sports President, Dick Ebersol, recently paid $50,000 at a charity auction to have Carly Simon tell him the name of the subject person in her song, "You're So Vain." Only Simon, Ebersol and that person know the identity, rumored to be Warren Beatty, James Taylor or Mick Jagger.

boxed Archie Moore and played at **YANKEE STADIUM**. We are sort of kindred spirits, but he on a national scale, and I was just a local guy doing stuff for a good cause, for some publicity. It became sort of a mission for me. Who am I going to help this year, and what am I going to do? The radio station benefited from it. I benefited from it. And, the charities benefited from it. But now, I'm too old and can't do this stuff anymore.

Thomas Edison sold the concrete to the Yankees that was used to build <u>YANKEE STADIUM.</u> Edison owned the huge Portland Cement Company....Edison's middle name was Alva, named after the father of one-time Cleveland Indians owner, Alva Bradley.

SHE'S SO PRETTY SHE'D BRING A TEAR TO A GLASS EYE

RENEE HERLOCKER

Renee Herlocker, 25, was a Broncos Cheerleader from 2000-2006. With brown eyes and brown hair, Renee can be found modeling on the pages of national magazines. She is currently the marketing associate with TIVIS Ventures as well as Sports Shares.

I come from a huge football family. We've had season tickets since 1963. South Standers in the old Mile High. Back in 1968-69, my mom was one of the original members of the Broncettes, the original Broncos cheerleaders. Later, they were called the Pony Express, then the Denver Broncos Cheerleaders. My mom was still in high school when she was a Broncos Cheerleader. She was knocked out by Floyd Little in a game. He picked her up off the ground, patted her on the back, and headed back to the field.

I was 18 and had gone to the University of Northern Colorado and made the dance team. I missed Denver, so I moved back home. I started coaching at Overland High School—their Varsity Pom coach. I wanted to learn the choreography. I'd never been on a professional audition. I had a short little haircut, did my dance resume, went out and did my thing. You see all the girls who have been on the team previously. A bit of an intimidation factor. You get to know them later and don't know why you are intimidated. Tryouts are just a two-day process. First day is the basics, and if you make the finals, you come back the second day for an interview. I think I was fortunate, a fresh face. I made it my first year trying out. Teresa Shear, the director, would call your number and name, and you'd run out to the middle of the field. Now everyone just stays in line. I remember being No. 5 that year. They called me second. I was in shock. People were pushing me year. They called me second. I was in shock. People were pushing me out onto the field when I was selected. The first person I called was my mom. My dad was being all shy on the phone and all quiet.

My first game as a cheerleader was at Mile High. It had such energy. We needed INVESCO Field, but Mile High had the energy. We have to be at the game four hours before game time, and we carpooled to the first game. We had one big room for all of us to sit in. It was like an old room with fake grass, and one bathroom for 26 girls. I can remember crying during the **NATIONAL ANTHEM** that first game. I was thinking about my grandparents who had passed away, wishing they could have seen me there.

Rookie year, there are lots of embarrassing moments. Falling in front of 76,000 people, mid-dance, builds character. Sometimes it's the little things. On September 10, 2001, I was to lead the team out for the National Anthem. I led the team to the wrong place on the field. I had to snake back and pretend everything was cool. Embarrassing is not really the right term. Funny is better. Funny is when we are in our snow suits. There is not a lot of give in the suits. Needless to say, you still are in cowboy boots. The grass is slick. You want to look good, but you have to be careful. If you fall, you fall....

My rookie year, in the first preseason game, it was 120 degrees on the field. We were doing a pregame routine to "Surfing USA." Each group had a surfer. They raised me up on a boogie board where I had to "surf." Two minutes before pregame started, one of the girls who was to hold me up got heat stroke. She was sick. She was weak and had trouble lifting me up. The boogie board started to teeter. I started to go down, and I grabbed her head on the way down. It was forever a huge joke. I almost ate it on a surfboard in my first cheerleading appearance....

Last April, right after auditions, three of us got to go to Walter Reed Hospital in Washington, D.C. Jake Plummer and John Lynch went with us. The soldiers had just arrived in the U.S. from Iraq and

Before Super Bowl XI, there was no **NATIONAL ANTHEM**. Vikki Carr sang *America The Beautiful*.

Afghanistan. That experience was so humbling. One of the guys I met there was having major surgery on his legs and hips. He had over 18 surgeries. When I was picked to go to the Pro Bowl, he had also been picked to go out there and we saw each other there, too. We went room to room at the hospital and listened to their stories. To put a face with those stories is very interesting and makes it personal. It's hard to look them in the eye, knowing they are in pain. I remember being in one of the rehabilitation rooms, and I was talking to a soldier and his wife. I could hear someone on a treadmill. It kept going faster and faster. I looked back and the soldier on it was sprinting—with two prosthetic legs! I can't even run a mile without complaining. I wanted to know what drove him to do this. He said it was painful and he wanted to rehabilitate so he could go back and fight with his brothers. Makes you think about your own life and how trivial things can be....

We went to promote the NFL Mexico in Mexico City. The Eagles played the Patriots. We flew into Mexico City and did mall signings. We went to these malls. Fans were everywhere. We were in these vans, mobs of people shaking the vans. We had to have man-made barricades to escort us to our cars. You'd have thought we were the President or something. It was kind of scary at times. I never thought something like that would happen to me. Who wants my autograph? It was crazy....

Tommy Maddox:
The promise of a lover, the performance of a husband.

IT'S A HARD WAY TO MAKE AN EASY LIVING

CHRIS VALENTI

Chris Valenti, a native of Golden, has worked for the Broncos for 10 years in the Equipment Department, the last three as Equipment Manager. He understands the value of preparation, planning, and the needs of professional athletes.

The **SUPERSTITIONS** we see with players are usually with their routines. They have to do with what music they listen to, who helps them get their equipment on, and what time they do all those things. I know that Bill Romanowski used to listen to John Denver before the games, which is surprising. A typical game day for me means arriving at the stadium six hours before game time. We put the jerseys out onto pads. Over half of the players use double-sided tape on their pads to keep their jerseys down. It's a two-person project to put the jerseys on the pads. We have to turn the jerseys inside-out, put the tape on the pads, then put the jerseys on the pads. Once you do that, it takes a second person to get the pads and jersey on the players. We put all the jerseys where they need to go in the lockers, names out, programs in place, everything the way the players want it. There are three of us to help get players into their equipment. Three of us for 45 players on game day, 53 total on the roster. About half need help getting into their pads. The players come to us when they're ready.

I usually get a letter from the "uniform police" regarding any uniform violations. A player can get fined for that. The majority of the

> **SUPERSTITIOUS** ex-Denver Broncos player Terrell Davis demanded that the name tag above his locker always read "Joe Abdullah," and Broncos center Tom Nalen won't wash his practice gear during the year because he feels that he's giving the equipment "natural seasoning" to shield "evil spirits."

pregame violations have to do with the players' socks. They have to be pulled up and they often leave them down. Other problems are untucked jerseys and pants not hitting the socks in the right place. The rules are set by the NFL and they are strict.

Reebok supplies all the teams. When I started, there were four licensee companies involved. In 2001, Reebok took over the entire league. They created Onfield Apparel to supply the clothing. All of the team owners are partners in Onfield Apparel. It covers uniforms, outerwear, performance wear and more. Shoes are still player by player—Reebok, Nike, **adidas** or Under Armour.

It's hard to balance between too much equipment that impedes their performance and not enough to be protective. Ed McCaffrey wore the oldest set of shoulder pads. They looked like a kid's set. They weren't what we wanted him to wear, but it was what he was comfortable with. He didn't like extra weight. He'd trim out all the extra weight. On the game jerseys, the numbers are sewn on, and he'd take out the mesh they were sewn too on the inside of the jerseys to reduce the weight. He took out inside layers of materials on the pants. He figured the reduced weight made him faster. He was big in the trend of cutting Xs in the front of his shoes. He'd wear a smaller size shoe and cut an X over his big toe. Those shoes would last three games, max. Some guys wear a new pair every game. Some guys, like Tom Nalen, wear Matt Lepsis' shoes from the previous year. He likes them broken in and wears them all year. Last year we had to glue new cleats on the shoes, because he wore them out. He doesn't like new shoes at all.

Champ Bailey has chrome plates on the bottom of his shoes. He picks which color he wants based on his mood on game day.

My first year was the first year with the new uniforms. The backlash was done before I got here. Everyone was used to them by the time I got here in June 1997. I love the new logo. Throwback jerseys are always fun. We used to do them on Thanksgiving. It was a chore for

> **adidas is named after its founder, Adi Dassler. adidas is never capitalized. Dassler's brother started the Puma shoe company…A Nittany lion, a cougar, and a puma are the same animal.**

us. We had to change everything. Some teams would just change the jersey. Our uniform change was drastic enough that we had to change everything from undergear to helmets and socks. Helmets are the biggest chore. The players need to wear the throwback helmet in practice to break it in, and that didn't happen much. It takes a couple of weeks to break in a helmet.

Quarterbacks first got headsets in their helmets in the early '90s. Plays come in from the sidelines. It's against the rules to communicate with the quarterback from the booth. Using the headsets speeds up the game. The communication is encrypted so no one can listen in. Technical difficulties happen a few times a year, but there's no real backup plan. If they have a problem, then they send players in with the play or have the QB come over to the sideline. It can usually be fixed for the next series of plays. The majority of the issues come from other frequencies bleeding into the quarterback's receiver from the marketing or catering radios.

Training camp is always fun with the rookies. Players stay in the dorms and hassle the rookies. Flour and syrup poured on sleeping rookies is common. Rookies also have to provide breakfast for the veterans on Fridays during the regular season. Breakfast is already provided, so it's above and beyond. One rookie forgot two weeks in a row. They drove his Lincoln Navigator onto the hill behind the practice field and left the radio and lights on with the doors open. He couldn't leave practice to do anything about it, so the battery finally died. He brought breakfast the next week, of course. The team provides breakfast and lunch for the players all week, and dinner, as well, for the coaches Monday through Wednesday. The coaches typically work 15- to 18-hour days. Coordinators seem to have the most to do.

UPON FURTHER REVIEW

Every time they kicked an extra point, there'd be a fight in the South Stands, and the police would come and usher off the six or eight guys who were fighting. Five minutes later, because half those fans were drunk, they'd grab another group. They'd be kicked out for the rest of the game, but they'd probably come back next game and start over again. For one game, my cousin and I went all the way to the top of the South Stands—56 rows up. This guy was sitting up there. He had a beer, and he looked at how far it was down the stairs, and decided there was no way he would be able to make it down there in time to get to the bathroom. He just whipped out a cup, urinated in it and threw it over the side of the stadium. My cousin got up and started running down the stairs. I asked him what happened and he told me. You couldn't do that today, because the stadiums are sold out, but in those days, there was nobody there to monitor it. The announcers used to talk about the fans in the South Stands being the noisiest fans in pro football. There were only 15,000 people who would sit in those stands, but because the stands were made of metal, if you stomped your feet, you could generate an ungodly noise. We used to do that all the time, and we took great pride in how much noise we could generate. It was very, very noisy. We were trying to disrupt the timing of the visiting quarterbacks. Sometimes it would work. I think the "South Stands" evolved because of the nature of the composition of the stands where you could generate that noise. Because we were in a pit, the acoustics were perfect for amplifying all that noise we'd be making.

——STU ZISMAN, University of Northern Colorado professor

I remember being at a Divisional Playoff Game at Mile High Stadium in 1992 when the Broncos played the Oilers. There was so much excitement in the stands when Elway scrambled for a first down on a last chance fourth down play, and then again when he passed to Vance Johnson on the left sideline to get another clutch first down. I tried to listen to Larry Zimmer in one ear and pay attention to the sounds of the game in the other. As we attempted the field goal, the whole stadium became hushed, as did Larry over the air.

Fellow fans around me clutched each other and clenched their fists in anticipation. It was a moment full of energy, hope and passion after we drove down the field for a chance to win, and then it was a moment of anxious anticipation. I remember thinking that as hard as it was to be a high school freshman, it had to be a lot easier than being a field goal kicker in this kind of pressure cooker. As the football sailed slowly through the uprights, the hush turned to a roar, and I heard Zimmer's unsure voice: "It's.............................GOOD!" It seemed like a lapse of 10 years between those words, one of hesitation and the other of utmost confidence. We could all breathe again once they were uttered. Fans all around me gave high-fives. The guy next to me gave me a hug and picked me up while everyone pounded the seats and stomped the steel stadium aisles making the deafening sound of Rocky Mountain Thunder. Only Mile High carried this unique sound and this magic. The best part of a victory was walking out down the ramps with everyone chanting, cheering, pumping their fists, singing "HEY" and making some more thunder. It always gave me tingles. It was a special place that brought thousands of people together to share in the love of a team and a game seeming to exist in an almost alter reality, if only for a few hours.

——CINDY FLETCHER, 30

Fans don't seem to cheer as much now. I guess it's because there is too much corporate seating and not as many dedicated fans. They are there for the winning seasons, but not when the team is down. I'm there regardless. Mile High used to be just plain loud. People cheered all the time. People watched the games intensely and really got into the action. I can remember a game versus the Pittsburgh Steelers. It was so loud my ears were ringing when I left. It was that way more often than  not. The new stadium seems quiet. The Patriots game in 2005 is the only time it has seemed loud at the new stadium. There has always been a sense of community at the games, but not as much in the new stadium as in Mile High. A lot of the community has moved to the local bars on Sunday afternoons. There are still die-hard fans out there. I enjoy the passion of the visiting fans, too. They are the most passionate of fans, as they've made the trip.

——JAMES CANTOR, moved to Denver in 1981

I started my Masters program at the University of Colorado in 1976. I was ready to finish my program with a video program since that was my course of study. I wanted to get much closer to the Broncos. In talking to my advisor, we thought that if I could get on the field, I could really make a special presentation. I wrote a letter to Bob Peck, the Broncos' Director of Public Relations. I met with Mr. Peck at their old headquarters. He was terminally ill with cancer then, which I didn't know at the time. I sat with Mr. Peck and chatted about football and my education. He thought it was a terrific idea. I left the office knowing I had secured passes to take pictures from the sideline. I took my 35mm camera, and showing my pass to get in with the media was a thrill. To be on the sidelines and see the intensity of what was going on the sidelines—amazing! The language was such that you couldn't repeat it many places. The players really taunted each other. I was on the sidelines for four games. The players were very intense. The second game I was on the sidelines for was against the Cardinals. I learned how to follow the press corps. Terry Metcalf broke from his slot position and you could see how the play was going to unfold. It looked like he would get the ball. That was the first test for the Broncos that season. Terry was hit by Joe Rizzo, and was hit hard. Watching the defensive players cover the field was exciting. Rubin Carter was part of that defensive team as well.

——JOHN POLLICE

We owned a bar and put a quarter from every beer we sold into buying tickets in the early days. I always told my husband that if we didn't save enough from the bar for Broncos tickets, we have to forgo the house payment to be sure we had our tickets. Our tickets were in Section 517 at Mile High. We could go down and visit with fans on the other levels of the stadium. We can't do that in the new stadium, which is disappointing. The people in front of us had their tickets for a year longer than us, and we used to share champagne with them when the Broncos won. Mile High was a very friendly crowd. There was a sense of community in Mile High Stadium in the early days. We always got to know the people around us, and we saw them at every game. There were no rowdy people and no one caused any real trouble. Once in a while there were some problems. One game versus the Raiders we saw someone fall off the deck to the next deck lower. We could bring food into the early games and everyone always shared with each other. Later, when we moved to another section, we noticed that we had different people around us at each game. It wasn't quite the same atmosphere when you didn't know the people around you. We don't enjoy going to the games as much now because of the new stadium. The fans aren't as friendly and there are lots of new people, and some security issues. Things changed after 9/11. It was important to support the team in the '70s when the team was really bad. We didn't have the other pro teams and the Broncos were all that we had. The owner took good care of the fans in the early days, too. It's always fun to be at the games when they have the older players out and to see them again. A lot of them are active in the community still, and some are on TV or radio doing broadcasts.

————**LINDA HOUPT**, born and bred in Colorado

I attended my first ever Broncos game on January, 17, 1984. My wife, Anita, was exactly seven months pregnant with our first son, Robert Christopher Manning, born April 17, 1984—yes, the same son with his picture in *Sports Illustrated* almost 21 years to the day later. She gave me, as a Christmas gift, tickets to the AFC championship game against the Cleveland Browns. These weren't just any tickets, but they were South Stands tickets—the area of the stadium that rumor had it you didn't want to be during a rowdy game like this one was bound to be. We arrived very early at the game and made our way to our seats. In stark contrast to my fears, I was amazed with the care everyone treated my Anita. They worried about her and her obvious condition, making sure she was comfortable and not in harms way. The game started and everyone was riveted to the action on the field. Were the South Standers crazy? Of course, but in a good "Mile High" sort of way. The first half was an amazing display by the Broncos creating a 21-3 halftime lead. In the second half, however, we saw that erode as Bernie Kosar led the Browns' attack, tying the game at 21-21. Then, John performed his magic and scored with five minutes remaining, 28-21. Bernie wasn't about to stop and started to drive the Browns down the field. As the tension grew, we could sense that everything was coming down to this last "drive" by the Browns.

We all remembered with irony "The Drive" just a year earlier when John had the same five minutes left and how it propelled the Broncos to one of their six Super Bowl appearances. Bernie took the snap at the 5-yard line and handed off to Earnest Byner who scooted to his left and cut back going in for what appeared to be the game-tying touchdown. On the 3-yard line, Jeremiah Castille stripped the ball. There it lay on the 3-yard line while Earnest dove into the end zone. A mad dash ensued with the Broncos recovering the ball. All of this happened facing the South Stands, less than 15 yards in front of my wife and me! I had just witnessed history: "The Fumble!" The stands erupted and Denver went on to win that game. In retrospect, I had to admit that although the South Stands were/are crazy, a better group of fans does not exist in the NFL. They treated my very pregnant wife with as much care as one does when making sure your eggs aren't broken before you buy them at the grocery store. I was proud to stand shoulder to shoulder with them as the Broncos beat the Browns. As we left the stadium, I turned to my wife and said, "I have to become a season ticket holder"—a pledge that I have been fortunate enough to keep.

———**ROBERT MANNING**, Monument, Colorado.

My husband asked me to marry him on a Sunday and said we would get married on that Wednesday at the justice of the peace. This is the second marriage for both of us. On Wednesday, he called and said, "Lou, we are not going to get married today." I was crushed. But then he said, "How would you like to get married at Mile High Stadium this Saturday?" I couldn't believe it. He knew someone who worked there and would let us do it. There were a few stipulations—we could only bring 10 people and we couldn't step on the lines, as the Broncos were playing San Diego the next day on national TV, and they had just finished painting the lines. We got married in the South Stands with six people and the priest on November 7, 1998. We didn't step on the lines! They rolled out the red carpet for us. I got married in blue jeans, a John Elway jersey and a white veil. My husband was wearing blue jeans, a John Mobley jersey and a top hat. I carried an orange and blue carnation bouquet from a local supermarket. We celebrated in a sports bar after that. My wedding ring was a Broncos ring from Trice Jewelers. The next day right before halftime, the CBS announcers were talking about how sacred the Broncos fans felt about

Mile High, and they showed us getting married. That was our 15 minutes of fame! It was the most memorable, coolest time in my life.

——LOUISE MORALES, Married since 1998

On Valentine's Day 2006, I took my girlfriend, Heather, to dinner at Morton's. Later that evening, I drove her to INVESCO Field, site of our first real date, three years earlier. As the snow lightly began to fall, we kissed near the bronze horse at the top of the stairs and I wished her a happy Valentine's Day. I spun her around, took a knee and asked, "Would you do me the honor of being my Valentine for the rest of my life?" Of course, she said, "YES!" Six months later, friends and family gathered at INVESCO Field for our wedding. It was only fitting to be married there as every pivotal relational event occurred on those same grounds. Pictures were taken on the 10-yard line, followed by a ceremony in the Club Level Lounge, beneath the pictures of Terrell Davis and John Elway. The wedding party wore navy blue with orange flowers for accents. The wedding officiant sported a black and white striped tie with a whistle around his neck. I, of course, wore a Broncos tie. From the wedding vows, to the orange-covered reception tables, to the orange and blue M&M party favors, every detail exuded a football theme. Not just any football, but Broncos football. With promises of my bride being a supportive cheerleader, and me being a leading quarterback through **INJURY** and health, we became one with the following ring exchange:

> As deep a love I have for the orange and blue,
> I pledge this and more to you.
> With this ring, I promise you a no trade clause.

As we rode away on our blue motorcycle, sporting Elway jerseys, we realized this was the start of our family legacy.

——MONTE DEAN, Centennial, Colorado

> **Almost every good football team at any level in America is one play away (injury) from being average. Average time lost due to injury in high school football is six days. Healing time due to injury to a high school cheerleader is 29 days. Among the sixteen most popular college sports, spring football has the highest injury rate.**

I remember the construction of the North Stands in 1975 at Mile High Stadium. The seats were to be in by the first game, but they weren't. We had to come up with 9,000 chairs for the first two games. We came up with about half of them for the first game and didn't quite make it to 9,000 for the second game, either. We had people sitting on the concrete slabs. The stands were built, but there were no seats. We went out with tape and taped off their 18 inches of space. The seats were in for the third game, fortunately.

———GAIL STUCKEY, worked for the Broncos from 1975-2003 as the Director of Ticket Operations and Director of Stadium Operations

I can remember when I was just a shaver in the early '60s, playing Little League football. The league and coaches used to take us to a Broncos game every year. We would get to Mile High early and get to watch the player warm-ups and sometimes even get to go down on the sidelines. The players would throw us their broken chinstraps and once in awhile autograph them for us. One game we were down on the sidelines and the **PUNTER** was warming up. We stood there watching him kick the ball for what looked like a mile in the air and a long way down field. I can still remember the sound of his foot hitting the ball. WOW! Our eyes were as big as saucers, and I'm sure our jaws were on the turf. I think he got a kick out of it, too—no pun intended.

———DEAN DUNKIN, Technology Manager, Born in Denver

…You could walk all over the stadium in the old days, unrestricted before the game and at halftime. You could really see the players during warm-ups. Elway's passes were like laser beams, with very little arc to his passes. No elevation, then a SMACK when the receiver caught it. I was at the "Blizzard" game with my daughter. We could barely see the players, but we stayed for the entire game. I was wearing a cowboy hat and by the end of the game there was a foot of snow on top of it!…The current orange color on the uniform changed the complexion of the team. The new orange isn't the same orange as when we had the Orange Crush. People embraced that

> **Joe Theismann holds the NFL record for the shortest PUNT that wasn't blocked—one yard.**

color and were passionate about it. They painted their cars and houses that color!

————JEB BARRY, 59, Denver

Everyone always talks about the cold at Broncos games, but no one really talks about the heat. Sometimes sitting in those stands, on the east side, facing the sun during a day game, it can be brutally hot. It can go from one extreme to the other.

————PAUL CLARK, southern Idaho native

I was a high school student in the mid '60s and a Broncomaniac even then. I worked at a McDonald's restaurant in West Denver, and one of my responsibilities as a substitute maintenance guy on the weekends was to wash the white Marlite ceiling every Sunday morning. Fortunately, this was in the days when the restaurants had walk-up windows and no seating areas. I had to be at the restaurant by 6 a.m. to get my standard work done. Then I started on the ceiling by 9 a.m. so I could be finished before noon, change clothes and meet my buddies to go to the home games. Invariably, I'd fall behind on my work, and I had to plead with the manager to let me finish the ceiling during the week so I could leave the restaurant for the game.

At that time, high school students could buy tickets for end zone seats for $1.50 during the week before the game. Needless to say, this was before the perennial sellouts. In fact, I recall quite clearly the season ticket "box score" on the front page of the *Denver Post* when the Phipps brothers were trying to bolster ticket sales and make sure the Broncos could stay in Denver. Fortunately, the Phipps' plan worked, and we've all been the better because of it. There were several of my friends that went to those games, but I was the designated ticket buyer. It was my responsibility to go to downtown Englewood to Kaufman's Tall & Big Men's Shop on South Broadway to purchase our $1.50 tickets. I never figured out why Kaufman's was the distribution point, but they were, and I made many trips there in my old '53 Chevy to snag our precious Broncos tickets....

While there are many memories of the games and players from those early years, there's one episode that for some reason remains the most vivid. In the beginning, the Broncos had marginal success against the San Diego Chargers. With John Hadl as quarterback, and Lance Alworth—the receiver known as "Bambi"—San Diego was always a tough match-up. San Diego's coach was Sid Gillman, and the Broncos fans roundly disliked Sid for the misery he heaped on their beloved Broncos whenever they played. In '65, prior to coming to Denver for the Denver half of the home-and-home series, Sid made several disparaging remarks about the Broncos that were reported in the Denver papers. While there was never love lost between the Denver faithful and Sid, the rhetoric created a fan frenzy before the start of the game, and the crowd was especially noisy, encouraging their boys to exonerate themselves. At halftime, much to everyone's surprise, Denver had the lead. Along with hundreds of others, our group of rabid fans assembled at the railing at the bottom of the South Stands in Mile High Stadium. My recollection is so clear it could've been yesterday. While the San Diego team walked beneath us into the visitors' locker room, we screamed and hollered for all we were worth, heckling the Chargers and their coaches, and particularly Sid Gillman for selling our Broncos short. But the memory that's the most prominent is Sid stopping below us and looking up with a sarcastic grin on his face and saying, "There's always the second half." The reality of his point took hold immediately, and we swallowed our bravado and retreated to our seats. The Broncos lost by two touchdowns.

———GENE VAN HORNE, Castle Rock, Colorado

I don't think I've missed a home Broncos game since I was old enough to walk, except when I was away at college. Mile High had a smell about it. It was the anti-corporate crowd that made it special. My appreciation for the Broncos is hard to put into words. The Broncos are a common denominator I've had for my entire life. It has kept all of my friends together from the time we were in high school.

———AARON KRAMISH

I can remember a regular season game against the Chargers at the end of a season. If we won, we'd wrap up the division. The weather the day before was beautiful. I woke up game day and it was snowing like crazy. I was very disappointed. I figured my buddies wouldn't make it across town, let alone to the game. My buddy called and wanted to know if we were still going to the game. He got to the house before noon. We loaded up for the tailgate. It took us 90 minutes of driving in a blinding snowstorm to get to Mile High. It had

snowed so hard that the steps in the stadium had basically become ski ramps. We bought a couple of beers. My buddy slipped and slid all the way down the ramp and only lost half his beer. He combined the two cups and chugged them before he came back to his seat! Against Houston, we sat in the fifth level. Everyone had their bags of shredded Yellow Pages. We dumped them and they fluttered through the air. The glitter they shot out after the Super Bowl reminded me of the homemade confetti from that Houston game. Bob Martin and Larry Zimmer truly were part of the fabric of Broncos Nation. In those days, the announcer always became tied into the team. Dave Logan and Scott Hastings were memorable during the Super Bowl, too. They are part of the whole experience.

——**DR. LEONARD GRAF**, 48, Aurora, Colorado

My neighbor would paint himself up before the games. They'd dress up dolls with the plastic helmets from the gumball machines. At a game versus the Jets, during the tailgate party, they had a doll with Vinny Testaverde's jersey and helmet on it hanging by a noose. We were yelling, "J-E-T-S SUCK" and had a great time. They had a fly-over with Blackhawk helicopters instead of the jets as they usually would, because we were playing the New York Jets.

——**JOEL TAYLOR**, Denver native

I was at the University of Denver stadium the first time an AFL team beat an NFL team. It was a preseason exhibition game, and was a year or two before the leagues merged. Denver played the Detroit Lions. Because they were still playing baseball at Mile High Stadium at that time of the year, they played the game at the University of Denver. The stadium is long gone—burned down 25-30 years ago. There was a lot of excitement because it was the first time an AFL team had played an NFL team. The old DU Stadium was just plank boards—it didn't have seats—and it was pretty well filled up. It was a very exciting time for Denver fans. We weren't very good in those days. Right from the get-go, it became obvious Denver might win the game. Denver, at that time, was not one of the stronger AFL teams.

The Detroit Lions just thought they would come out here and throw one on Denver, and they just didn't play very hard. To Denver, it was a real challenge to get to play an honest-to-God NFL team, so they really went at it hammer and tong. I'm a native of Denver and don't read much from the national media. I read them all on the Internet now, but in those days, the Internet didn't exist. I don't know what the national reaction to the game was. Of course, the Denver media just went bonkers. It was played up heavily in the *Post* and *News* and on the local TV stations!

————**DAN GREEN**, 59, Denver

A film clip of John Madden that was played frequently in years past showed Madden on the sidelines ranting and raving, waving his arms, etc. In 1978, I was in the West Stands for an early in the season Broncos-Raiders game. The Raiders' bench was on the east sideline. Don't forget that the Broncos and Raiders had played on January 1, 1978, in the 1977 AFC Championship Game, won by Denver. Denver was moving right-to-left from my vantage point—toward the north—when the following occurred: Quarterback Craig Morton lofted a long pass to Riley Odoms down the east sideline at about the Raiders' 35-yard line. As the ball was coming down Odoms basically grabbed the Raiders' defender, threw him down, made the catch and went out of bounds. Madden went nuts, rushed to the official, gestured and hollered until the ref threw a flag. Madden, satisfied, calmed down. Then the official made the pass interference sign, and pointed to OAKLAND. It was a riot! Madden really went nuts, for good reason, in my opinion. I believe this sequence to be the famous clip of "Madden goes crazy." …Another time, my dad took me to a Denver-Oakland game in the late '60s. It was announced that Raiders' quarterback Daryle Lamonica was injured and would not play. Denver fans were hoping that without the "Mad Bomber" the Broncos would somehow have a chance. Of course, George Blanda shredded the Broncos and the Raiders won easily. The memory that sticks about this game is that of a fan in the same section yelling—make that bellowing—"Put in Lamonica!" after yet another long pass completion by Blanda. The comment cracked up everyone within earshot, and my dad laughed about that even 30 years later.

————**SPENCE WOOD**, Golden, Colorado

It was the Monday Night game when John Elway's number was retired. The Broncos were playing the Miami **DOLPHINS** and there was a huge ceremony with fireworks planned for the retirement at halftime. I was selling programs under the South Stands as a fundraiser for my kid's high school band program. Whenever we did this before, we would sell programs up until halftime, and then they would cut us loose. This time, the programs were a special edi-tion featuring a salute to John. Many people were buying two or more. The producers had doubled the number of programs to sell, and we would be called upon to continue sales until well after the game was over. Additionally, they had us wear tall, red and white striped hats (Cat-in-the-Hat style) and large, colorful smocks with vendor buttons all over them. As halftime approached, I made sure that our stand was covered by others and snuck off toward the gate to the field where I would be able to see the ceremony up close. As I approached the gate, a security guard motioned me to the side of the narrow sidewalk. As I stood to the side of the fence, I watched in awe as players who were in the "Ring of Fame" passed me as they entered the field to the sidelines for the ceremony. After they passed me, I walked up to the gate to get as close as I could. To my surprise, the security guard opened the gate and motioned me in! Thinking that he was looking at my hat and vendor buttons as some kind of pass, I said: "I don't know if I should be allowed in." He smiled and again motioned me in, showing me where I could stand on the sidelines and not be in anyone's way. I will never forget the roar of the crowd as John and his family were applauded. It was amazing to see the fireworks and players all saluting the greatest Broncos of all-time. And I had a front row seat! I eventually returned to my program stand and continued to sell programs. Unfortunately, the Broncos were defeated by the Dolphins that night. Several minutes before the game

> The undefeated 1972 **DOLPHIN**s (17-0) beat only two teams with records over .500. They were actually three-point underdogs to the Redskins in Super Bowl VII.

ended, I saw a man wearing a Dolphins jersey running full speed down the concourse toward the exit gate. A few seconds behind him were some very agitated Broncos fans screaming: "Fish fry! Fish fry!" It looked like the Miami fan had a good lead and I don't think they ever caught him—at least I hope they didn't!

———JEFF BAKER, Centennial, Colorado

Why did the
South Stands drink
chunky beer?

Chapter 5

Fandemonium

If There Were Sponges That Cleaned Up Broken Dreams, Woolworth's Would Still Be In Business

SHE LOOKS MAEVELOUS

MAEVE DRAKE

Maeve Drake has been the Broncos' reception-ist for 14 years and has heard every imaginable story a fan could come up with in order to gain access to the players and coaches. One day, when answering the phone, she said "Denver Bonkers" rather than "Denver Broncos." The caller was Pat Bowlen.

I had a gentleman come in one year, saying he had an appointment with Mike Shanahan. His secretary didn't have him down for an appointment, but the man was adamant he had been communicating with Mike all week about it. It turns out he had been communicating with him telepathically all week! He finally told me it was telepathic. I called security to escort him out.

When Jason Elam hurt his back, I got calls from hundreds and hundreds of people who thought they could be an NFL kicker. I had one gentleman come in wearing kicking shoes, wanting to try out. Some of the people were in their 50s even. People were just lining up thinking they could do that.

I've had people come up and ask if my desk is a bar. One of the funniest stories is from 1990 or so, right after Karl Mecklenburg retired. A guy kept calling, because he wanted to try out for the Broncos. He wanted to take over Karl's position. He kept telling me how good he was and how big he was. It turned out that he weighed 175 pounds. I told him that the majority of our staff probably weighed more than that.

I always get calls from people who want to give the coaches advice. I always ask what NFL team they work for. They've never coached, but they still think they know more than the coaches. I'm really the gate-keeper. I've been here so long, I can tell when people aren't the people they say they are. Pat Bowlen is always getting calls from junk bondsmen from New York. I always take messages for those.

When I don't want to give out my name to callers, I tell people I'm a temp. It works every time.

After we changed the uniforms in '97, I received hundreds of calls. One guy threatened to come out and shoot me, because we had changed the uniform. My only role in that was that I was the only person he got to talk to. I'm not easily intimidated, so I've not had to call the police. You have to have a sense of humor or you'd last 10 minutes here. You get very frustrating calls. Every year I hear from a lady in California who is very educated, very well spoken. She always asks for Mr. Bowlen, and she tells me she is the heir to the throne in England. She calls every year. During the Super Bowl years, we had lots of strange calls. I once had a woman call and ask which players on the team were single. She wanted to date one of them. It didn't matter which one, any of them would do. When Terrell Davis was playing and having migraines, people would call with remedies—stuff like putting stones on his head, using the urine of a pregnant calf—all kinds of strange stuff. People walk through the front doors all the time. I'm the only one in front of the locked doors to the rest of the staff. I guess I have to "take one for the team."

I had a guy call to tell me that every time he watched the Broncos, they would lose. He said that if John Elway would give him an SUV, he'd stop watching the games. We have little kids call and want to talk to John Elway. We encourage the kids to write a letter. I probably get 100 crazy calls a day during the season. The number goes up when the team is playing well. When they're playing bad, people call in swearing and calling us names. During the Super Bowls, I lost my voice from being on the phone so much. It was so busy, I couldn't leave my desk.

Jake Plummer is one of the nicest players. People used to call when he had the beard and complain—how it was such a bad example to have a beard and long hair. One lady called three times a week. I finally said, "Jesus had a beard and long hair. Do you not like him, either?" Some people do have legitimate complaints. They just want someone to listen, even though you can't help. They want to talk and talk. If it is legitimate, I'll ask them to call me back at a less busy time so I can manage the switchboard. I try to get them in touch with the right people when it's warranted.

People call and act like we owe them a favor. They want to know the schedule before it comes out or something like that. They want immediate gratification. I'm always nice to the callers. I've been here long enough to handle the calls well. Some people threaten me about calling my boss before I even say a word. One lady was furious, because I wouldn't give her Jerry Rice's address. She wrote a letter to my boss, Chip Conway. He gave me a better score on my review after that because he realized what I have to deal with on the phone. I don't let callers swear at me. I don't have to listen to that. Some people call up almost hysterical about stuff. We always get disgruntled calls after a loss. They blame everything on the quarterback. It's always his fault. They think I have some sort of control over the game, or like the team wanted to lose.

The Lewis and Floorwax radio show calls me pretty often. We joust on the air. Sometimes they don't tell me who they are. They asked if I was related to some Hollywood guy who had a deep voice, too. It was really busy that day, and I don't know that I ever figured out who it was. I asked if the guy drank a lot of whisky and smoked a lot of cigars. I didn't know I was on the air!

I answered the phone once "Denver Bonkers" and it was Pat Bowlen.

I love the people I work with. The NFL is like a large family. After this many years, the people are part of my football family. The team has been very nice to me, and I think they appreciate me. My saying is, "If you aren't going to do something that is going to save the world, you should be in a business that entertains people!" No one enjoys my humor more than I do.

HE'S GETTING HIS GOLF BALL RETRIEVER REGRIPPED, AS WE SPEAK

JOHN BRENNAN

John Brennan, 62, is president of SportsFan, a chain of sports apparel stores. One of his stores and his warehouse are—quite literally— within a 7-iron shot of old Mile High Stadium.

We've had a number of famous customers, but none more so than John Elway. A lot of the announcers come in, including **BRENT MUSBERGER**. They're usually looking for gifts for their kids.

During the Three Amigo days, during a Sunday game with lots of snow, Vance Johnson came in at about 10:30 in the morning. He was looking for a pair of nylons to wear under his uniform to keep him warm that day. We didn't have what he needed, and in the snow, he couldn't go anywhere else. It was before the days of Under Armour.

When we first moved into that location in 1986, there wasn't really much going on in that neighborhood. Our building had been empty for two or three years. When things were slow in our warehouse and retail store, we'd crack out the 7-iron and a bucket of golf balls and whack them into the old Mile High Stadium. It became a tradition. When a celebrity came into the store, we'd invite them to the back of the warehouse to try and put a golf ball into Mile High. It took a decent 7-iron to reach it from there. We always wondered what the groundskeepers thought when they would be mowing Mile High and come across golf balls.

> **BRENT MUSBERGER** was the home plate umpire when Tim McCarver made his professional baseball debut for Keokuk (IA) in the Midwest League in 1959.

I can remember our warehouse manager, Tony, running out of golf balls. He went down to the Mile High parking lot to pick up the balls that didn't make it into the stadium. One of the groundskeepers came over with a golf ball and said, "Are you looking for this?" Tony told him, "No, I'm looking for a Titleist!" He promptly scooted back up to the store. The back of the warehouse was on a hill next to the stadium, about a 50- or 75-foot vertical drop to the stadium from there. In order to get it into the stadium, the shot had to have a good bit of loft on it. It was only about 150 yards to the edge of the stadium. A good hitter could get it in with a 9-iron even. The store was on the west side of Mile High. We were doing this before the luxury boxes were built. The boxes made it a tougher shot.

We've had a number of players come in and either admire their own memorabilia or buy someone else's. Typically, the lesser-known players come in and want to outfit their family and friends in their jerseys for the games. One of the reasons we carry so many jerseys is that many places only carry the popular players' jerseys. We do have guys come in and buy 15 or 20 jerseys for their families.

In the late '80s or early '90s, one of our vendors called and said that John Elway had an agreement with them that he had to do a certain number of autograph signings with them and that he owed them a signing. I told them we were definitely interested in hosting one. It was 10 a.m., and they said he'd be there at 3 p.m. It was the last day of this contract. On such short notice, I had no idea how we could promote it. I called one of the radio stations and told them the story. They made an announcement, and within 30 minutes, we had a line outside. By 3 p.m., there was a line blocks long. His draw was incredible. His secretary came by first, and said that he was contracted to do a one-hour signing and that was it. She wanted him to leave at the end of the hour, but they didn't want anyone mad that he had to leave after an hour. We set up a table and people lined up. We could tell that only the people in the store would be able to get autographs. We shut the doors and told the people outside that only those inside would get autographs. I expected a really ugly scene, but no one left. After his hour, he walked out the front door. The people out there weren't mad at all. In fact, they cheered him when he left. It was cold—10 or 15 degrees. That was just the kind of thing that seemed to happen with Elway all the time.

I'm in the shop every Sunday. On game days, we set up a tent at the bottom of the hill, in front of the main entrance to INVESCO. We get there at 8 a.m. and stock the tent with merchandise. Around 10 a.m., the crowd starts going in. Broncos fans are some of the best, without a doubt. We sell all sports, and the football fans are beyond any kind of comparison with other fans. They buy, and they buy heavily. If it has to do with the Broncos, they really don't care about the price. They want the best, the best looking, the most authentic.

We have a steady contingent that comes from an incredible distance. We have one family that comes from near Little Rock, Arkansas. We have a parking spot for them. They're hardcore Broncos fan. They set up a tailgate in our parking lot and cook ribs for our guys in the tent. There is a Broncos bar in Billings, Montana, called Tiny's Tavern, owned by Roger Knutsen. He has season tickets, too. They come to every home game—a huge group from Billings that comes every Sunday.

Raiders fans need braces just so they can hold their heads up.

YOU TALKIN' TO ME?
NO, HE'S TALKIN' TO YOU.

JACK KAUFMAN

Jack Kaufman is semi-retired and drives a taxicab. He had a record shop in downtown Denver and worked at a radio station. He has been with Yellow Cab for 36 years.

In 1981, I was sitting in my cab at the Fairmont Hotel in Denver. A guy walked up to the first cab in line and wouldn't get in because the cabbie was smoking a cigar. The second driver didn't know how to get to the place the guy wanted to go. So he gets in my cab with two women.

Well, I play the trumpet and I carry the trumpet in my cab. I asked the riders where they were from, and the guy said "Canada." I played "O Canada" and "Canadian Sunset," and we talked for awhile. While we were driving out to a pizza place, he told me he worked at Mile High Stadium. I told him that he was a little old to be selling peanuts, and he then told me that he owned the Broncos. We got to the restaurant, and I still didn't believe he owned the Broncos. I get riders all the time who tell me they're people they aren't. It didn't make sense to me that he'd take a cab instead of a limo. He asked me to come back and pick him up in about 40 minutes. He gave me $20 on about a $4.20 cab fare.

While he was having pizza, I went to the union hall and found out he really did own the Broncos. Later, he wanted to go to the Colorado Mining Company, which was one of the No. 1 restaurants at the time. All the celebrities used to go there. I picked up **ELVIS** Presley there a

> Do you know what Jerry Garcia said to **ELVIS** when he first saw him in heaven?
> "Hey King! Guess who your daughter married."
> That's a true story—Give or take a lie or two.

couple of times. Elvis used to order a peanut butter and banana sandwich there. It was a huge sandwich. Elvis gave away five or six Cadillacs when he was here. He gave one to my neighbor, Bill Kennedy. Anyway, Edgar Kaiser got back in the cab and asked me what I was doing Saturday night. He asked me to be his guest for the Broncos game. The only problem was that the game was in Miami. He said he would fly me down there on his private jet. We dropped the girls at the hotel and then I took him to the Colorado Mining Company Restaurant. He asked me if I knew how to play the National Anthem on my trumpet. He asked if I wanted to come in and eat with him. We went in to eat and Dan Reeves was there with some other coaches. Edgar again asked me about going to the game in Miami. He told me a plane would be waiting for me at Combs Field, the private airport.

Meanwhile, I'm afraid to tell anyone because I'm really not sure it will work out. I got my softball practice covered on Saturday and went to the airport. I didn't even tell my girlfriend I was going because I didn't want to look stupid. Sure enough, they were waiting for me at the airport! The Kaiser family was on the plane. They owned Kaiser Aluminum, and Edgar Kaiser was the owner of the Broncos!

Gail Stuckey, who was in charge of tickets for Denver, was on the plane, too. I got down to Miami and they put me up in the hotel with the ball team. I called my girlfriend to tell her where I was. We had been dating for eight years and I'm still dating her now. I told her "We can't go out tonight because I am in Miami." She hung up on me, so I call her back collect so she knew I was in Miami.

I brought my trumpet to the game. I was sitting next to Edgar in the owners' box. I'd play "Charge" every time the Broncos scored. I had played tunes on the Gulfstream on the way down there, too.

I knew Bob Martin from earlier, like 1953. I was a promotions guy for several record companies. Bob was a DJ, then owned his own

DENVER BRONCOS DENVER BRONCOS DENVER BRONCOS DENVER BRONCOS DENVER BRONCOS

It is true that NBA Coach Pat Riley never played college football, but was drafted by the **DALLAS COWBOYS**. His brother, Lee, played seven years in the NFL. It is not true that Pat Riley combs his hair with a pork chop.

station before going to Newsradio 850 KOA. The TV guys knew who I was and saw me on TV and talked about me on TV back in Denver. I had 30-40 messages on my answering machine when I got back to Denver.

When I got home and went to my softball game the next day, the team was bugging me and asking for my autograph. Monday morning, I was sleeping and Kaiser Industries called me and said the Broncos organization wanted to see me at 9 a.m. They called again, but it seemed like a big hoax. I hadn't been drinking, so I couldn't think of what I did to be in trouble. There was a third call, so I went down to Broncos headquarters to see Grady Alderman, the general manager. Matt Robinson came out almost crying. Robinson had just been cut by the Broncos. I went in and sat down, and they asked me to work for the Broncos! They wanted me to be a "high priced gopher." They told me I'd be taking care of various things. Since I knew the city, I would help the new players around and escort the Kaiser people around, too. Edgar had a couple of limos and wanted to get rid of them, so I kind of fell into his lap. They had run a background check on me during dinner.

Of course, I was pretty well known from the trumpet, and had been on a number of TV shows. Still, I was dumbfounded by the whole thing. I'd been a Broncos fan a long time and now I was working for them! The managers and my co-workers at Yellow Cab couldn't believe it. I told them I'd need a cab full-time instead of just for a shift.

I ended up working for the Broncos for three years. I kept working for Yellow Cab, too. I did a lot of things for Edgar. He really was pretty shy. He'd practice before the media spoke with him. He was a really good guy.

I was there when they did the Elway deal with the Colts. I had to keep quiet about it, and the press knew that I knew what was going on. I knew everything that was going on.

One of the players, Bob Swenson, was a holdout linebacker. They sent me to him with a contract to get a signature. The media followed me out there. I kept my mouth shut and didn't leak to the media. That is probably why they kept me around. Swenson signed for the Yellow

Cab charge and tipped me $500! He bragged about it to the *Rocky Mountain News* even. He didn't sign the contract at the time, but he tipped me instead. He eventually did sign with the Broncos, but I never did get the $500!

Tom Jackson is a really good guy. One day he brought all the linebackers into the main complex and asked me to lead them into the office playing "When the Saints Go Marching in." The players were in full uniform and I walked across the street like the Pied Piper! They were dancing in back of me as we walked across the street from the practice facility to the management offices. We marched through all the rooms and offices. Then they all stopped and started doing calisthenics. It was like Snow White and the Seven Dwarfs. I dealt with a lot of players. Tom Jackson is probably my favorite.

Carroll Hardy worked for the Broncos, too, when I was there. He's the answer to the big trivia question, "Who is the only player to ever pinch-hit for Ted Williams?" I think he lives in South Dakota now.

I had a field pass when I worked for the Broncos. I could sit in the owners' box, but I felt uncomfortable up there. I used to go to the South Stands and play "Charge" with Barrel Man. Guys from the band would join me, too. I aimed the trumpet up into the stands when I would play "Charge." The players said my timing was bad, as it would interfere with the players calling signals. I tried to do it on defense mostly. On offense, I'd do it only after a play, and always facing the stands, not the field.

Lyle Alzado did me a favor once. He was good friends with a comedian that was on tour—Joan Rivers. I got a call in the offseason from Yolanda from the Broncos office. She said that Joan Rivers had broken her ankle in the mountains. She called Alzado, who asked me to go get her. I took her to the Broncos' trainer and back to the hotel. She said "I owe you," gave me two tickets to the show with her and the Smothers Brothers and tipped me very nicely.

ROLL OUT THE BARREL, MAN

TIM McKERNAN

Tim McKernan is Barrel Man. He was born in Tacoma, Washington, and grew up in Southern California. He has lived in Denver since 1967 and worked as a mechanic for American Airlines.

I grew up an **L.A. RAMS** fan. I moved to San Francisco before I came to Denver. I couldn't stand the 49ers, so I'd go and watch the Raiders. I became a Broncos fan as soon as I came to Denver. On my first drive into Denver, I picked up Newsradio 850 KOA and Bob Martin broadcasting a game. I went to a game at Mile High Stadium and instantly became a Broncos fan. I bought my first season tickets the next year.

Being Barrel Man is a 24/7 thing. To be associated with the Broncos is an honor that I just can't explain. It's more than an ego booster—it has become part of my life.

The barrel was found at work. They were getting ready to throw it out. We took it down to the paint shop on our lunch break and painted it up to look like an Orange Crush can. It was '78. I had always led cheers in my section at the game, and I didn't want Orange Crush to die after the Super Bowl. At first, we were going to make a drum out of it. I was headed to San Diego to a game, and my family was going to watch for me during the game. I told my family to watch for a guy beating a drum that looked like an Orange Crush can.

> The **RAMS**, who began as the Cleveland Rams, were named for the Fordham University team.

At Mile High, we sat in Section 117, in the North Stands, right behind the goal posts. We were about 15 rows up. Once I started wearing the can, the team really gave me free rein of the stadium. I'm not officially a member of the Broncos organization. I've never been hired by the team. I did have Newsradio 850 KOA as a sponsor for a couple of years. But, the team has been very accommodating over the years. I ended up in the hospital twice and the team sent flowers both times. The Broncos made the team hotel available to me for away games, at the team rate even. They recognized me as one of the top fans.

Anyway, my brother had bet me $10 that I didn't have the guts to wear the barrel. It was more of a dare than a bet. Of course, I did it. That was against the Chicago Bears, on a Monday night—October 16. I had to wear the barrel in the snow. It was to be a one-game deal. I didn't wear it to the next game, and the fans in my section wanted to know where the can was! The next home game was against Green Bay, and I wore the can. CBS did a special on the Broncos fans and their tailgate parties. I got dressed in the barrel and got my free beer and pork sandwich at the tailgate party. Walking toward the stadium gate, a guy touched me on the shoulder. I found out later it was **PAT SUMMERALL**. He had a cameraman and said they were doing a special on Bronco-maniacs. He told the cameraman to keep me on camera.

The coldest game in the barrel was at Kansas City in '83. At kickoff it was 24 degrees below zero, with a wind chill factor of 42 below. By halftime, I was spending most of the time under the hand dryers in the restrooms trying to warm up. The Kansas City fans had gone home by halftime. I changed out of the barrel and watched the rest of the game in the cold. It kept getting colder.

The rumor was that all I wore under the barrel was my boots. I'll leave that to everyone's imagination. I did typically wear shorts—orange shorts. You never know what other fans are going to do, so you have to be prepared.

> **PAT SUMMERALL**'s real first name is George. He is called Pat because when he was a kicker with the New York Giants football team, the newspapers would print: "P.A.T.-Summerall." P.A.T. stood for "Point After Touchdown." Summerall played minor league baseball against Mickey Mantle.

There are 21 barrels. I'm wearing No. 21 this year. We've donated some of the barrels to silent auctions. We put barrel No. 18 on eBay. It was from Super Bowl XXXII. It sold for $30,000! The Wild Horse Casino in Cripple Creek bought it. Barrel No. 1 is in the "Hall of Fans" section in the Pro Football Hall of Fame in Canton, Ohio. The backup barrel I had for Super Bowl XXXIII is hanging on the wall with a cardboard insert of me in it. I was inducted into the Hall of Fans with the first class in '99. It was unbelievable. It was probably one of the most exciting times of my life. It ranks right behind the birth of my kids and my wedding. There were 31 fans that year, including a Cleveland Browns fan, even though the Browns weren't in existence that year.

The feeling of Super Bowl XXXII is indescribable. I was on my knees almost praying that Brett Favre wouldn't complete that last pass. When the pass was knocked down, I jumped up and there were TV cameras right there. They interviewed me on the spot, wanting to know how it felt. I was crying. I couldn't explain the feeling. It was emotionally draining. There was a big party after the game. Tailgaters were handing out toasted cheese sandwiches to everyone!

The ticket to the first AFC Championship game I went to was $6.60! After the first Super Bowl in '77, the Broncos left the field with their heads hanging. One of the fans started chanting "We love the Broncos." It resonated throughout the Superdome. I still get emotional when I talk about it. The players lifted their heads and walked off the field proud.

In Billings, Montana, there is a restaurant and bar that is a Broncos bar. Broncos fans watch the games there. The menu in '98 had the Super Bowl team from '78 with icicles on it with the caption, "The year that Hell froze over." The entire bar is done in orange and blue. There are lots of Broncos fans up there. They see the team as the "Rocky Mountain Broncos." Those fans always want pictures with me, Barrel Man. I'm in a bunch of Christmas card photos with people.

I stand the entire game when I'm in the barrel. When I first started out, I'd put the barrel on at 8 a.m. and wear it all day. Now my stamina is not what it was. My doctors insist I get out of the barrel at halftime. The year 2007 will be my 30th season in the barrel. I will likely retire the barrel after the 30th season. I'll still go to the games, but not with the barrel. I'll still be Barrel Man, though. I retired from my day job after 39 years.

I got married at INVESCO Field. It was gong to be a small wedding until the news media got hold of it. We got married in front of the horses in 2003. My wife's name is Becky. There were over 500 people at the ceremony, and then we had a tailgate wedding reception with many more. I wore the barrel with a tuxedo jacket for the wedding. My wife wore a fur jacket. Some former Broncos players were there along with other fans.

My oldest son made the statement a couple of years ago that my personality changes when I put on the barrel. He says I strut like John Wayne. I have a different persona when I put on the barrel. Fans' personas change when they put their team's outfit on.

Being Barrel Man is like being a celebrity. Some have called me an icon. Some have said I'm the most famous Broncos fan ever. It's flattering. The picture sessions start immediately when I go to the tailgate parties. My kids are pretty proud of me being Barrel Man. They were embarrassed about it at first. My daughter was going to UNC and the professor in a psych class brought up Barrel Man in a discussion about deviant behavior. Her roommate jumped up and told the professor, "Ask his daughter. She's in this class!" The kids are proud of me, though.

I was in the Barrel for the Snow Bowl. I turned my ankle in the third quarter. One of the secrets to being in the barrel is to keep moving to keep warm. Late in the fourth quarter, I had to change into regular clothes. I was kneeling on the stairs in San Diego once and a young lady came along and gave me a swift kick. I rolled to the bottom of the section in the barrel! I've slid down aisles from slipping on the ice at Mile High. I rode a tricycle at a charity event and got flipped off the back. I fell off a stage at a Broncos rally. I've never been seriously injured, though. I've had frostbite a number of times. No one knows what I'm wearing under the barrel, but I do wear a hat and gloves to try and keep warm.

In Giants Stadium, they made me stand in one place the entire game because the Giants didn't want me wandering around the stadium getting the Broncos fans wound up.

NOSTALGIA ISN'T WHAT IT USED TO BE

RUSTY MORSE

Rusty Morse moved to the Denver area in 1958 from Iowa and is one of the top sports memorabilia collectors/dealers in the nation. In 1986 he published the first checklist of Broncos football cards.

In college I spent my first semester at the Coast Guard Academy and was the fourth-class manager for the football team there. The coach was Otto Graham who is a football Hall of Famer. He's also in the basketball Hall of Fame. I was involved with football, and in the '70s I was a social worker and started following the Broncos. And ever since, I've been in the field of sports collectibles. It was so obvious when John Elway came along that he was going to be big in the world of collectibles. When Elway came in, it was clear that the Broncos were going to go on to Super Bowls. So when the Topps football cards came out—the '84 Topps set—I could buy a case of those the year after for about a third of what it normally cost and that case of football cards would have 20 Elways, 20 Marinos, and 20 Dickersons. And for 50 or 60 bucks, that was a deal. My partner and I bought 2,100 cases of the '84 cards. That's a semi-trailer load. We put them into storage and eventually sold them for a substantial profit. There is a baseball card of Elway, too. That card is extremely valuable. One collector—Bill's Sports Collectibles—bought out the entire inventory as soon as Elway came to Denver. He owned them and essentially owned the market. He didn't realize it, so he sold the card to a lot of Denver people for five bucks. The price nationally was up over $100.

The interesting thing about collecting football material is that many of the people that are in the business of sports cards are so focused on baseball, and they look on the football cards as sort of a step-child.

You can't find many football cards before 1988. That's because Topps had an exclusive contract that expired in the late '80s. Now we have a lot of companies producing football cards. Prior to 1988, any football card with an individual player on it had to be published by Topps, because of their contract. That means that the old cards prior to the late '80s are all Topps or the really old ones were made by Bowman and Fleer.

When you're running a store, people come in and offer you things. Someone came in and had a first-year pennant from 1960. Someone brought in a football from 1960-61 with all the signatures of all the players on it. The first year of the Broncos, every time they kicked a field goal, the football would go into the stands. But the general manager of the team would go retrieve it, because of the cost of balls. And it became such a problem that they made a dummy football with signatures on it, and they would take the real football from the fan, and give them this dummy football. Someone brought in a Broncos program from the first season. We put it on the wall for $50 and it would sell. There has been a Super Bowl pennant for every Super Bowl the Broncos played in, including 1978, when they printed up pennants that said World Champion Broncos, in case they won the Super Bowl. Well, some of those pennants didn't get destroyed. We had a 1978 pennant and sold it for $50.

The first-year pennant has a team photo on it and has this Bronco on it. The guy on the Bronco is actually picking his teeth. And the pennant is not really orange, it's kind of an off orange-yellow. That pennant sold in 1992 for $175. The AFL material is really scarce. I don't think I've seen five of the AFL logo pennants prior to 1967. They're just really scarce.

The one thing that nobody seems to be able to find is the famous striped socks of the first year. And also a football helmet of that period would be extremely rare. Fred Gehrke, who was the general manager of the Broncos, essentially designed the first helmet with a logo on it, which was the Rams helmet. He is featured at the Hall of Fame in a display with a copy of that helmet. He individually painted all the helmets of the Rams.

TAILGREAT

CARLA PATTY-WEIS

Carla Patty-Weis, 44, was born and raised in Centennial. The mortgage loan processor became a Broncos fan in 1983 and a season ticket holder in 1993.

I became a hard-core Broncos fan in the mid '80s. Friends and I would get together every Sunday. After "The Drive," we all went to the airport and waited for hours for the team to get in. As I am only about 5-feet tall, I couldn't really see much. The guy in front of me was 6-foot-2, and he offered me a lift. He put me on his shoulders, and we cheered our hearts out. I couldn't speak or yell anymore when we got done.

Sundays actually start on Saturday for me. I paint my fingernails orange and blue. Game day we start around 7 a.m. and drag everything up from the basement to take to the tailgate party. We usually cook based on the where the opposing team is from—BBQ when we are playing Kansas City, fish when against Miami, Cajun when we are playing New Orleans. We cook everything in the parking lot. We deep-fry turkeys at Thanksgiving. Eleven of us tailgate together. We're from all over the area. They all are fans I met in the parking area. We won the "Most Valuable Tailgaters" award last year. It was an honor for a group of rag-tag tailgaters out in Lot N.

I'm a huge, huge John Elway fan. He came to the Broncos when I first started rooting for them. We are about the same age. I outbid two guys on an autographed jersey. I spent a ton of money, but it was worth it. I bought it at an auction with the Denver Board of Mortgage Bankers. The money went to a home for battered women. The bidding was heated, and I kept giving the other guys a dirty look. The bids were going up by $25, then by $50 each time. I spent $650 on the jersey! I was so proud to outbid the two men on it. Money wasn't the issue. It's a prized possession and is in my living room along with my John Elway **_SPORTS ILLUSTRATED_** magazine and my other memorabilia.

My uncle and my dad got season tickets first. I saw a lot of passion for the Broncos in my father when I was in high school. When they couldn't go to the games anymore, they passed the tickets on to me. The older I've become, the more passionate I've gotten for the Broncos. Guys look at me like I'm nuts when I talk football with them. I attended Football 101, and realized that I knew way more than they were teaching. I don't know where the passion came from, but now I bleed orange and blue!

I dislike the Chiefs more than the Raiders. I can't stand to see that sea of red. Their fans travel well with the team, and it makes me mad to see them at the games. I have a sign for the Chiefs game. It says, "BBQ the Chiefs." It has an Eddie Kennison rat being held over a campfire.

SPORTS ILLUSTRATED was first published in 1954 and its first swimsuit issue was in 1964. The _Sports Illustrated_ Swimsuit Issue has 52 million readers, 16 million of them are females... 12 million more than normal....In 1955, SI selected horse owner William Woodward as their Sportsman of the Year. Woodward's wife shot and killed the unfaithful Woodward before the issue went to press. SI then selected World Series hero, Johnny Podres.

THE KING OF FANS WAS A PAWN FOR THE BRONCOS

FRED PASTERNAK

Fred Pasternak owned three pawn shops in the Denver area. He prides himself on his game-day outfit, consisting of orange pants, a Broncos shirt, orange suspenders, and Broncos cowboy boots.

When the Broncos came here in '60, I went down to the stadium and bought myself and my father season tickets in the South Stands. My priority number is 2088, and my dad never got to go to a game. He died at age 54 before he got to go to a single game.

This was before they had a net to catch the field goals and PATs. So when they kicked a field goal, it was the most dangerous thing on earth. One time, a ball was coming towards us and it bounced off two or three guys' hands. It landed on the bleachers and a bunch of us dove for the ball. There was a pile of humanity with everyone grabbing for the ball. I had my hands on the ball for a split second, but someone pulled it away from me. Then a guy grabbed my head with both hands and pulled real hard. He thought my head was the football, because I was bald! I've been bald since I was a kid. And he grabbed my head! The next year, I changed my seats to the sidelines. I didn't want to take a chance of getting hurt in that south end zone. They put up a net a few years later, so they don't have that problem anymore....

I had a pawn shop, Pasternak's Pawn Shop. In those days, the Broncos didn't make the money they make now, and I did a lot of business with Broncos players. In fact, I've got two fur coats my good friend Rick Upchurch hocked. One of them is still in my closet with his name in it. It is a men's mink jacket, and I wear it all the time. The other one was a full-length coat with his name in it. I donated that to the Channel 6 auction, and it brought in $3,000 for charity.

Rick Upchurch was dating Condoleeza Rice at the time. She was in graduate school at the University of Denver. Upchurch was the only serious boyfriend that she ever had. Upchurch said, "She thought Jim Brown (the Cleveland Browns' Hall of Famer) was the greatest thing since sliced bread. She loved the way he played the game, because he was aggressive, and he went after what he wanted. And that's the way she was, she went after things she wanted. She knew how to strategize and get control." Well, he's coaching Little League Football now, in Pueblo, Colorado. I loved him dearly. He was one of my best customers.

Paul Smith died; he had cancer. What a guy. I remember taking my son, Paul, to the airport one day to welcome the team back from a road game. Paul Smith put his hand out, and I put my little one-year-old son in Paul's hand. Paul used to hock. In fact, the pawn shop still has his Super Bowl ring. He died, and his wife and in-laws are fighting over who gets it. But I'm out of the pawn shop. I retired 10 years ago....

I've had season tickets for about 36 years. I had 17 season tickets awhile ago. When I got divorced, I had them in the name of my pawn shop. I lost all 17 tickets because my wife got the pawn shop. I was just sick, because they were great seats. But a friend of mine has been selling me his tickets for the last 10 years. He gets them and then brings them to me and I buy them—so I'm still covered. In fact, my seats are better now than what the pawn shop seats were!...

I go to Kansas City every year to watch the Broncos. One year I had just bought a new car—a Mitsubishi 3000 GT. A cop caught me in Burlington at 130 miles an hour—unbelievable. And he asked me, "Why are you going so fast?" I didn't know what to say, so I said, "Do you see that plane? Our wives are on that plane, and we have to pick them up at the airport in Kansas City." And I said, "You're really screwing up my time." He didn't like that too much. It cost me $438 cash! We went on to Kansas City, and I went much slower.

I've been to all the Broncos' Super Bowls. The first one was when we were playing Dallas, and I guess that was when Rick Upchurch was with the team. We got killed bad. Just standing in **NEW ORLEANS** at the Superdome when they played the National Anthem was the biggest thrill of my life. And we got beat by Dallas bad.

I have to go to the game. I can't watch it on television. I went to one game when it was 19-below-zero. Of my 17 season tickets, I was the only one who went. We were playing Kansas City in the early '60s. I wore a snowmobile suit and Mukluk boots, and I put them on the catalytic heater to keep my feet warm. The rubber melted to the heater, and I couldn't get them off my feet.

At half-time of a **NEW ORLEANS** Saints game in 1968, Charlton Heston drove a chariot and rode an ostrich while filming a scene for the movie *Number One*.

The difference between T.O. and government bonds? Government bonds mature.

YEAH, THAT'S THE TICKET

WALTER WEINGARTEN JR.

Walter Weingarten Jr. is 64-years-old and goes by the nickname "Sunny." He contracted polio during the second worst epidemic of the 20th Century. He has used a ventilator or respirator for 55 years and has had an iron lung for 35 years. Mr. Weingarten has been a Broncos fan since the team's inception and in 1965 became the first disabled patron to purchase season tickets.

Having the Broncos in my life started in the early 1960s. I was unable to finish high school at that time. I had some serious medical problems due to polio. I had been home-bound for a long time. I had to have something to keep me going. I was really in survival mode, but I knew I would get better. I used to listen to the Broncos games on the radio and watch them on TV. It was my life-blood. It's what kept me going, kept me alive. I loved reading the articles from the old writers of the '60s. The writers were very in tune with what was going on. It wasn't as extensive in those days, but was what I needed.

After the first five years of the Broncos struggling, I had a lot of empathy for them, with my own struggles. The first ticket I bought was in '61 versus the New York Titans. Later they were the New York Jets. In 1965, I started with season tickets. That got me out of the house. That was very difficult, and still is.

The '60s were difficult for Broncos fans. The team was one of the eight charter members of the AFL. None of the teams really acquired quality players. Some teams did better than others. In '66, the AFL merged with the NFL. Floyd Little was our first No. 1 draft choice, and he was one of the great players of the '60s. The entire decade was full of a lot of turmoil. Lou Saban joined the team as coach in '66 to bring the team together. In 1967, the Broncos ownership wanted to sell the team. **BIRMINGHAM, ALABAMA**, wanted the team. The Quarterback Club was formed and they helped raise money to pay off the mortgage of the old stadium. The city took over the stadium and remodeled it, and the team stayed in Denver with new local ownership.

In '66, the Broncos played the Houston Oilers in the opening game in Rice Stadium. They played the entire game without a single Denver first down. We didn't get to play in the **ASTRODOME** because the Oilers couldn't pay the rent.

I'm not sure why I decided to start collecting my ticket stubs, but now I have every ticket from every game I've attended in the last 46 years, except one—Opening Game '63, against the Kansas City Chiefs. It was on a Friday night at the University of Denver stadium. The Bears had priority on the stadium then. I also have a program for every game I ever attended. They are all organized in file folders. I've kept all the newspapers, too. I have Super Bowl scrapbooks, one for each Super Bowl. I guess I am clinging to something that is a major part of my life. They are mementos that show that I really did go to the games.

During my first season as a season ticket holder in 1965, a season ticket cost $24.50—$3.50 per game, for seven home games. It wasn't mandatory to buy the preseason games then. Parking was $3 and hot dogs were 50 cents. Popcorn was just 15 cents. Now my season tickets are $90 per game plus $300 for a parking permit. That comes to

> **The New England Patriots once played a regular-season home game in BIRMINGHAM, ALABAMA, in September 1968.**

> **When the ASTRODOME opened in 1962, it was hailed as the Eighth Wonder of the World. Oilers owner Bud Adams said the rent was the Ninth Wonder of the World....On June 15, 1976, the Pirates were "rained in" at the HOUSTON Astrodome. Ten inches of rain flooded the Astrodome parking lots and access roads. The teams made it to the park but the umpires, fans, and stadium personnel did not.**

$110 per game now. With polio, it's hard to go to the games. The cost of tickets may be the bigger obstacle, however.

I sat at the bottom of the South Stands at Mile High, Section AA. I still see people at the new stadium that I sat with for 35 years at Mile High. People remember me sitting down there. In 1982, my parents' home was broken into. They stole my AC/DC television set, which I would hook up to my power wheelchair. I could watch the instant replays then. Rocky the Leprechaun heard about it and took a grocery bag and passed it down the line to collect money to replace it. By the time it got to Row 12, it was full with $500 in it! I bought the best color 10-inch AC/DC TV I could. It was very emotional to have that many people in the South Stands give me that much money to replace my television set.

The entry to the locker rooms was near the South Stands at Mile High Stadium. There was one very vocal fan who didn't like the officiating. He leaned over the railing to yell at the officials, and leaned a bit too far. He fell 12 feet onto the turf. I saw a lady sitting in Row 12 during a Monday Night game in 1974. She was wearing a fur coat. Every time the Broncos would score a touchdown, she would open up her fur coat. She wasn't wearing anything under the coat! Security tried to find her, but couldn't. Maybe they didn't try very hard. I remember another lady in the 1960s at a game versus the Chargers. She got through security and onto the field. Right before the ball was snapped, she ran into the play. Fortunately, she was not seriously injured. She was arrested, though. It was weird to see a fan right in the middle of the play. There was some excess drinking in the South Stands, but mostly it was families. There were lots of kids then, as the tickets were inexpensive. You don't see a lot of kids at games now.

The design of the tickets now is more artistic than in the early days. The early tickets were simple—just words. There was no Ticketmaster then. The first tickets looked like a movie ticket—heavy paper with words typed on it. The ticket style remained pretty much the same for many years. I was in Row 6, Seats 1 and 2. I was the very first disabled person to buy season tickets. That gave me Priority No. 1 for those season tickets. I'm Priority No. 3635, otherwise.

I sat on the committee for INVESCO Field for Disability Access. We were to oversee all the changes and improvements for disabled access. In Mile High, I couldn't even use the restroom. I use a reclining wheelchair and a ventilator. At the new stadium, they've covered everything for disabled fans. I ran into Pat Bowlen before the new stadium was approved, and told him I was going to do something about the shortfall and be sure the new stadium was friendly to the disabled fans. It is. Of the 76,000 seats there, we were allowed 760 disabled spaces and attendant seating. That is quite a change from the 50 spaces that Mile High Stadium had. The 1998 law requires 1% of seating be reserved for disability seating, on all levels.

Game preparation has gotten more extensive for me over the years. My circulation has gotten worse, so it takes about an hour-and-a-half to get dressed. It involves a lot of layering—a layer for about every 10-degree drop. Against the Colts a couple of years ago, it was 18 degrees, and my ventilator got water in it from the rain and snow. I have it better protected now. I have breakfast at 10 a.m. I pack a lunch and leave about 12:30 p.m. By the time I get to the field, I'm already exhausted. Luckily, I have an outstanding attendant, Larry Long, who takes care of me. He gets me ready. He's been with me for eight years. I can't just put on my jacket and grab some money and go to the game. My preparation is probably more extensive than any of the players. I usually have to go right to bed after the game. It's a very exhausting day, but well worth it. It is worth the sacrifice.

Attending the Super Bowl games was very difficult. I had to drive to them and, with the ventilator, that was difficult. Everybody has a hobby, an interest—the Broncos have been mine. I also coach my son's Little League Baseball team. Super Bowl XII, the Broncos' first, is the one I remember the most. We cheered for 15 minutes after the game was over, even though they lost. It was a wild season. Fans went nuts over the merchandise and missed work to go to games. You can only do something for the first time once, so it's always the most exciting. I have an autographed football from each of the Super Bowls the Broncos have played in. After 40 years as a fan, I've acquired quite a few things, some of which are quite valuable. I'm hoping to set up a dedicated room for all of it.

THERE BUT FOR THE GRACE OF ELWAY: TWO MISTAKES FOR "THE MISTAKE BY THE LAKE"

The next week was the Broncos game—*the drive*. When Kosar hit Brennan for that touchdown pass with about five minutes to go, I always think I jinxed it because I yelled out to my dad, "We're going to the Super Bowl." It was just one of those great moments. Then Denver got the ball at the two, and it was like, "There's no way, against our defense, that they'll be able to come back." But, they did. And, they won that one in overtime. I worked myself up into such an emotional state that I really made myself sick. I couldn't go to school the next day. All of my friends thought I was ducking out. They wanted to give me a hard time—ride me about the Browns loss. But, I seriously worked myself up so much emotionally that I got a fever, and I didn't go to school the next day, because I was legitimately sick.

—**MATT PENCEK**, 35, Tonkaville, Pa.

Sundays are special in Cleveland. You wake up early. You have your breakfast. You go to mass, and then you get in the car and go downtown. That's just the way it is from week-one through week-seventeen.

The Drive. My mom and dad are already trying to get hold of a travel agent—we're going to the Super Bowl! What a lot of people don't know is if we had just a little bit of luck on that drive…. Elway was in the shotgun at about their forty-yard line. He sent Steve Watson in motion. The center snapped the ball a split second too soon. It hit Watson on the hip. Elway had to scramble to fall forward to get the ball. If that ball's on the ground, I believe Carl Hairston or one of our guys up front like Reggie Camp, falls on that ball. People don't remember that. If someone's got film, I'd love to watch it again. If we fall on that ball, we're going to the Super Bowl. But, Elway, being such a great athlete, was able to reach down and grab the ball, literally, off his shoe tops. He ended up completing a pass on the play, and the rest is history....

———CARMEN ANGELO, Browns Fan

A lot of people I know become fans of the teams where they live. I have, for better or worse, never been able, or desirous, of doing that. I've always followed the Browns. I have emotional highs and emotional lows, but, to me, that's better than not caring. The "Drive" and the famous "Fumble" happened. My wife had to take the kids and leave the house 'cause I was unlivable for three or four hours.

The worst people in the history of the world were Adolph Hitler, **MICHAEL JORDAN**, and John Elway!

———MARSHALL BASKIN, Los Angeles resident since 1976

I was working security at 'The Drive' game. After the game, it was like you had hit the crowd in the face with a sledge hammer. They were just stunned. I couldn't believe it. At that particular time, doing my duties, I was circling the field. When they started that drive, I was on the Denver sideline. I was going, "Oh my God, these guys are driving the ball down the field." I was coaching high school at the time. At the end of that game, I learned a lesson. When the game was coming close, prevent means 'Prevent me from wins." I guess that was the one thing I thought, "Marty, why did you go into a prevent? You should have been after Elway from the very first snap when that ball was on the two-yard line. You should have been after him the whole time instead of dropping everybody back and only sending four." You don't give Elway that much time to throw the ball. I was there at the end when Denver kicked the winning field goal, but I didn't really pay attention to it, and I haven't had a chance to watch it on the video to see if it was actually to the left or to the right of the upright. All I know, is when I saw the ref's hands go up, I thought, "Oh, it's a done deal. It's a done deal."

The only thing Earnest Byner is known for is The Fumble, which is unfortunate, because he is a very personable, kind-hearted, big-hearted guy...he was a heck of a ballplayer. He would block, run, whatever. I

> **MICHAEL JORDAN was given his first set of golf clubs by fellow University of North Carolina classmate, Davis Love, Davis Love, Davis Love....The Roman Guy.**

hate the fact that his career is always going to be noted by The Fumble. I hate that rap on him because Earnest was better than that. I always tell everybody, "You can say what you want to say, but, first of all, he didn't fumble the ball, he was stripped. Second of all, if Webster Slaughter had completed his route and not wanted to be a cheerleader, Jeremiah Castille wouldn't have been there to strip him of the ball."

I was watching ESPN, and they were reshowing that game. Jeremiah Castille said "Webster Slaughter broke his route off." That's what made him realize it was a run 'cause Webster had been burning him all game. He said Webster cut his route short and turned around to be a cheerleader. Earnest was maybe a foot away from being in the end zone. Castille said, "Byner had been running people over all game, and I had to make a decision. Do I hit him head on, or do I just try to go for the ball and hit him on the side. With him running people over all game long, I'm going to the side and hit him." When he saw Slaughter cut his route short, he was able to see Byner coming, where if Webster had run his route completely, by the time he got there, Byner would have scored, and the Browns would have gone on to the Super Bowl.

———CURTIS FRANKLIN, 48, Cleveland

I remember being at 'The Drive' game. I was in high school at the time. I remember going with a friend, his father, and a bunch of other people. We tailgated out in the Municipal parking lot. My friend's father said that the best way to be warm at game time is to take your jackets and shirts off before the game. So, there we were in freezing cold weather, with no shirts on, just a tee shirt—that's it, playing catch football and grilling hot dogs. It was absolutely freezing, but then when we put on our jackets, we thought, "Wow. This really works." We were so stupid. I remember thinking we had that game in hand. We've got the dog bones tied around our necks, our faces painted, and each play, we'd say, "We've got to get them on this play." It was just how noisy the stadium went to absolutely how quiet it was! Walking out of the stadium after that loss, there wasn't a single person talking. I remember one guy said, "I can't believe it." Everybody looked at him like, "Yeah. No kidding. You don't need to say that."

———SEAN SAMUELS, 35, Browns fan, Phoenix

SO SAY YOU ONE, SO SAY YOU ALL

 I moved out here in '73, and every day in the paper, 12 months of the year, were stories about the Broncos. It wasn't like that in Detroit. The Broncos had the orange pumpkin looking uniforms with the blue helmets in '77. My father was working in the automobile business and got two tickets to the game against Oakland in January '78. I ran down on the field like everyone else and celebrated. It was just a bunch of guys. Athletes weren't as highly paid as they are today. You'd see the players in the community then. It was a different time. It was the ultimate—like your first kiss, your first date, holding hands for the first time. As time went on, the expectations got higher, and the team didn't live up to those expectations. Dan Reeves came along and was a tough coach. In '83, they made the great trade that brought John Elway to the team. They practiced up in Greeley at the time. People would follow the team around to see where Elway got his hair cut! That is the kind of impact that the Broncos have on this city, this state. The first game Elway played for the Broncos, he lined up behind the guard instead of the center….Cable TV wasn't around. There weren't as many choices. You had to either watch TV or listen to the radio to get your information. If you wanted to go 100 m.p.h. down I-25 during a Broncos game, you could. There wouldn't have been anyone on the Interstate. A lot of people thought that maybe Elway couldn't win the big one. When the 49ers blew out the Broncos, it was one of the saddest days ever. The hangover was unbelievable.

——TOM MANOOGIAN, a.k.a. Lou from Littleton, Newsradio 850 KOA

I used to take my wife, my brother and his wife on the bus from a Longmont bar to all the games in Denver. In '77, we went to the AFC Championship Game where Jim Turner kicked the field goal that beat the Raiders. After that game, the crowd went berserk! Fans rushed the field and tore down both goalposts, and they stayed at

Mile High for hours! Anyway, we also celebrated in the stands as long as we could, and finally had to take the bus home. This is where the story starts. I was a purchasing agent for a mechanical contractor in Fort Collins. A salesman from a pipe company in Greeley stopped by the next morning and told us he had just talked to a guy in Fort Collins who was at the game. He had stayed at the Mile High parking lot for hours after the game. On his way to his Volkswagen bus, he saw, laying in the corner of the parking lot, a goalpost with one upright still on it! He asked some people if they would help him tie the crossbar to the top of his bus, and they did. The guy drove all the way on I-25 from Denver, half sloshed, to Fort Collins, 50 miles away! The guy thought he would saw up the goalpost and use it to make mailbox posts, but he found out that he could not cut it, because it was made out of a very hard lightweight metal that he could not cut with a hacksaw. When he told me this, my heart stopped, and I said, "Look, if he'd give me a six-foot chunk of it, I'll pick it up and have it cut to whatever he wants!" He agreed. I mounted a two-foot piece. We had been to the playoff games versus Pittsburgh and Oakland, as well as the Super Bowl, that year. So, I had the three tickets decoupaged and superimposed them on the goalpost. I hung it on the wall in my family room. The next summer, my company was one of the sponsors for KUAD radio in Windsor. A

salesperson came by to talk about an ad, and I told her about the piece of the goalpost I had. She said, "That is amazing. I go to CSU, and I'm working for KUAD part-time. My name is Lana Miller. My dad is Red Miller, the coach." I said, "Wow! I'll tell you what I will do. If he will sign my goalpost, I will give him another piece of it." The next day, she called and said, "My dad says if you'll bring your family to the practice field next to Moby Gym at CSU today, he'll sign the goalpost." So, we did. Not only did he sign it, but he had all of the team members who played in the '77 Super Bowl sign it. To this day, it hangs proudly on my wall next to the piece of my actual seat from the South Stands of old Mile High.

————GALE RUSSMAN, a Broncos season ticket holder for 39 years

Our group started in the '60s. Some union workers and I were building a missile base. We were working so much overtime we didn't get to go to the games a lot. We had tickets later with some other friends that still go to the games. My son and I moved up to Club Level seats in the new stadium. We don't tailgate anymore, and we lost our parking space when we cut back to two tickets. Club seats are nice. There are a lot of great fans there. A lot of them are corporate seats, but there are some regulars near us. At one of the games, there was a drunk Kansas City fan who kept standing up and getting in the way of watching the game. He made a couple trips up the stairs and would stand in front of the lady in front of us so she couldn't see. She finally got tired of him and gave him a swift kick to the backside and sent him tumbling down the stairs!

I can remember when they declared Orange Sunday. I bought an old van that we decorated, put an awning on it, and did it up to tailgate with. The town used to decorate for the games. As we've grown, some of that has gone away, but it's still pretty strong. They should

have Orange Sunday every year, especially for the Sunday Night and Monday Night games. The fans locked onto the Broncos because of timing. The town was the right size and was just ready for a pro team. The organization was solid. For a long time there was a waiting list for season tickets, and for many years you couldn't buy a ticket at the gate. It was just a prime time for the Broncos to be here. I don't think anyone ever regretted having seats at Mile High. It's about the people, the team and the players. I've been going to the games with my family—wouldn't trade that for anything. It's an experience that you can't understand unless you do it. We've had friends who have gone to every game and every Super Bowl. Friendship is still more important than money or anything there is.

——BOB SCHWARZ, 74, Denver

My husband and I have a Super Bowl party every year at our house. For the Super Bowl versus the Packers, I decorated the house inside and out. I was up every hour to check and make sure no one had stolen any of the banners and flags outside. We had one Packers fan come to the party. We made him sit on a tiny stool with a cheese grater in the corner of the room farthest from the TV. After the Broncos won, we went running out of the house with horns and cowbells, crying because we were so happy. My neighbors were surely wondering what their crazy neighbor was doing. I ended up with a bruised hand because of the cowbell. The Packers fan at the party gave me his jersey, which I stomped on and rolled around on, but he wouldn't let me burn it. I got my husband out of bed early and headed to the parade to see John Elway raise the trophy. It was so crazy there. We thought we had an excellent spot picked out, but they moved the rails on us and we had about four inches of space to stand in. There was a young man in front of me who let me put my camera on his head and use it as a tripod. There were 600,000 people there. As a Broncos fan, there is nothing like it. I would say the mood was euphoric. Everyone was smiling. Everyone was a best friend. It didn't matter if you were 30 or 60, everyone was a Broncos fan that day.

——CARLA PATTY-WEIS, 44, Centennial

I've had season tickets for 15 years. I saw going to the games as entertainment and a chance to be together with family—time with my brother-in-law and with my kids. In the old Mile High Stadium, you could get very close to the sideline where the teams came out of the tunnel. We would try to get near the fence and see the players close up. I can remember seeing John Elway on the sidelines with Steve Watson—close enough to see that Watson's fingers were distorted and bent. I remember one time in particular against the Vikings, screaming at Elway as he tried to get out of bounds. He got hit hard at the sidelines and landed right in front of us at the fence. We pretty much had a good time at all the games. I always enjoyed watching Elway play. I really like the characters, though. Guys like Tom Jackson, flipping off John Madden. Karl Mecklenburg's intensity. I remember watching Howie Long chase Elway. It was like a bloodhound chasing a rabbit. I think he lived to chase Elway. For me, the value in sports, especially football, is in the teamwork and sacrifice involved. Football teams have to work towards the common goal. Broncos fans are people who value family, hard work, sacrifice and discipline. I've had a chance to show my kids that by showing them what the teams go through to achieve that.

—————WALTER CURTIS, 58, refrigeration mechanic

It was the '77-'78 season, and I had just graduated from high school. The Orange Crush Defense was the rallying phrase for the first Super Bowl season in the Broncos' history. My friends and I had liberated ourselves and moved out of the paternal nest and were now on our own. I lived in what we called the "Duplex" and my parents called a "Commune" on East Colfax and Josephine. It was Party Central and our Broncos fan headquarters. Orange Crush soda had grabbed on to the name for the Denver defense and was happy to lend their name to get the free advertising. I owned a white 1966 VW Bug that became the Broncos Bug as the Super Bowl approached in '78. We purchased and consumed many six packs of Orange Crush soda. I drilled holes through the cans and stacked them on my antenna and all over my Bug. I drove around for weeks thinking it was the coolest thing ever. As game time approached for the Super Bowl with the Dallas Cowboys, we were at a fever pitch, hoping Craig Morton—I think they called him "Weak Knees" Morton at the time—would make it through the game. When it was apparent that we—the Broncos—

were going to be defeated, you would have thought there'd been a death in the family. We were depressed for weeks. The cans came off the Broncos Bug and all was doom and gloom at the "Duplex." We would have more Super Bowl defeats to follow before the "Glorious" victory in '98 over the Green Bay Packers, which no one gave us a chance to win. We may have moved out of the "Duplex" and moved on to our adult lives, but we never forgot that first Super Bowl or the heady days of the '77-'78 season. Going through those crushing Super Bowl defeats over the years only made it all the more exhilarating when we finally won 20 years later. I was brought back to those Orange Crush glory days and was tempted to cover what was now a station wagon with soda cans, but my children were doing that to their cars, carrying on the tradition of Broncomania!

——**BILL DAWKINS**, Aurora, Colorado

I was in the Navy, stationed aboard U.S.S. Midway, out of Yokosuka, Japan. I was home on leave and was at a bank getting some money. This was in '90, and at the bank was a defensive coach for the Broncos. I got the nerve to start talking to him, and he asked if I was a Broncos fan. I informed him that I indeed was and would be watching the Broncos in Tokyo against the Seahawks. "You're going to fly all the way to Japan to watch us play?" he asked. I replied that I didn't have much of a choice, as I was stationed in Japan and was home on leave. He got my name and told me to report to the main ticket booth with a friend the day of the game. I asked why, and he told me I would find out then. Well, I did, and next thing I knew, I was watching the game on the sideline with the Broncos. It was great. There weren't a lot of Broncos fans there that day, but we won. I made sure all the people within hearing range knew that from then on, the Broncos owned the Tokyo Dome, and all others had to pay rent. It's a wonder I didn't land in a Japanese jail cell. A few months later, I was in full combat in the first Gulf War. Now, I have a helmet I bought at an Army surplus store. I sanded it to bare metal and painted it in Broncos colors. I call it the "NO LIMIT SOLDIER HELMET" and it goes with me to every game.

——**NICK A. ADLON**, Sheridan, Colorado

Super Bowl XXXII came around and my son, Howard, suggested we drive to San Diego and get tickets when we got there. We left that night, and drove through the night, but we didn't find many Broncos fans in San Diego. We camped out and then went to the Gaslamp District. We found someone selling tickets, but they were $4,000 each! We watched the game on the street in our RV in the Gaslamp District. People walking by joined us. Before the game, there were no Broncos fans. After the game, there were lots of Broncos fans! There was even a parade after the game. I have a Broncos room full of memorabilia. A few years ago, a gentleman made a picture using commemorative envelopes of the games. It has the names of the quarterbacks and coaches. He made 500, and mine is number 50. Each of my five kids buys me stuff. My customers gave me stuff, too, including some of the Orange Crush cans and bottles. I have four Elway signatures and footballs from Super Bowls, as well. I have an orange bowling ball from the '77 season. It's never been used. At Christmas, I make a "Broncos Tree" with Broncos bulbs and decorations. I've made a Broncos baby quilt and my Broncos room has Broncos wallpaper. One of the most enjoyable games we ever went to was when the NFL players were on strike and the subs played. The atmosphere was very relaxed. We beat the Raiders. Nobody booed at all. I don't think you should ever boo at the games.

————MARGIE CARLISLE, Denver resident since she was 10-years-old

Everyone in my family is a die-hard Broncos fan. During the Super Bowl years, my sister was living in Florida. We would call back and forth several times during each game all season long. We swore we wouldn't cry at the end of each of the Super Bowls, but we always did together over the phone. After the second Super Bowl win, my sister came to visit in August. Since we never got to watch the games together, we decided to have a Super Bowl party. The entire family came, and we all dressed in our orange and blue, ate orange and blue food, had orange and blue balloons, pompons and flowers. We put the video in and cheered just like it was a live game! The only difference was that we were able to watch the commercials and were much, much more relaxed. My sister and I still cried at the end—only we were together this time.

———KATHY DILLON-DURICA, Fort Collins, Colorado

The first Broncos game I went to was when they went to the Super Bowl in 1977. I lived in Reno then and they became my team. My family and friends were Raiders fans. I've been to every Super Bowl the Broncos have been in. I've only missed three or four Super Bowls at all. I was in San Diego, at a restaurant the night before the Super Bowl. Brett Favre was there with his family. He was wearing an orange T-shirt. I new then he was going to lose. We were right in the corner of the field watching Elway spin into the end zone. I had a nice leather jacket made with both Super Bowl patches on it that I wore to Atlanta. I told the manufacturer of the jacket we were going to three-peat. He said if we did, he'd take the jacket back and make it reflect that for free. My business is better on Mondays when the Broncos win. It's like someone died when they lose. People don't feel like coming to work or buying anything. Life is good when the Broncos win.

———"DEALIN'" DOUG MORELAND, took three hours to get to the Monday Night Snow Bowl and walked the final mile in the blizzard to make it to the stadium before kickoff

In approximately '80 or '83, Joe Bell, a copy editor for the *Denver Post*, was the ultimate Broncos fan and kept voluminous statistics of each and every thing the team did. The Broncos organization said his stats were better than many they kept themselves in those days. Joe was somewhat physically handicapped and the sportswriters at the *Post* assisted him in putting together a book, which was called *The Broncos Bible*. It was never a great financial success—not many copies were sold—but it was greatly admired and loved by the Broncos fans who did happen to get a copy. Joe went on to Kansas City and became copy editor of the *Kansas City Star*, but he never quit being a Broncos fan, which I'm sure he kept quiet in the Kansas City newsroom. The book was done in chapters from 1960, when they were founded, up through whatever year the book was published—'80 or '83. Each chapter had several interesting stories about what went on in that particular season. It was heavy with statistical material, which was for only the dyed-in-the-wool sports addicts. They are now in rare supply. A good friend of mine who runs booths at estate sales and antique shows claims they sell for $25-$50 when you can find one. I have two or three somewhere in a box and didn't realize they were worth that much. As I recall, we sold them for $5.95. Bob Martin, radio voice of the Broncos, knew and liked Joe Bell. He did radio commercials and on-air interviews for him.

———DAN GREEN, 59. owner and publisher of *The Record Stockman*

When I heard they were going to sell stuff from Mile High Stadium, my vision was to get one of the fiberglass benches off the South Stands and stick it in my back yard. When I heard they were selling the chairs, I thought, "Oh, man, I got to figure out how to do that." It wasn't cheap—$200. I spent a good portion of the day in my car going down there when they began to tear Mile High down. There were about 70 giant orange trash receptacles around the stadium, and they said 'Mile High Stadium.' They were huge, monster receptacles. There was one sitting outside the southwest entrance to the stadium a few days before I picked up the chairs. Workers were ripping out the other side of the stadium and there wasn't much activity there. I thought, "Wow, what a cool big trash can to put in my garage!" I sat in my truck out there for over an hour until I saw this other guy come up. He walked by. He turned around. He walked back. He walked by again. I thought, "Who is this guy? Is he security? I'm just going to drive up there and throw one of those trash cans in the back of my truck and drive off. I'm going to do it. I'm going to do it." Then, this guy came up, took the garbage can from under me and drove away. He had been staking the place out, now knowing that I was there at the other end of the parking lot. I was like, "You bum! You took my garbage can!" Here we were—two psychos out there trying to steal a garbage can that said 'Mile High Stadium' on it. It took several weeks to demolish the stadium. The press boxes caught on fire one day. I was driving by and saw the fire trucks. That was pretty freaky—like the stadium was upset. It was sad. I walked around there for a couple of hours a few days shooting pictures from all different angles. I took a whole video tape of going to that first preseason game—walking between the old and new stadiums. There was a dirt sidewalk from where we parked and you got a vision of the old and the new. The fact that they weren't going to call the new building "Mile High Stadium" was pretty chintzy in my book.

——MIKE FABIAN, die-hard Broncos fan

In late December 2004, I was walking into a bar to meet a couple of friends and slipped on the icy sidewalk. I broke my clavicle and shoulder. I'm 6-foot-4, so it was a long fall. I was on my way in, not out, so I was clean and sober. I ended up at Rose Medical Center. My friend, Josh, a big Broncos fan, gave me a ride home from the hospital. The medical center gave me a CD with copies of my x-rays. Josh thought it would be a great idea to have Steve Antonopulos, the trainer for the Broncos, sign my x-rays. His nickname is "Greek,"

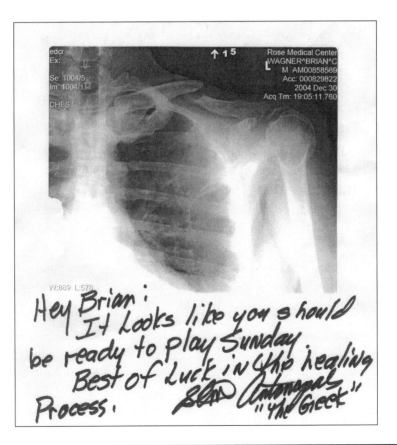

and he's been with the team for years. Josh got it signed, "Looks like you'll be ready for Sunday's game.—Greek."

——BRIAN WAGNER, a Broncos fan since the age of 6

Guys from the Broncos bus group all met and watched the Super Bowl against Green Bay in a friend's basement. It brought us together with our Broncos Pride. That is where the spirit of the bus came from. After college, we came back together and decided we needed to find a way to go to the games and represent the team well. We started toying with the idea of buying an old school bus. We looked for months and couldn't find one that was the right price. We wanted to restore and paint it. We finally found one in Indiana, but didn't go buy it. Jeter Thomas and I were sitting at lunch in downtown Denver arguing whether or not we had exhausted all our resources. We walked outside and a bus drove by that was for sale! We went and looked at about 10 buses. We found a 1990 bus for $3,000. I don't think the owner realized it was newer than all the others. He painted it orange for us for $300. We drove it around the block picking up our friends. We'd work on it every Saturday. We have Astroturf on the inside, as well as a flat-screen TV, and we turned some seats around. We have a huge grill and get a great turnout at every game. We're proud of the bus. We had an incredible turnout at the AFC Championship Game in 2005. It wasn't just Broncos fans, either. Everyone was sharing in the excitement. We created a stuffed doll of Jerome Bettis and tied it to the front of the bus. We had a sign that read, "Our bus is bigger than your bus," and even the Steelers fans liked that. They were taking pictures with it. It was amazing to see the kids coming up in Elway jerseys wanting to hit the Bettis doll with a broom. The bus is a lot of work, but with support from others, it has gotten a bit easier. People come by and ask how they can help. They donate stuff for the bus—parking tickets and more. It has taken on a character of its own. We're looking forward to more and more seasons with the bus!

——CHASE BOSWELL, Broncos fanatic

The South Stands fans are the down-to-earth, working people who care about stuff and are not afraid to show it. We always made a lot of noise pounding our feet on the metal stands in Mile High. I miss the old stadium. The new ticket prices have out-priced the working people. The fans aren't the same. It is a whole different crowd of people in the new stadium.

When I go to the games, I always pack a bag with certain things in it. I take a small TV to watch the replays, and my headphone radio to listen to the Newsradio 850 KOA broadcasts. I'll have one ear on the radio, one on the stadium. I always wear certain clothes and do my hair a certain way. I always eat the same thing, drink the same drinks. I usually have waffles and some juice before a game, and half a glass of milk. It's a ritual. Everybody says the players are the reason, but I believe that if I do something different, it has an impact. Since my surgery, it is hard to get around. I am in Section 132, Row 11, on the aisle, and it's hard to walk up and down the stairs. In the old stadium, everyone sat in the same seats for years. Everyone huddled together to keep warm. It was like a big family. The new stadium mixed up where people sat. The 2005 playoff game versus the Patriots was the first time the crowd was really noisy in the new stadium.

I scrimp and save all year to be able to afford my tickets, and I won't give them up. I'm surprised at how many people sell some of their tickets. There just isn't a consistent group of fans anymore.

The chance to go to Broncos camp got me through my surgery. I was in the hospital for quite awhile. A bunch of the players sent me cards and flowers. They send me Christmas cards, too. The team is just wonderful—from the coaches to the storekeepers to the owners. They really care about the fans.

My house is a shrine to the Broncos. I have stuff in my office, my house, my car. I started out as "Bronco Baby," but with the different accents and such, it turned into "Bronco Betty." I accepted that. No problem.

———BRONCO BETTY, Hasn't missed a home game since 1960.

DENVER BRONCOS DENVER BRONCOS DENVER BRONCOS DENVER BRONCOS DENVER BRONCOS

Name the Raiders coach... win valuable prizes

Chapter 6

On the Road Again

Today We Ride

RAIDERS FANS ARE PROOF THAT HELL IS FULL AND THE DEAD ARE WALKING THE EARTH

MIKE KIRSHBAUM

Mike Kirshbaum is 40-years-old and was born in Glenwood Springs. He works for a monthly magazine in Denver. Although a die-hard Raiders fan, he has never been to Oakland. He doesn't know that "there is no there there."

I became an Oakland Raiders fan because my brother, who is three years older and 100 pounds heavier than me, used to beat the pudding out of me. Gregg was a Broncos fan and took extreme pleasure in beating me up, especially when my Mom wasn't around. I figured I needed to get back at him, so I rooted for the Raiders just to make him mad.

We'd play backyard football—Raiders versus the Vikings in Super Bowl XI. We picked teams based on who thought each team would win, and I was the only one in the fifth grade who thought the Raiders would win. They all told me how stupid I was, but the Raiders won that Super Bowl. I couldn't wait to get to school on Monday.

There are a number of Raiders fans in Denver. The second-highest selling NFL gear here is Raiders' apparel. There are some Raiders bars around. I had a Broncos fan threaten to kick me out of a bar when I was rooting for the Chiefs once. He told me to go back to KC. I go to the games and root for the Raiders. I've never rooted for the Broncos. I can't even root for them if it is beneficial to the Raiders. It's like grabbing a knife and saying you are going to cut off your toe. You might grab the knife and take off your shoe, but you can't cut it off.

My coworkers' first reaction to me being a Raiders fan is that they immediately don't like me. They find out later I'm pretty unbiased in analyzing games and they realize I'm OK. I went to University of Northern Colorado in Greeley. As the Broncos camp is there, I used to deliver pizzas to the Broncos players. One time, I remember an offensive lineman opening the door. He wasn't a Bronco yet. I told him to enjoy his pizza, and said "Go Raiders!" He understood and still gave me a tip.

Typically Broncos fans are more intelligent than Raiders fans. They are definitely less violent, and they believe way too much what the Broncos PR machine tells them. Broncos fans never say "We should be better." Raiders fans will tell you if the team is awful.

I spent a game with Jim Otto, Al Davis and Morris Bradshaw at Mile High Stadium in the press box. That is where my seat was to cover the games. They thought it was great that I was a Raiders fan. You aren't supposed to cheer in the press box—I had a real hard time with that. Bradshaw noticed and commented that it must be hard for me not to cheer. The Raiders lost that game. I interviewed Art Shell after the game and he didn't seem too upset about losing. I couldn't understand it. I was basing my whole next week's mood on the game, and yet, it didn't seem to bother him.

I remember in '77 when the Broncos beat the Raiders in the AFC Championship Game. I was 11 at the time. Tom Jackson put the ball in John Madden's face and said, "It's all over, fat man!" I'm thinking that for not winning anything prior to that, they were pretty cocky.

GASSIN' UP

I wasn't a Broncos fan until I moved to Denver in grade school. I've never met such passionate fans as in Denver. I've been a Dallas and Kansas City fan, and the Broncos fans are the most passionate. I'm still a Broncos fan today. My wife, Christine, and I have season tickets and fly from Chicago to Denver to go to the games. We split those tickets with another couple, but we also go to a game at Arrowhead Stadium in Kansas City each year. It's not as fun as being in Denver. Denver usually wins those games, though. The K.C. fans treat us pretty well. They aren't mean spirited. There's a little trash talking, but it's all in good fun. The Broncos get in your blood. It's hard to explain what drives us to travel from Chicago to Denver four or six times a year to go to games: it's just how we are. Broncos fans are hard core and dedicated. Steve Foley is probably my favorite player. He wasn't a big player size-wise, but his heart and passion as a player was special. We're going to six games this year and trying to go to two more. We have Denver tickets in Kansas City on Thanksgiving Day. We also purchased **COLTS** season tickets, so we can potentially see Denver play there in the playoffs. It was less expensive to get season tickets than to pay a broker for them. I think Denver will be playing Indy in the championship game this year.

———CHAD GILBERT, 41, Crystal Lake, Illinois

The fact that the Denver Broncos had colorful characters helped through the bad years. These guys are for real—it's our little cow town perception across the nation that made it "us against the world." We were collectively, as a group of 75,000 people in Mile High Stadium, screaming that it was us against the world....We had a great time at the Newsradio 850 KOA tailgate party at Super Bowl XXXIII. It was a rowdy time in Ft. Lauderdale, Florida. There were huge party boats behind the restaurant. Everyone on the boats was partying. The women were showing their body parts willingly. It

> Tony Dungy, Indianapolis **COLTS** coach, is the last NFL player to throw and make an interception in the same NFL game. He was a defensive back and a backup quarterback for the Steelers.

became a contest between the women on the boats and women on the docks! The view was perfect. The night before, Eugene Robinson was arrested. That made us wonder about our prospects for the game. There were a ton of Atlanta fans there, of course. But there were also a lot of Minnesota fans there, as they thought they would beat the Falcons and had already headed to Florida. All the true Broncos fans were up in the second deck of the stadium. It was a phenomenal experience. Knowing this was it for Elway, I felt an immense amount of pride to be from the Rocky Mountains and to be a Broncos fan.

——DR. LEONARD GRAF, optometrist

After the Broncos beat the Packers, I was there to introduce all of the players at the Capitol Building for the parade. The thing that stunned me was the number of people at the parade. It was much bigger than any parade before. Some estimated it at over 600,000 people. It was a hot, beautiful day, and I was looking at the crowds that were 12-, 13-, 15-people deep lining the streets in downtown Denver. From the curb to the buildings, there were masses of people. It was like a movie. I've never seen anything like it in my entire life. It seemed like everyone we had seen on the street was now in front of the Capitol Building. The energy of introducing players and talking to the crowd was overwhelming. There were adults, kids, grandkids, dads—all generations at this parade. When you see over half a million people, it's cool and a little scary!...

We did our radio show from Canton, Ohio, for John Elway's induction into the Pro Football Hall of Fame. We drove there and stopped in places like Lubbock, Texas, and Memphis, Tennessee. Everyone respected and loved John Elway. We were removed from the true Broncos fans because of our route there. We got up our first morning in Canton, and the entire RV park was full—hundreds of RVs. I'd say that 97 percent of the campers had Broncos' flags flying on them. It was Broncos Central in Canton. I bet a caravan of them would have been 12 miles long. You could tell from the number of Broncos fans that this induction was going to be all about John Elway, even though there were other great players being inducted, too. Everything was about John Elway. John's daughter introduced him at the Hall of Fame induction and spoke about him. I think 90 percent of the people at the induction were Broncos fans. Elway was the first Broncos player inducted into the Hall of Fame.

——SCOTT HASTINGS, former NBA player who became an announcer for KFAN Radio and the Broncos

I went to a Thanksgiving game in Dallas a few years ago. I was standing next to a Cowboys fan and he told me that the Broncos suck. I asked him why they didn't fill in the hole in the stadium roof. He told me is was so that God could watch His team play! I said that was awfully nice of them since the Broncos had played there only four times. He didn't find that very funny.

——TIM MCKERNAN, Denver, a.k.a. Barrel Man

As the Raiders left the field, the fans were throwing snowballs, really iceballs, at the Raiders players. One of their players snuck through the fence and went up into the stands and started beating the heck out of the fan...a Raiders fan walked into the men's room and yelled something to the effect that "John Elway is a donkey &%*#." The Broncos weren't playing well anyhow, so the men in the men's room just pummeled him. Unfortunately, that kind of stuff happens sometimes.

We drive 600 miles one-way to see the games in Denver. We got snowed in one year in Rawlins, Wyoming. They had a blizzard. We went through the Yellow Pages looking for a Broncos bar so we could watch the game. We found one. The owner answered the phone and told us to come on down. They had a big spread of homemade foods and Broncos banners all over the bar. We made some new friends and had a great time watching the game. The bar owner gave us one of the banners, from the back-to-back Super Bowl wins.

People realized how dedicated we are. It took us 14 hours to get to the game driving through a blizzard, and then there were a bunch of empty seats. We drove 600 miles and the people in Denver didn't drive across town. We started driving down in 2000 when we moved up there.

I can remember as a kid having big orange foam hats, drinking Orange Crush, and watching the Broncos play. We had an orange Pinto. We were recently at a department store and they had a rack of Orange Crush T-shirts. I bought them all and gave them to my friends. Orange is in, even for the "regular" people, so it's good for Denver fans!

——CRAIG CORDELL, Season ticket holder who drives 1,200 miles roundtrip from his Idaho home.

I was living in San Diego during Super Bowl XXXII. My whole family was raised Broncos fans, and we're all still Broncos fans. My family came out for the game. We were out at the nightspot Jimmy Love's the evening before the game. We were in the downstairs area as a group. The next table over was a group of Patriots fans. I met a young man named Woody who was very handsome and had a good conversation with him. He had come down there looking for a restroom. His friend in front of him stopped, and Woody bumped into him. He said to Woody, "Look, there's your wife," and it was me. We hadn't even met, yet. We talked about football. Woody lived in L.A. at the time, so his family had flown out to see Woody and then drove down to San Diego. If it weren't for the Broncos, we wouldn't have met. Woody and I got married in 1999. He's still a Patriots fan, but we do have Broncos season tickets. We have one child now, and one on the way. Had the Broncos not gone to the Super Bowl, I would have never met my husband.

——KATIE (ZURCHER) HINES, Denver

We also go to FanFair every year. It is a highlight for all of us. We missed it last year because we went to Disney instead. When the kids found out they missed FanFair, they were really mad at us. We joke that our retirement will be spent in INVESCO Field's parking lot. My game room is totally dedicated to the Broncos—collector's plates, trading cards, autographed **FOOTBALLS** and more. My son is

> NFL **FOOTBALLS** are made in Ada, Ohio. Each team uses one thousand per year. The balls are made from cowhide, not pigskin. The balls used by kickers are different and are marked with a "K".

trying to get my trading cards. He wanted one of my John Elway rookie cards, and I traded him for an autographed Jake Plummer card. We were here in New Mexico during a fire that caused us to have to evacuate our home. I was rushing through the house at 2 a.m., grabbing the most important things. I didn't have a lot of room to take things. When we tried to get out of town, it was a long five-and-a-half hours to drive a 20-minute drive, I realized I forgot to pack coats for the kids, but I did have my Broncos trading cards and my Elway autographed football! That made my mother really proud.

——MANDI GEORGE, New Mexico resident

After the Broncos defeated Cleveland at home, my friend and I decided we were going to Super Bowl XXII in San Diego even though we had no tickets. Off we went in my bright orange 1976 Chevy Vega. Super Bowl or bust. After stopping in Laguna, California, we picked up another friend and headed for **JACK MURPHY STADIUM** the day before the game. We found some tickets and paid $300 apiece, which seemed like a huge sum of money. There was a pep rally going on at Sea World that afternoon. We eventually made it there, but were turned away at the gate because they said it was full. As we started to leave, we noticed then-Congresswoman Pat Schroeder and a small group of well-dressed people heading for that same gate. We followed them even though we had on all our Broncos gear. At the gate, she told them who she was and that she was to deliver a speech at the pep rally. They opened the gate and let all of us in and escorted us right up to the stage. We had front row seats. The best thing, though, was that I was standing next to Floyd Little and gave him a high-five.

——STAN ROHRIG, Arvada, Colorado

The game that sticks in my mind the most was against Green Bay. We tailgated and sat in the South Stands. It was the "Snow Bowl." The snow was blowing straight into the stands, and we couldn't keep our eyes open long because of the blowing snow. We made it through the

> **QUALCOMM was formerly JACK MURPHY STADIUM,** named after a local sportswriter who was instrumental in helping San Diego obtain the Padres franchise in 1969. Jack Murphy's brother was Bob Murphy, New York Mets announcer for 40 years.

third quarter and then had to leave. I've never been that cold in my life....I saw the Broncos play in Pittsburgh in '88 and sat near the 50-yard line. I walked in wearing a white sweater with a very small Denver "D" on it. I got to my seat and all around me were iron workers wearing helmets. One of them saw my sweater. He told me I had two options—take the sweater off and wear it inside out or take it off and throw it on the ground. The only thing that kept them from pummeling me was that my dad was an iron worker, too....In '74, I was a sophomore in college in Michigan. The Broncos played in Detroit on Thanksgiving. My cousin had season tickets, and we went to the game. His seats were right below the press box in Tiger Stadium. The Broncos beat the Lions. My aunt and uncle were at home cooking a turkey. They were listening on the radio and the radio announcer kept saying that there was one Broncos fan in the stadium and that he was right below the broadcast booth. He said that was the most obnoxious fan. That was me! The Lions fans were throwing beer on me, and we were high-fiving each other. It was a BLAST! They dumped beer on me at the end of the game.

————STAN SCHWARZ, Colorado resident since 1955

Both of my children never thought their dad actually worked. They saw football as just playing. During the big snow storm in 1982 that shut down Denver, Coach Reeves had the players go in for practice anyhow. The offensive line used to drive in together. It took them two-and-a-half hours to get there that day. They were at practice for only 20 minutes when they were sent home. They couldn't make it home. The next day, they snowmobiled David home to get clothes, then to the airport to get to a game. Channel 9 landed its helicopter at my house at the request of the Broncos. I was pregnant and in a new subdivision, so they worried about me being there by myself during the snow storm. They took me and our black lab, Zack, to Craig and Susan Morton's house. We stayed there for a couple of weeks before the snow was cleared enough to get home!

————CECILIA STUDDARD, married to Dave Studdard,
a Denver Broncos offensive lineman for 10 years

In '88, I was going to college at the University of Puget Sound at Tacoma, Washington. I went to the Broncos game in the Seattle Kingdome with a friend who had tickets. I wore a Denver Broncos divisional champions jersey to the game. Midway through the second quarter, three drunk, angry Seahawks fans picked me up and held me over the third railing at the Kingdome. They "politely" asked me to remove my jersey and to quit being so obnoxious. Through artful negotiating, they allowed me to keep the shirt on, but I was subdued throughout the rest of the game.

———GREG BUTLER, Denver

After I left Denver for California in '84 and then came back 20 years later, I felt like it was a lot more sophisticated. I've probably been to seven or eight Raider games in Oakland. That's an atmosphere that if I was never in again, it wouldn't bother me. I took my 8-year-old son there for his first professional event ever. There were people there— the man looked like an accountant and the wife looked like she could have been a nurse. They were two seemingly mature adults who had on professionally-printed t-shirts that said, "F--- the Broncos." My son looked at that. Then, he looked over at me. How do you explain to an 8-year-old kid? At eight, he's old enough to read. You walk out of their stadium after a loss, and you want to get out of that stadium as fast as you can because they're pretty lathered up. I had a liquor bottle land maybe 15 or 20 feet from me as I was walking out of the stadium. It had been thrown from the top of the stadium. That's the kind of stuff they do. It's a really strange environment up there. When we went to Oakland, I did not wear any Broncos gear. I had given my son a really nice Broncos leather jacket and he wanted to wear it there. I told him to remember what our experience had been at that stadium before and to decide for himself it he wanted to wear some-thing Broncos there. He thought about it and decided not to.

———RICHARD AGREN, Denver

Chapter 7

Playin' Favorites

Put Me In, Coach

MRS. MORTON, DO YOU NEED MORE TOWELS? NO THANKS, MY SUITCASE IS FULL

RANDY WRIGHT

Randy Wright, a graduate of Colorado State University, currently lives in Alamosa, Colorado. His story is one that makes us all believe our actions do have an influence on the great game of football.

It was Week 7 of the '77 Denver Broncos football season and the dreaded Raiders were in town to face the 6-0 Broncos. Denver had beaten the Raiders badly, 30-7, in Oakland two weeks earlier, and everything looked good for a repeat performance.

I live in Alamosa, but I was going to school in Fort Collins at Colorado State University, and my parents were coming up for the game. They would be with some of our family's closest friends. Both couples were staying at the Marriott Hotel on Hampden. Since I hadn't been home in awhile, I decided to surprise them with a visit. In those days, if you asked at the desk what room someone was staying in, they would actually tell you. Armed with my parents' room number, my college roommate and I headed for the Marriott elevator and up to their room. When we reached the room, I had decided to mildly scare my parents with a little yell as they opened the door, a simple practical joke. Or so it was planned. The lady who opened the door looked like the wife of my parents' friends and, like planned, I yelled! The only problem was that it wasn't them. She slammed the door, scared out of her mind. I felt horrible.

My roommate and I wandered the hall for a couple of minutes making sure we had the room number they had given us and wanting to apologize to the lady. About that time a hotel security guard showed up. He, very nicely—though I'm not sure why, looking back at it—asked what we were up to, and if he could help us. We explained the situation and he took us back to the elevator where he called the front desk and again asked for my parents' room number. The correct room was across the hall from our earlier victims, and escorted by the security guard, we soon found out that no one was there. All that for nothing. There was no such thing as a cell phone and no way to get in touch with them. I could have just waited for them to show up, but under the circumstances, we were too embarrassed to hang around. We headed back to Fort Collins.

My parents and their friends went to the game the next day and watched the Raiders beat up on our Broncos, 24-14. Craig Morton had a terrible day. My weekend wasn't getting any better. But it got worse. When I finally got in touch with my parents and told them of our debacle, my mom's voice got excited.

"That was the room across the hall from us?" she asked.

"Right across the hall," I answered.

"Do you know who was staying in that room?" Her voice wasn't pleasant.

"No," I said.

"That was Craig Morton's room!"

My heart sank. My Broncos had lost to the Raiders. Craig Morton had been a big part of the loss. And it had been my fault! I know how that Cubs fan felt when he caught the foul ball, costing his team the game.

I don't know who the woman was. I assume it was his fiancée or wife. I didn't know which it was at the time. I don't know if she was even supposed to be there. None of that matters. But after all these years, I just wanted the chance to apologize to the Mortons and to all the Denver Broncos fans who had to endure a home loss to our nemesis, the Raiders.

THE FOURTH ESTATE DOESN'T TAKE THE FIFTH

SAM ADAMS

Sam Adams is a columnist for the Rocky Mountain News. *He was the beat reporter covering the Broncos for both the* Denver Post *(two years) and* Rocky Mountain News *(two years). He is originally from Cleveland and was a huge Browns fan. "The Drive" is painful to this day.*

One of my favorite stories is training camp in 1994 in Greeley, Colorado. I'm covering the team and stop into a sports bar one night. Elway and some of the players are there. They have a Pop-A-Shot basketball game. I challenge Elway to a game. There are some kids there who see us, and they come around. Elway is the hero of heroes to them. We flip a coin. He wins the flip and I go first. I put up 82 points. The last three or four baskets I made I was looking at him and talking instead of looking at the basket. I think he got 36 points. I told him that this almost made up for "The Drive." For two weeks at camp, he'd walk by me shaking his head, telling me he wouldn't forget the game. Not too many people get to beat Elway at anything, and I beat him at Pop-A-Shot. He's competitive at everything, even if he's not good at it....

I used to play cards with the players on Tuesdays with Shannon Sharpe. I wasn't supposed to be in the locker room on their off-day, but we played anyhow. We'd bet on boxing matches, too. We'd have to pay the other person in coins—rolls of quarters, rolls of nickels. They had to go in a Tiffany's bag. They could afford to go to Tiffany's to buy something to get the bag, unless you won the first bet, then the first loser had to go get the bag. I paid in quarters. I lived in an apartment, so I had quarters for the laundry. Keith Burns, Shannon Sharpe, and me. We did this until Sharpe went to the Ravens.

We were in Kansas City in 1999, the night before a game. Mike Shanahan is a big boxing fan. He had a fight piped into the ballroom at the hotel so the players could watch the fight. Oscar de la Hoya versus Felix Trinidad. Big fight. Everyone thought Oscar was going to win except for Sharpe. When Trinidad won, Sharpe went nuts, dancing around and collecting his bets. Shanahan lost to him. It was fun to see these guys enjoying themselves outside of football. It was nice to see Shanahan enjoying it with his players. Sharpe made Shanahan sign the money he won....

Being in the locker room after Super Bowl XXXII, after the other media had left, was great. Elway was one of the only ones left. He had a little glass of what looked like champagne. He got to his locker and sat down. He was looking at me and laughing. Greek, the trainer, came out to get the injury list. Elway told him his shoulder, knee and side hurt. It was after the Super Bowl, so it didn't really matter. Looking at each other, they just start hugging and celebrating.

A week later, I was in Del Frisco's Steakhouse on a weeknight. I walked into the cigar room with my buddy. Elway was there. We talked to him for awhile. He said his side still hurt. I said, "Well, that guy flipped you around like a helicopter!" He gave me the scoop and told me that the Broncos would be the "Team of the Year" for the ESPYs. He was right. I was with the *Rocky Mountain News* then, so we broke the story the next day, before it was announced. The Broncos flew to New York the next day to the ESPY Awards. **ESPN** was upset that we knew ahead of time. I never revealed my source. It's funnier now than it was then, of course....

I had a good relationship with the team. I tried to always be fair with the team. I just wrote a story about Rod Smith. He came in undrafted in '94 and made the practice squad. Practice squad players didn't go to away games. He wanted to go to the Chiefs game since he was from K.C. He didn't want to ask Wade Phillips, the coach. He was afraid to ask and asked me to ask for him. I told Wade he should talk

ESPN debuted September 7, 1979. ESPN2 debuted October 1, 1993. *ESPN, The Magazine* made its first appearance on March 11, 1998.

to Rod. That was in 1994. I found out 12 years later he did go on the trip. He's a big star now. He's the Broncos all-time leading receiver....

I played golf with Mike Shanahan once when I was doing a magazine story on him. I'm a terrible golfer, but he's pretty good. We played at Castle Pines. My awfulness reared its head throughout the front nine. It was driving him nuts to have to play with me. I could see it, but he was being very nice about it. We stopped to get a hot dog at the turn. We came out and got on the 10th tee. I looked at Mike and told him that I was going to sit that hole out. Bill Rader, the team chaplain, was playing, too. He yelled out to the other players that I was going to sit out this hole and eat my lunch. A couple of holes later I hit a ball and it landed in Ed McCaffrey's backyard. I didn't hit out of his yard, though. We got to the 16th hole, the toughest par-3 on the course. They all bogied, and I parred it. I almost had a birdie. I shot over 100. Mike almost had two holes-in-one. Very close. A strong breeze would have pushed one of them in the hole.

Another great memory is when the Broncos played Houston—"The Drive in Denver." I was in the press box, because Rick Reilly from *Sports Illustrated* needed a stringer to get quotes from the losers' locker room. They were paying good money to go get quotes. The game was just about over. With four minutes to go, the media went down to the field, in the end zone area. I started walking towards Houston's sideline, headed to the loser's sideline. Houston was winning, but Elway was marching them down the field. The Broncos kicked a field goal and won the game. I went to get quotes from the Houston team. Rick couldn't understand how I knew the Broncos would win. I said, "I'm from Cleveland!" I knew with five minutes to go what would happen. I had seen it before. Once you saw it happen once, you felt like it could happen again anytime Elway got the ball. "The Drive" in Cleveland was the beginning of Elway's drive to the Hall of Fame.

JOHN ELWAY IS JUST A REGULAR GUY WHO SOME DAYS WORE A CAPE

LUKE STAHMER

Luke Stahmer is the Director of Corporate Partnerships for the Colorado Crush, the Arena Football League team owned by John Elway. He first started working for John Elway right out of college. He graduated with honors in astrophysics and thought about being an astronaut, a pilot or joining the Navy.

An intern position came up where I would sell tickets over the phone. I was overqualified for the job, and my resume made it to John Elway's desk. The team was initially based in the Broncos marketing department....The team practiced at Dove Valley. A few of us were scouting out the scene before the Crush season started. Practice was coming to an end and Elway picked up a ball and told me to go for a pass. All I could think was that John Elway was going to throw me a pass. I guess it hadn't quite sunk in, yet, that I worked for Elway, especially not when he wanted to pass a football to me. It was the coolest thing ever. I ran 20 yards. He threw a rocket right at me. The ball hit me square in the forehead and knocked me to the ground. Everybody saw it happen. Trainers came running over with their bags. Everyone was laughing. I picked the ball up and ran to the end zone to do a touchdown dance. That was the beginning of my relationship with John.

The first year the team was in business, John was very involved with the team. He flew with the team on the commercial flights. We were on a Frontier Airlines jet flying to San Jose, California. He has his own jet, so he didn't need to fly with us, but he wanted to be closer to the team and coaches. We were on the plane, Elway on the aisle and me in the middle seat. A woman came down the aisle. Elway was reading the paper with sunglasses on. She walked by a couple of times, and then stopped and asked him if anyone had ever told him he looked like John Elway. Before John could say anything, I told her that I got that all the time. Everyone cracked up. She walked on by thinking I was crazy. She turned a bit red and never came back. Frontier flies the team as part of a partnership with the team. It's not a chartered plane, and Frontier doesn't have first class, so we sit with all the other passengers. It was the last time Elway flew with us. There were 49ers and Raiders fans at the airport when we got there. The fans hated him so much we had to call security. The fans were screaming and yelling, not wanting him there....

I get so many autograph requests, because John Elway is my boss. It's funny how quickly word travels, especially since the Crush won the World Championship. I wear my championship ring. It's a big ring— like the NFL uses. It's the same mold that the Patriots used one year. I'm small, so it's not like I look like a football player. It's nice to have a keepsake like that. I use the ring to my advantage. It's a good ice breaker with the women. I'm proud of what the Crush have done. People have opened up doors for me I never dreamed possible due to my relationship with John. I'm on a first name basis with the Governor of Colorado and have met the President of the United States. Tours of the Capitol, tours of NORAD. It's neat to see how people still clamor around him. People still come up to him and tell him their greatest day was his big win over Green Bay—not when they had kids or their wedding day, but that Super Bowl win.

John and I don't talk football a lot. When we're in the office, it's like working for anyone else, like working with a fraternity brother. He pushes us to go further and harder. We're very competitive in the office. It always seems to be a race, whether it's at lunch or completing a report. John works out in the weight room with the players and gets a bit competitive there. I've stopped working out with him. He can bench twice my weight, even now. He's still physically very fit. John's executive assistant is Kathy Hatch. She's like the office mom. John loves to scare her. He hears her coming to her desk, and he'll hide behind a desk or something and jump out and scare her. You never know what to expect from him. One thing that does catch up with us is when we're on the road. We were in Philadelphia, and Jon Bon Jovi had started an arena football team, the Soul. John worked with them to develop the team. They came to our facility and put on a concert. In Philadelphia, Bon Jovi decided to put on a special party for us at the Ritz. We were hanging out at the hotel and John brought some guests along for the trip. Al Gore and Bruce Springsteen were there. It was just a simple party, hanging out, enjoying ourselves. Word had spread that John was in town. Veteran's Stadium was due to be imploded the next morning. We had to leave the hotel with 100 people at the door in the way, a cloud of smoke coming from the Vet. Traffic was a nightmare, too. It was hard to get to the game on time. It was an eye opener to see the attention. I got him in the minivan and to the game. He really doesn't like taking a limo. He actually prefers to drive himself in a regular car. The first time John met Bon Jovi in person, Elway was just in awe. We all were. The attention they get is unreal. People just flock around them. We were at Sky Bar in L.A. with them once. Heather Locklear walked into the bar and wanted to meet Elway. The sports celebrities are really like a big brotherhood. They all get along and like to talk with each other.

What's the definition of gross sports ignorance?

144 Kansas City Fans!

YOU'RE IN GOOD HANDS WITH ALL-STATE, ALL-PRO JOHN ELWAY

RAELEE FRAZIER

Raelee Frazier makes life casts for historical figures. Her work can be found at the Denver Art Museum, the Smithsonian Institution, and the Colorado Sports Hall of Fame.

I've made 25 baseball Hall-of-Fame players' hands. I used to make ethnic featured mannequins for museums. Obviously, I would have to do body casts and such to do those, and the hands were part of it. Thus, I became known for doing hands of celebrities.

I met a gentleman by the name of Chris Tucker at an art show. He was working with the hitters' hands in baseball. He said, "What if I can get John Elway? Wouldn't it be great to do John Elway's hands?" This was between Super Bowls when he was already a star. I said, "Of course."

It took Chris quite some time to convince Kathy Hatch, who is John Elway's administrative assistant, that this was a worthy project and not something really weird. We had to go through his agent. We did 32 of them because it was Super Bowl XXXII. He was going to use a few of them for his foundation and for his family. We gave him four, and then we did another one for him because they were much more popular than he thought they would be.

All 32 of them sold in two weeks—for $12,500. Channel 9 did a special story on the project and individual fans called about them until they were all gone. We wish we could have made more. We probably weren't very smart about the price we charged. Obviously, we had to make money on it, but we weren't out to be greedy.

A couple of the people decided they wanted to resell theirs, so we put them on the market and gave the money to charity. Some went as high as $50,000! The first set was available at the John Elway Foundation and sold for $40,000, and then they sold two at $25,000 for a charitable auction. These were bought by businesses. Probably two-thirds of the people who originally bought them are just people who really admired John Elway. One woman bought two sets—one for her and one for her husband. It was amazing. I was dumbfounded that one individual would have that big of an impact on a community at that time in his life. The man who bought the last one for $100,000 at Craig Hospital went out and checked out all the items there, and this was what he wanted.

John Elway opened up his office, and I set up all my equipment there. The reason some people will not do this is because they have to shave the backs of their hands and fingers on up to about two inches above the wrist bone. John was somewhat concerned as to what the guys in the locker room would have to say, but he came in and, sure enough, he had already shaved. I had been concerned because he's a real hairy guy. He walked around checking out the pans and was a little tentative about the wax. I always put their little finger into the wax a couple of times to show them it's not going to burn. Then, I started drawing around his hand on the football. He was very receptive to instruction. He said he felt like it was an art project. As I'm pulling the hair off his arm, he said he understood why he couldn't be an artist because of the pain involved. He was very quiet, but very watchful and curious as to how this was going to turn out. It probably took an hour to do this.

I tell the players I can only give them a product at the end if they give me their full cooperation. If they don't do this, then the piece at the end does not look good. To a fault, John did everything I said for him to do, and well beyond. He got his hand so deep in the wax on the first hand that he got it up on the hair. When I had to pull that wax off the hair, he was a little concerned. I have a video that was made by Channel 9 when we did this—they actually won an Emmy for this video.

John was a very gracious person. He was not arrogant. I'm surprised people would pay that kind of money, but that re-enforces why people like him. I've seen John Elway a couple of times since then, and he's surprised, and maybe a little embarrassed. He really appreciated the wax hands. He said it was a little bit of an 'out of body' experience to see his own hands on a football like that.

I've done Dan Marino, Joe Montana and **TROY AIKMAN**. Joe Montana was great to work with—almost a real cut-up. He brought his father along, and he brought us some wine. He was very entertaining and loved the process and was really gracious. Montana's hands are in private collections. We have not done as much with Montana's as we've done with Marino's. Like Elway, he used his for charitable auctions. Aikman was distant. He was not as communicative, but he was following my instructions. He has fabulous, huge hands. Out of all the athletes I've done, I would say Andres Galarraga, the late Buck O'Neil, Aikman and Elway have the biggest hands. A lot of baseball players have small hands, but none of the football players had small hands. Pee Wee Reese had very small hands. Al Kaline had small hands. Greg Maddux has very small hands, and he was a real sweetheart.

I've never been a sports fan, but this has been wonderful. I've traveled across the United States to get all these guys and, because of the stories, they tell, it is a reflection of American history. It's not all statistics; it's stories of what happened to them on the road and what happened between this player and that player. It's a mirror of our society since 1940.

My set of Ted Williams' hands is in the Smithsonian in the American History Department. Most of the baseball players I've done were well beyond the height of their career. In Elway's case, I think if someone is that much of an influence on a community, to be able to capture them at the height of their career is great. I had made historical figures for 20 years before I started doing hands. This was my commitment to history.

> **TROY AIKMAN** wrote a book that had nothing to do with football. It was a kids book called *Things Change*, and it sold an astonishing 200,000 copies....When Aikman was a Henrietta, OK high school student, he was the boys state high school typing champion.

HE SLAM DUNKED TOUCHDOWNS, SPIKED JUMP BALLS AND BIRDIED DOGLEG PAR-3s

LONNIE WRIGHT

Here's a story about a man who played for both the Nuggets and Broncos...and he wasn't the organist. Lonnie Wright played collegiate football at Colorado State University. He was a defensive back for the Denver Broncos from 1966 to 1967 and played in the ABA with the Denver Rockets (now the Nuggets). He has worked at the New Jersey Medical School for 33 years. He directs a number of summer programs geared primarily for minority students—to get them interested and motivated towards medicine. He is on the admissions committee, among other committees. He also makes public appearances on behalf of the school and helps with the recruitment of students.

I got to Colorado State University primarily because my father liked Jim Williams who was the basketball coach at the time. I was recruited more heavily for football than for basketball because I always had a football body. I had a real bad knee at the time, and I decided to play basketball because I thought it would be less stress at the time. I wasn't aware that colleges would operate on you for free. I thought the expense would be incurred by my parents, so I took what I considered the easy way out and decided I would play basketball. I subsequently got operated on after my first year in college.

Jim Williams and the Colorado State University basketball team went to **MADISON SQUARE GARDEN** in New York. They invited me and my family over for a game. I always had a fear of

> The official name of Boston Garden was Boston **MADISON SQUARE GARDEN.**

flying, and I told them to send me the prettiest brochures you could because I didn't want to take a lot of trips. My father really didn't want me to be around the streets in Newark, so he thought I could be a better man if I got away and lived on my own in Colorado. I don't think any of us had any idea how far that was away.

When I got there and looked around, it was strange because I had come from a predominately all-black high school. In '62, when I arrived at Colorado State, there was a total of about 10 African-Americans on campus and very few in town. It was a cultural shock to me, but I knew I was there for a purpose and I knew it wasn't going to be forever. After getting situated, I really enjoyed it and loved it. After the first summer when I came back home, I stayed out there during the summers and worked in Colorado. I did not play football at Colorado State.

My first pro team was the Rockets, now called the Nuggets. That was the ABA. When Spencer Haywood came out of the Olympics, we were still the Rockets. It's an interesting story how that whole thing evolved with me. After not playing football for four years in college, I was approached by several professional football teams. Denver wasn't the first football team to contact me. Dallas contacted me first. Their player personnel director, Gil Brandt, always felt that basketball players were better all-around athletes. He had a history of selecting basketball players. Pete Gent, a tight end with the Cowboys, was also a great basketball player at Michigan State, and they approached me first. I had some interest from the Buffalo Bills and a few others, and then the Denver Broncos jumped in. At the time, I hadn't even signed a football contract. Then I was a fifth- or sixth-round draft choice of the **ST. LOUIS HAWKS** about a month later.

We played Houston with Elvin Hayes and Don Chaney in the NCAA Tournament my last game of my senior year. Gil Brandt met with me after my last game of eligibility. He had a sizeable check. It took

> **In March 1954, the Lakers and the HAWKS played a regulation, regular season NBA game using baskets that were 12' high rather than the usual 10'...the next night they played each other in a doubleheader. True facts, believe it or not!**

everything I could get to refuse the check. That Monday, I got back to the lecture hall for my class and there he was with a little bigger check. I refused that, as well. Then Denver came into the picture saying they would match anybody's bonus money. I thought that if I signed a football contract, I had their bonus money in hand. If I got cut, and I was initially hoping to get cut, then I could go back to St. Louis and start playing basketball. I looked like a dog on defense, just so I wouldn't get hurt. But I started getting into it, and four or five games into the season, I started at defensive safety for the Broncos.

It was strange when I had to tell the people at Colorado State that I wasn't going to play basketball there—that I was going to the Denver Broncos football camp. They didn't understand the reasons why, particularly because I had signed a football contract before the NBA draft, and I'm sure it hurt me in the draft. I thought the money was there because I was out a year after Joe Namath signed an unheard of $400,000 multi-year contract with the Jets. The football people were floating a lot of money around, but very few dollars were offered in basketball.

My idea was that if I got cut—I had their bonus money—then I would go to St. Louis and try out for basketball, which I had been doing for the last four years. But, pride gets in the way, and you start learning and trying, and you start getting acclimated back into football and you start learning it and start enjoying it as well. I played that year and played a second year with Lou Saban.

I played with the Broncos for two years. After the second year, Saban let me go in the expansion draft to Cincinnati. I had a basketball camp in Fort Collins, Colorado when **PAUL BROWN**, the coach of the Bengals, contacted me up there and wanted to know what I was going to do. I said I'd really like a no-cut contract, and he actually laughed at me on the phone.

> **The Bengals, owned by the PAUL BROWN family, were named after the Massillon (Ohio) High School Tigers, whom Brown coached before he became head coach of Ohio State and the Cleveland Browns.**

During the second year of football, I also played basketball from December through April or May, with the Rockets. I took two weeks off and joined the Rockets. I had been approached by Bob Bass and a few other people who had known about my reputation at Colorado State and they said, "Why don't you come out and think about playing a half year of basketball?" I had to get permission from Lou Saban, obviously. He said it was a good idea and to just keep in shape.

Some guys had played in both the NFL and Major League Baseball, but nobody has played, from my understanding, football and basketball. I had gotten letters from the baseball Mets, even. At one time, somebody said, "Why don't you try out for the Triple-A baseball team in Denver?" I didn't do that. One reason was that Paul Brown laughed at me on the phone. And, my second year, after playing a half a year of basketball, the Rockets came in and gave me a no-cut contract for a number of years, so my decision to go back to basketball at the time was made for me. Then, I got back into things and played five years with the Nuggets and then one year with the Miami Floridians.

First, there was a war between the ABA and the NBA. When they went to solve all the issues and allow the ABA to be absorbed by the NBA, there were certain qualifications that the ABA had to make. Since Houston already had the Rockets, we could no longer call ourselves the "Denver Rockets." As a result of the merger, we became the "Denver Nuggets." Our team drew very well. We had Spencer Haywood right out of the Olympics and Trinidad Junior College. That year, we won the division, but we didn't win the championship. We had an 18-game winning streak. The ABA played in the old downtown arena, and the Coliseum was always packed. The ABA had Julius— Dr. J.—Zelmo Beaty, Rick Barry, Larry Brown, Doug Moe, Charlie Scott, Connie Hawkins, Roger Brown—you name it—we had it in the ABA. Our coach was Bob Bass. The year we really took off was the year when Joe Belmont took over as the head coach.

I went back to Colorado when I was inducted into their Hall of Fame at Colorado State about 10 years ago. I'm also in several other Hall of Fames. At the Meadowlands, I was introduced at halftime of the Giants and Miami Dolphins game and went into the New Jersey Sports Exposition Hall of Fame. Then, I'm in the High School Hall of Fame here and also in the Pro Sportswriters Hall of Fame and the Newark Athletic Hall of Fame.

I've been blessed, there's no question about that. I still talk to a few friends in Colorado. Most of my adult friends are either in the West—in California or in Colorado—and I keep in touch with them. I just talked to Floyd Kerr yesterday and congratulated him on his induction into the Colorado State Hall of Fame. He's the AD at Oregon State. I keep in touch as best I can, but I don't try to dwell in the past. I keep trying to keep looking forward.

Denver was a beautiful city. I had all these intentions of going back to Denver and living there. I loved Denver. I really loved the town— when you're coming from an inner city like I'm from with the hustle and bustle of East Coast living, it was such an absolute delight to live in Denver.

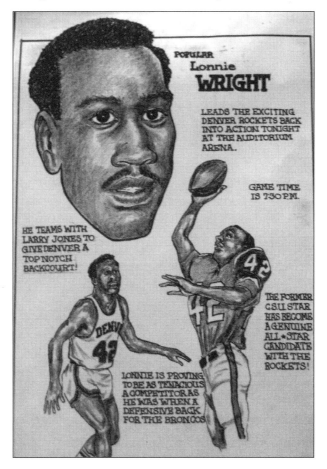

SCHLERETH WAS A VISIONARY WITH ESP...MAYBE IT WAS ESPN

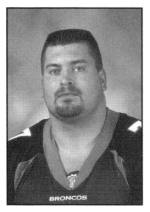

MARK SCHLERETH

Mark Schlereth, born in Alaska, was an offensive lineman for the Broncos from 1995-2000 after playing six years in Washington. He currently does analysis on ESPN, co-hosts on NFL Live, and writes for ESPN the Magazine. *Mark currently resides in Denver with his wife and three children.*

When I signed as a free agent in Denver in 1995, I had failed my physicals in Chicago, Indy, and Atlanta. I just wanted to play football somewhere. I came out for my physical and passed. I was shuttled back to the airport by the Broncos staff. I called my agent from a pay phone—no cell phones then. I was on the phone with my agent, and he told me not to get on the plane, to stay there. I went to a coffee shop and asked if I could use their phone so I could talk to my agent again. The coffee shop people got totally excited about it, and I wasn't even with the Broncos yet. I talked on the phone with my agent to negotiate the deal. I ended up going back to the hotel and signed with the Broncos the next day.

During training camp, we went to Japan to play the San Francisco 49ers in a preseason game. All I remember about the trip was that it was hot at the practices and the locker rooms were tiny. After the game, we headed right back to the States. We had a layover in L.A. and got back to Denver at about 4 a.m. We walked out of the terminal and there were probably 30 fans waiting for us at the airport. Those same fans are the ones I later got to know over my six years in Denver. They're great people. They're passionate fans who you see at the tailgate parties, at the airport. We had a special bond, a special relationship. They make food for you and take care of your family. We used to crash tailgate parties now and then. Fans loved that. Fans would invite us over after the games. I always appreciated the fans, the food and the hospitality.

There are several die-hard Broncos fans who have been there for the duration. They were always at the airport when you took off and again when you landed. They always dressed to the nines in Broncos gear. They truly love the Broncos. At first, you think they're nuts, then you grow to appreciate their passion for the game, and that they really care about the guys. They have your best interest at heart. Bronco Betty was one of those who lives and dies by the Broncos.

There were 600,000 people at a parade and pep rally after the Super Bowl. The fans really, really wanted the Super Bowl after losing four previous Super Bowl games. It really dawned on me how important the game was to the city. It was a back-and-forth game, and we were able to overcome penalties to win. The moment for me that was the most important was seeing John Elway come to the realization that he had finally overcome the monkey on his back, to see the ultimate joy and jubilation on his face. You could see the past disappointments roll off of him. Going to that parade and seeing the fans at the Capitol made me realize that the fans had lived and died by the Broncos and were feeling the same way that Elway was. You could see the pride that the fans had, the excitement for the team. The monkey was off their backs, as well. I hadn't been here during the tough times, so to see the reaction of the fans was wonderful. They lined the streets, high-fived us, gave us gifts. It was something special. I can remember thinking how special it was on that stage in front of 600,000 fans. I still get stopped almost weekly by die-hard Broncos fans. They always thank me for being a part of the Super Bowl win. Sometimes as a player you don't realize how much the fans appreciate you. You are so focused, both mentally and physically, that you don't have a chance to stop and appreciate how much your fans love you. The parade gave me a chance to pause and take in what the fans meant to the Broncos.

As a player, you notice your family in the stands, and the general atmosphere, but you rarely notice individual fans. It's not until after the game that you notice the fans hanging over the wall, hoping for a glove, a jersey, a dirty snot-rag—anything they can get their hands on from the players. They were there win, lose or draw. The South

Stands fans were right there when we went into the locker room. The 12th man has an impact, especially on goal-line stands. The deafening noise from the fans has a big impact. It really is impossible to function as a unit as an offensive team when the fans are that loud. The home fans help the defense tremendously.

When you're playing, most of the time you don't really think about the fans. In 2001, after I retired, I was able to go to a Broncos game for the first time as a fan. It was neat to see everything that goes on from a fan's perspective—the excitement, the disappointment. The myriad of emotions was very cool. It's been fun to be on the other side, and to be a fan.

DENVER BRONCOS DENVER BRONCOS DENVER BRONCOS DENVER BRONCOS DENVER BRONCOS

OPEN THE GATES...OPEN THEM WIDE THE FANS OF THE BRONCOS ARE COMING INSIDE

MICHAEL YOUNG

Michael Young is a 10-year NFL veteran. He played four years with the Los Angeles Rams, four with the Broncos (1989-92) and one year each with the Eagles and the Chiefs. He currently is Senior Director of Special Projects with the Denver Broncos and Executive Vice President of the Colorado Crush.

The first project I had when hired by Pat Bowlen and the Denver Broncos was to develop a corporate sales program. We felt we needed to rebrand ourselves. With all the new teams in Colorado, we were perceived as old and tired. Mr. Bowlen decided that he was going to change the uniforms. We developed a relationship with Nike, and he asked me to help with the re-designs, since I was a former player. I was very involved in the process, especially the logo. When the logo was presented to the public, he mentioned my role in the process. There were a lot of unhappy Broncos fans with the new uniforms. The old guard and long-time fans didn't like the new look. One of the things I said was that I didn't really feel strong in the uniform. Guys had commented that we were wearing weak colors. Lots of teams were going to black on their uniforms. I got a lot of letters after my comments were printed. Some of the letters were good, some bad. Some people wrote to tell me that I didn't feel strong in the uniform because I was weak.

One of the most creative letters I got included a tissue. The letter read, "This is what your new logo looks like." I looked at the tissue, and someone had wiped their bottom with the tissue and mailed it to me. I thought it was a very creative way to say, "Your new logo looks like crap." I saved that letter. Maybe we can put the letter and tissue up in the Broncos Hall of Fame.

My most memorable game with the Broncos was during the 1992 season, the game prior to the AFC Championship Game in Buffalo. We were playing the Houston Oilers. They had a great defense that year. Houston was up by two points. They punted and backed us up to the 2-yard line with less than two minutes left in the game. Elway came in with the play to the huddle, looked at us with huge eyes, and we could tell he thought we could score. He called "Ray 66." He looked at me and said, "Michael, I'm coming to you, and you BETTER catch the ball!" Everyone was looking at me in the huddle. Sure enough, it was a crossing route, about 18 yards out. I was covered, but he let it rip to me anyhow. I slid between two defenders and caught the ball. The media called that sequence "Overdrive." I'd never been called out in a huddle like that before. Of course, we ended up scoring and winning the game.

I first started working for the Broncos about two months after retiring from the NFL. The first big partnership I sold was with Anheuser-Busch. It was the first time that Anheuser-Busch would have signage at Mile High Stadium. It was a bit controversial at the time, because of the past relationship with Coors. I was so concerned about everything being perfect. The banners had to hang from the upper level, just above the suites. We were attaching the banners to the metal rails. I didn't trust anyone else to do it, so I was up there hanging them myself. It was a Saturday and I was in jeans and a T-shirt. They hadn't cleaned the stadium from the previous week's game, yet. I had to get on my stomach, and reach under the rail to hang the banners. I had a guy holding my feet so I wouldn't slip through and fall. By the time I was done, I was covered in soda, ketchup and mustard. There was a gentleman working near me, cleaning. I walked by him when I was done, and he had a puzzled look. He said, "Didn't you used to be Michael Young?" He had such a sad look on his face. He was baffled that the best I could do after playing in the NFL was to crawl around on my stomach in mustard, hanging banners. He really did think that was my job.

After the Super Bowl in New Orleans, where we got destroyed against the 49ers, we were in the locker room after the game and the interviews. John Elway and I were the only ones left. We were combing our hair in front of the mirror, and I asked how he felt. I could just see the disappointment in his face. He looked at me and said, "They will never forgive me for this." It shocked me that he said that. I tried to console him. We wouldn't have gotten that far without him. I always remember that because he was just devastated. Then, after the Super Bowl in San Diego, outside the locker room, I grabbed him, and told him that they have forgiven him now. He just smiled. He knew what I was referring to. Eight years had passed between those conversations. That whole thing stuck with me for a long time. He really felt he was carrying the hopes and dreams of the city of Denver. There wasn't much positive going on in Denver in 1988, so the Super Bowl was a big, big deal.

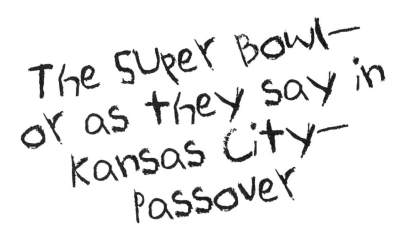

The Super Bowl — or as they say in Kansas City — Passover

TAKE THIS JOB AND LOVE IT

BILLY THOMPSON

Billy Thompson played defensive back for the Broncos from 1969-81. He joined the Broncos' front office in 1986 and has worked as a scout, in community relations and in player relations. He currently is the Director of Alumni/Community Relations.

T he 1977 season was a pretty magical year for the Broncos. We were picked to finish last in the division, but we knew we were better than the previous year, when we finished 9-5. We opened the season at home against the St. Louis Cardinals. They had a high-powered offense. They had flown into Wyoming to practice for our game. They were trying to adjust to the **ALTITUDE.** It was in September. We shut them out, 7-0, at Mile High Stadium. It was one of the tougher games we played, but one of the more enjoyable ones. We had shut them out at home, even after they did the extra traveling to prepare for the game. I knew then that we had a special team and that if we stayed healthy, we would do well. One of the key games that year was in Kansas City. It was one of the greatest plays I've ever seen. It will be entrenched in my mind forever. It was a very close game. I think we were up by a touchdown. It was fourth down, late in the game. K.C. lined up in a punt formation, but everyone knew they had to try something special. They came up with this play called the "Fumblerooski." The quarterback set the ball on the ground after the snap, and everybody ran one way, and one player picked up the ball and ran the other way. It was like fourth-and-20, so

> **Mountain climbers "pass gas" violently at high ALTITUDES. At 11,000 feet, the stomach's resistance to the expansion of gas is greatly reduced. Always try to be the lead climber. That's a free tip from your Uncle Rich.**

we figured he couldn't run 20 yards. He got past us and ended up headed for the end zone. Louie Wright came from "way across Georgia," from all the way across the field, and tackled him just before the goal line. We thought he had scored, so the defense left the field. It turned out he didn't score, but the ball was on the 1-yard line. In the huddle we were in total disarray. A lot of stuff was going on in the huddle, but we held them on four downs and won the ball game. We finished 12-2 that year and went to the Super Bowl. That was the greatest game I've seen the Broncos ever play on the road. It was an incredible goal line stand. Louie made one of the greatest plays I've ever seen. Rich McCabe, one of our coaches, always told us not to wait for someone else to be the hero, and Louie didn't wait. We only lost two games that year. One of those losses was to the Cowboys at the end of the regular season, and we lost to them again in the Super Bowl.

We played the Raiders in the AFC Championship Game. From the time I signed with the Broncos, the Raiders and Chiefs dominated the AFC West. The Broncos were the doormat then. That changed in 1977. That was the first year we beat the Raiders twice in one season. The AFC Championship Game against the Raiders was a very emotional game. It sent word around the league that the Broncos were here, and the status in the AFC had changed. No one has been as dominant in the AFC as the Broncos since then. It was a crisp, cold December game. The fans were just wild. The game wasn't even close. The fans poured onto the field and tore the goalposts down. A sold out house couldn't squeeze any more fans into the stadium. They really wanted to see us beat the Raiders. I went to school with Art Shell, who is now the head coach of the Raiders. He and I were pretty close. After that game, I talked with Art and we talked about how that game would change things for the Broncos. The fans were so excited about that game. I've never seen that happen since. They tore down both goalposts and tore up the grass. I've never seen Denver that excited before or since. It's a memory I will always cherish. It was all the pent-up frustration being released. It was really sweet.

Losing the Super Bowl was a mixed bag of emotions. We'd worked so hard to get there, and were the first Broncos team to go. We played with great, great tenacity. We were down by 10 at halftime. After the game, we were walking back to the locker room, and the fans were still cheering. I turned to Tom Jackson, and asked if we won or lost, because the fans were just going nuts. He said, "We lost, but we won." It must have been a 10-minute ovation.

It was very special to have played for only one team. It's rare now. There are so few who have done that. The fans really know you when you're able to do that. There aren't too many places I can go in Colorado where fans don't recognize me. That is special.

Pat Bowlen is one of the best owners in the league. He's the kind of owner you want to play for. He wants to win, and win fairly. He wants to be No. 1 on the field, and No. 1 in the community. He gives us the latitude to go out and represent the organization. I talk to other people around the league about how they work in their communities, and I believe we have the top organization in the league when it comes to community relations. A lot of players want to come to Denver to play, because we are a first-class organization with absolutely first class fans.

Green Bay—
Come smell
our dairy air

THE BIGGEST WAS LITTLE...
THE ORANGEMAN WHO WORE ORANGE

FLOYD LITTLE

The former Broncos all-pro running back recently wrote a book called Tales from the Broncos Sidelines. *He wrote about Lou Saban and John Ralston having different coaching styles and the psychological tests he had to take to determine which position he was best suited for. It includes the story about when Saban fired him for fumbling in a game and how he was able to keep his job.*

One of the best stories is that we were playing in Utah, against the New England Patriots. We didn't know which was the home team, so we both came out in red jerseys. We had to go change into Utah State jerseys. They were smaller than us, and we played terrible. Coach came in and kicked the table over and referred to us as gutless thieves. He said he'd be replacing all of us as soon as we got back to Denver. He said he could outplay us all and challenged us all to a fight.

Players now are more entertainers than actual football players. There are some real football players now, but not many. There are a few who could have played in my era. The game has changed, the players have changed. It's less about team now.

Denver has the most serious, knowledgeable fans in the NFL. They were there, win or lose. They'd be at the airports waiting for us, thousands of people. They were so sincere about their football team. We weren't even winning then, and they were still supporting us. They always told us to keep our heads up. That just doesn't happen today. Those fans loved their team, loved their players. The players stayed in Denver in the off-season then. The fans today don't remember the early days. They aren't supportive when you lose. I don't remember hearing fans boo then. It always took me forever to get to my car after a game. I'd sign every autograph. I was always happy to do so. I didn't turn anyone down.

My favorite game was the last game I played in Mile High Stadium. It was 1972, when they declared it Floyd Little Day. The fans donated a car, a boat, cash. I donated it all to the Boys & Girls Club. The mayor and governor were there. I even got a commendation from the President of the United States. I had my wife and daughter with me. The fans I played for came to say thank you for my efforts and my work. That's the game I remember most.

I always played the game the night before in my head. I always thought about my shoes. We used to have one pair of shoes, and if it was raining or wet, we'd have to go in and put longer cleats on the shoes. Players now have 12 or 15 pairs of shoes. When I played, I used to shine my shoes the night before a game. I'd take my shoes home, brush them off and polish them. I'd envision these shoes carrying me over the goal line with the ball. It gave me a chance to sit still for a few minutes and recap the new plays we had developed that week. I'd play every down in my head before the game. I'd vividly imagine us winning, including the score on the scoreboard.

The South Stands were a bunch of rowdies. They were die-hard fans, though. I do remember them throwing a snowball onto the field during a kick. They just erupted. They threw a loaf of bread at Lou Saban one game, because they were mad that he had gone for a tie instead of a win the previous game.

I want to thank all the fans for all their loyalty and support. Even 25 years after playing, I get such a warm welcome when I'm introduced. I know it's frustrating for them to not see me in the Hall of Fame. It's frustrating for me, as well. Both John Elway and **JIM BROWN** wrote in my book that it's a travesty that I'm not in the Hall of Fame. John Mackey even wrote a letter to the Hall of Fame and told them to

> The only person to score back-to-back fifty-point games in the history of Long Island High School basketball is **JIM BROWN**, the NFL legend. Brown was drafted in the 1957 NBA Draft by the Syracuse Nationals.

make room for me, and if they didn't have room, they could take him out. Great players on bad teams should still be in the Hall of Fame. Denver Broncos fans can write to the Hall of Fame, too. I'm still in the top 12 of all the other rushers that are in the Hall of Fame. There are 18 guys in the Hall of Fame with less numbers than me. I've met all the criteria for the Hall of Fame, with the exception of playing in the Super Bowl. Yards and Super Bowls are the qualifications. A lot of us who played hard, but not on winning teams, can't make it into the Hall of Fame. It doesn't matter if we led the league in a category. Major League Baseball has six qualifications. The NFL has just two. The Broncos have been to six Super Bowls, but have just one player in the Hall of Fame. If it's not me, that's fine, but the Broncos deserve another Hall of Fame inductee.

Raider fans give it the old college try. They get drunk, pass out and say they'll finish it tomorrow.

HERE ME NOW, LISTEN TO ME LATER

DAVE LOGAN

Dave Logan has been broadcasting Broncos games on News Radio 850 KOA for 17 years. He brings his love for sports and understanding of the game to Colorado listeners as co-host of the Sports Zoo, heard on KOA weekdays from 3-7pm. Logan has been "Colorado Sportscaster of the Year" three times and is one of the most accomplished prep football coaches in Colorado state history, with state championships with three different prep teams.

It was Super Bowl XXXII and we had been out in San Diego all week. Part of my responsibilities were to do "The John Elway Show" and "The Mike Shanahan Show" on tape and get them ready for Sunday. We had Elway set up for the day before the game. There were drapes to maintain some privacy. Normally, players don't say a lot about any secrets during a pregame show. He was in a very candid mood that day, though. It was a two-segment show, four minutes in each segment. His comments showed that he was very confident about their chances to win and how important the game was to the team and to him. He was very poignant and sincere with his comments. After the interview, I felt it was a great piece, because of his candid comments. Our engineer then said, "Uh-oh." He didn't think we had a tape of the interview! There was a technical foul-up between our San Diego broadcast point and the station, so we got none of it on tape. We had to figure out what to do. I walked in the player's lounge, and told John what happened. After about two minutes of a one-sided conversation, John agreed to retape it.

When I was doing TV in the preseason, they had to get someone to step in and do my job. One year they got the late Hank Stram. He at one point in a preseason game, had to pee so bad, he peed into a cup, in the booth, while he was on the air. I've never had to pee into a cup on the air.

The windows in the pressbox have never been shut during a game I've called in 17 years. If you're going to shut the windows, you should just call the game from the studio. Part of the lure of listening to the broadcast is feeling as if you're at the game. The elements are part of the broadcast.

A lot of broadcasters prepare scripted comments for various situations. I hadn't prepared anything for the Broncos maybe winning the Super Bowl. I thought they had a chance. It first hit me late in the game that they had a real chance to win. Terrell scored, and it was, 31-24, I think, with about two minutes remaining. When he scored and we went to a break, it hit me. The Broncos were two minutes away from their first Super Bowl win. There had been so many years in Denver without a win. For the people who had been Broncos fans for years and years, this was the ultimate. They had been fans, been ridiculed, suffered the losses. From that point on, it was a pretty emotional time. That was the most important game I've called.

I grew up in Denver and have always been a Broncos fan. We'd go down and watch Floyd Little. You grow up in a city, and you're a fan of that team. To come back and call my hometown team has been great. I enjoy the games immensely. I've enjoyed the ability to stay near the game I really love. I've been really blessed. It was either going to be broadcasting or coaching. It's been nice to be able to come back and live in the city I grew up in, with family and friends here.

When Elway took the victory lap around the field before his retirement, that was a special time. He hadn't officially announced his retirement. I remember saying on the air that if this was not Elway's last game at home as a Bronco, it sure seemed like it. It was the AFC Championship Game. Those were back-to-back Super Bowls. Those were pretty special times. Not many teams get to experience that kind of success once, let alone twice.

I'm a fan of the game, and of guys who play the game the right way. Elway was certainly one of those. As a broadcaster, the special moments will always be special, whether as a fan or as a broadcaster. Not a lot of guys in this profession get to broadcast those kinds of special moments.

I REMEMBER BOB MARTIN

I used to bowl on Sundays, so I'd listen to Bob Martin on the radio calling the Broncos games. My husband would listen to him while he worked in the yard, too. If the game was exciting, he'd run inside and watch the replay. We like to turn down the TV and listen to the game on the radio.

——MARGIE CARLISLE, former mail sorter at the Denver post office

Bob Martin was the announcer from the start. I had a store called Sportstown, USA. I knew Bob because I'm friends with Doug Moe and Larry Brown. People don't know how good Bob Martin was. He was one of the best broadcasters ever, not just as a local guy. He was also one of the most cerebral guys you'd ever want to meet. He was very cultured and was into the theater and was extremely well-read. I had some wonderful conversations with him. He was very understated—I'm not sure "shy" is the word. He had a very reserved personality and wasn't the stereotypical, outgoing sports commentator. Bob was so much more than a sports commentator. You can take the Vin Scullys and Red Barbers, and Bob Martin was as good as any of those guys. He was one of those guys who could have done something on a national level had he chosen to, but I don't think he ever wanted to. He did CU football; he did the Broncos; he did the Nuggets—he was just happy doing sports locally. He didn't care about getting a national position. He is still my favorite broadcaster.

——RICHARD AGREN, former professor at UNC

I loved listening to Bob Martin during the games. I was very sad when he got sick and passed away. It was a big loss for the fans and the community. Bob made the game so interesting to us. He explained everything—facts and figures. He helped us learn about the game of football and what was going on. He helped us understand the game better. That is what endeared him to me on the radio. He made it more personal.

——ELLEN LEVINE-JONES, attended North Denver High School

I was a play-by-play announcer, but did the color role with Bob Martin. That helped me understand what the play-by-play guy doesn't see. I would always try to pick up the things that I knew the play-by-play guy wouldn't see. Bob and I were very good friends outside the broadcast booth, as well. We liked a lot of the same things—good food, art, etc. The chemistry came across on the air. We were fortunate to be together in the golden time when the Broncos first started to gel and have winning seasons, the great success in '77 that carried into the mid '80s. There was a broadcaster who said, "I'm a much better broadcaster when we're winning than when we're losing." Bob was a true professional who worked hard in his preparation. We both had the same ideas of what a good broadcast should be. We were playing the Bears in Chicago in old Soldier Field. The broadcast booth was very low, right on top of the last row of seats. It was a really cold day, probably 15 degrees. Some guy in the stands threw a beer into the booth. It hit Bob right in the head, but he didn't miss a beat! He didn't say a word. In the third quarter, Bob walked over to this guy with a big cup of 7-Up and fired it at him, a direct hit right on the back of his head. The fan had to leave the game because the drink started to freeze on him! When I was working with Dave Logan in Kansas City, after a comment the fans didn't like, a fan threw a beer at Dave. Logan looked at him and went down in the stands after him. I don't think he ever found him. I had to handle the game myself until he got back.

———LARRY ZIMMER, Bob Martin's broadcast partner from 1971-89

Bob Martin was the kind of football announcer who was true to everything that took place on the football field. He never had an alibi for a player or the team. The officiating crew was correct with him until they reversed a call. He did a terrific job. You knew that you would get the best analysis possible when he called the game. We used to watch the games on TV and listen to Bob on the radio. He was that good. The Broncos fans have missed Bob since then, but he was in an era of his own. He provided great analysis and was always prepared for what was going on. Bob was at the "masters" level of commentators. He knew what to look for and let listeners into the play very well. Dave Logan has done a great job as well.

———JOHN POLLICE, a Broncos fan since the team's inception

A lot of people thought Bob Martin was arrogant, but he wasn't. He was a really big guy and he helped me a lot when I was young. I was a record promoter and he was a DJ. He'd always play the songs I took him. He was into sports then. He touted the first issue of *Sports Illustrated* magazine on the air. I had a dog named Geraldine then and I used to keep the dog in a fenced yard at the office. My dog somehow escaped. I called Bob Martin and asked if he could mention it on the air. Someone a couple of blocks away heard Bob on the air and brought my dog back. Bob Martin was a really good guy.

———JACK KAUFMAN, Yellow Cab driver

Bob Martin was a classy sports announcer. Zimmer did color with him. It's funny how the class of a person comes through in their delivery. Always crisp and clean, and emotional, but not overdoing it. They described the play on the field by telling you what happened, instead of screaming it at you. He was a key Broncos personality.

———JEB BARRY, Denver resident for 59 years

Gerard Warren suffers from Anorexia Ponderosa

SHORT STORIES
FROM LONG MEMORIES

I have to say that Tom Jackson was one of my favorite players. Between my junior and senior years in high school, I went to the Mile High Football Camp in Golden, and Jon Keyworth was the fullback at the time. He and a bunch of other Broncos players were there. Tom Jackson really made an impression on me just for who he was—the kind of person he was. He was dealing with high school kids, as I'm sure many players do. But he really made the connection with me. I like to see him do well and go as far as he's gone with his broadcasting career. The Orange Crush defense was just huge. They were really, really top flight. Karl Mecklenburg was another guy that I really loved to watch play. I especially respected him because he was taken so far down in the draft. He wasn't able to train for football—he was studying for exams and that said a lot about the intensity with which he played.

——ANDY FOX, 46, Kerrville, Texas

Randy Gradishar from **OHIO STATE** has never really been commended for what he did for the team and community, and really should be in the Hall of Fame. He has been left out. He was a remarkable football player. There was no better defensive core than that team. Joe Rizzo was from the Merchant Marine Academy. He was maybe the only NFL player to ever come out of there.

——JOHN POLLICE, 62

In the 1976 **OHIO STATE**-Indiana game, the Hoosiers scored first. Indiana coach Lee Corso called a timeout. During the timeout, Corso had his team pose for a group picture with the scoreboard—showing Indiana leading Ohio State 7-0—clearly visible in the background. Corso featured the picture on the cover of the 1977 Indiana recruiting brochure. Ohio State won the game 47-7.

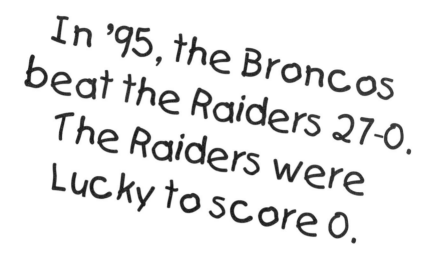

In '95, the Broncos beat the Raiders 27-0. The Raiders were Lucky to score 0.

DENVER BRONCOS DENVER BRONCOS DENVER BRONCOS DENVER BRONCOS DENVER BRONCOS

When Chan Gailey, the former Dallas Cowboys and current Georgia Tech head coach played Little League Baseball in Americus, Georgia, his coach was Dan Reeves.

If football is a religion, why don't the Chiefs have a prayer?

DENVER BRONCOS DENVER BRONCOS DENVER BRONCOS DENVER BRONCOS DENVER BRONCOS

The Chargers were originally the Los Angeles Chargers in 1960, the first year of the AFL. They were owned by Barron Hilton of the Hilton Hotel chain. Hilton owned the Carte Blanche credit card company and named the team Chargers to promote the credit card.

THE ORIGINAL, THE ONE AND ONLY, ROCKIN' 'N ROLLIN', FULL-TILT BOOGIE DENVER BRONCOS IMPOSSIBLE TRIVIA QUIZ:

- What former Broncos player—an active NFC player at the time—lost an 8-round fight to Muhammad Ali in the late 1970's?

- Condoleeza Rice has had only one serious boyfriend. Can you name the Broncos star that she dated while a student at the University of Denver?

- Name the only player to play for both the Broncos and the Nuggets.

- What current Broncos player has his baseball cap in the Baseball Hall of Fame in Cooperstown?

- What was unusual about John Elway's last college game?

- Ed McCaffrey's father-in-law was once often-written about in *Sports Illustrated*. Why?

- What former Broncos All-NFC defender was a *Parade Magazine* first team All-American basketball player?

- What recent Broncos quarterback's father was a first round draft pick of the St. Louis baseball Cardinals and was drafted five different times by Major League Baseball teams?

- This recent (1997-2001) Broncos running back still holds the record for most touchdowns in one Division I college game with eight. Who?

- How many Broncos…in the 47-year history of the team…never attended college.

You will find the answers to these questions contained within the pages of this book and its sequel.

August 15, 1983

Sports Illustrated

LOOKING LIKE A MILLION

Denver's John Elway Makes A Dazzling NFL Debut

This section contains all 19 covers of *Sports Illustrated* graced by the Denver Broncos, plus five others if you have time.

Credit: ANDY HAYT/SPORTS ILLUSTRATED. August 15, 1983.

Credit: *JOHN G. ZIMMERMAN /SPORTS ILLUSTRATED.* October 17, 1977

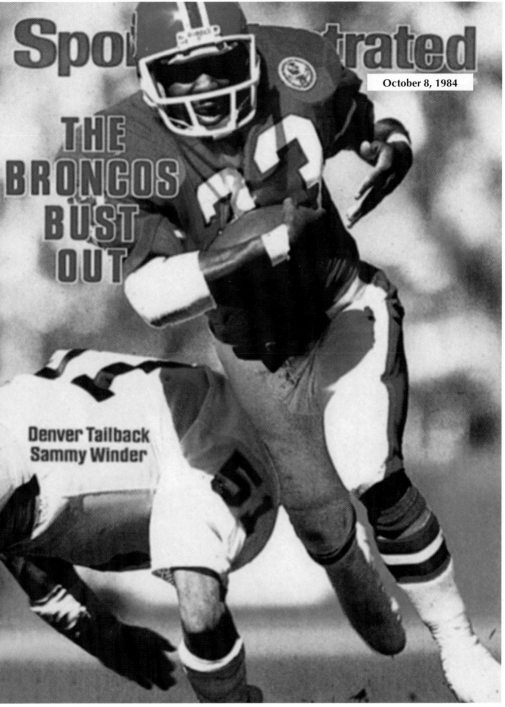

Sports Illustrated

October 8, 1984

THE BRONCOS BUST OUT

Denver Tailback Sammy Winder

Credit: ANDY HAYT/SPORTS ILLUSTRATED. October 8, 1984.

Sports Illustrated

October 13, 1986 $2.25

DENVER IS UNDEFEATED

ELWAY AND EVERY WHICH WAY

Credit: PETER READ MILLER /SPORTS ILLUSTRATED. October 13, 1986.

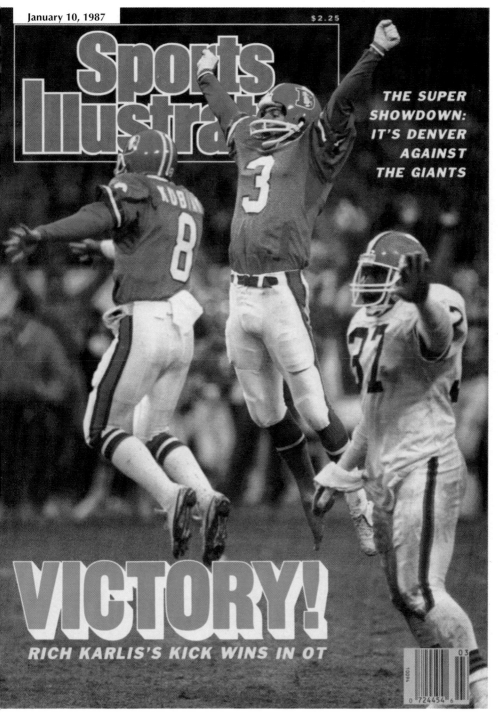

January 10, 1987

$2.25

Sports Illustrated

THE SUPER SHOWDOWN: IT'S DENVER AGAINST THE GIANTS

VICTORY!

RICH KARLIS'S KICK WINS IN OT

Credit: TONY TOMSIC/SPORTS ILLUSTRATED. January 10, 1987.

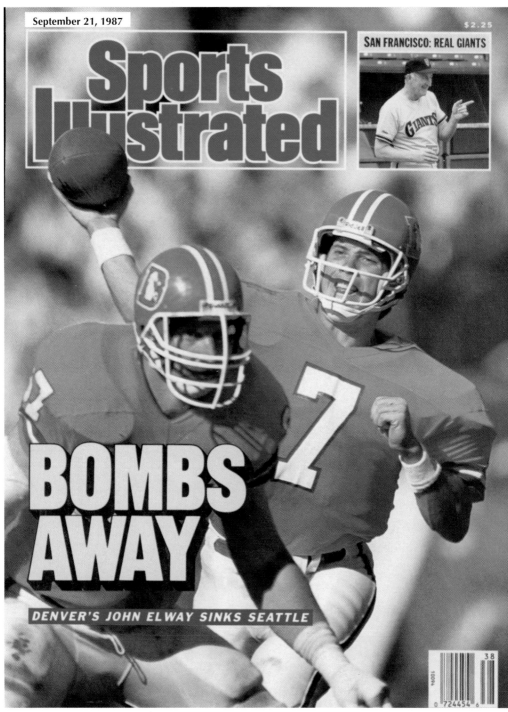

September 21, 1987

$2.25

Sports Illustrated

SAN FRANCISCO: REAL GIANTS

BOMBS AWAY

DENVER'S JOHN ELWAY SINKS SEATTLE

Credit: PETER READ MILLER/SPORTS ILLUSTRATED. September 21, 1987.

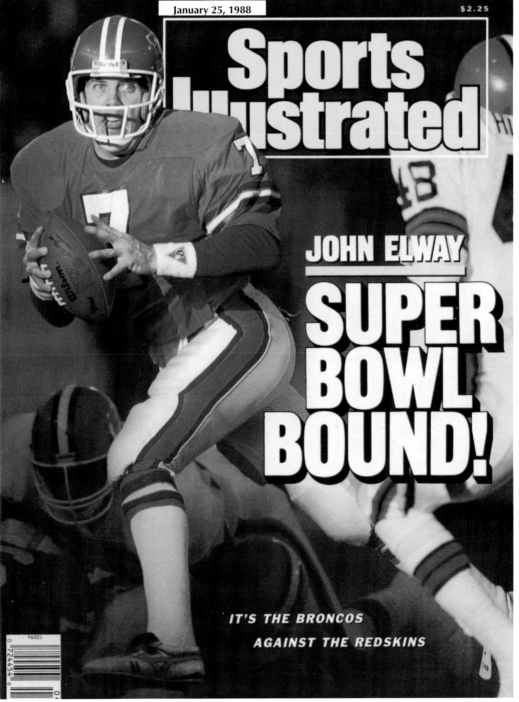

January 25, 1988

$2.25

Sports Illustrated

JOHN ELWAY

SUPER BOWL BOUND!

IT'S THE BRONCOS
AGAINST THE REDSKINS

Credit: PETER READ MILLER /SPORTS ILLUSTRATED. January 25, 1988.

August 1, 1988

$2.50

BOSTON'S RED HOT SOX

Sports Illustrated

TONY DORSETT

HAPPY TO BE A BRONCO, BUSTER

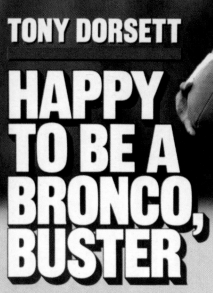

Credit: DAMIAN STROHMEYER/SPORTS ILLUSTRATED. August 1, 1988.

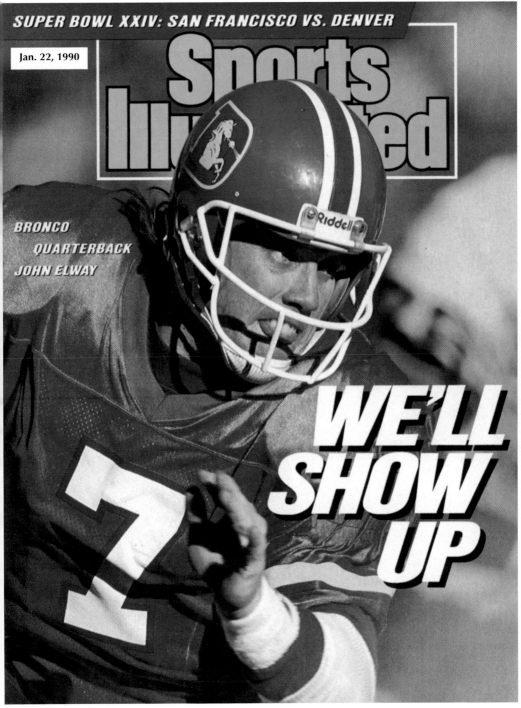

SUPER BOWL XXIV: SAN FRANCISCO VS. DENVER

Jan. 22, 1990

Sports Illustrated

BRONCO QUARTERBACK JOHN ELWAY

WE'LL SHOW UP

Credit: JOHN BIEVER/SPORTS ILLUSTRATED. January 22, 1990.

August 2, 1993

Sports Illustrated

Good Riddance   Grow Up

John Elway is ecstatic that he's still in Denver and his nemesis Dan Reeves is now in New York

Credit: SPORTS ILLUSTRATED. August 2, 1993.

Leading Off Their Sunday Best

Credit: BILL FRAKES/SPORTS ILLUSTRATED. December 28, 1998.

Fans in Denver, Green Bay and Miami show that where there's a will, there's an Elway . . . and a Favre . . . and a Marino. Photographs by **Bill Frakes**

Credit: BILL FRAKES/SPORTS ILLUSTRATED. December 28, 1998.

JOHN ELWAY
An Appreciation

················

BY
RICK REILLY

Credit: *HEINZ KLUETMEIER /SPORTS ILLUSTRATED.* Dec. 30, 1996–Jan. 6, 1997.

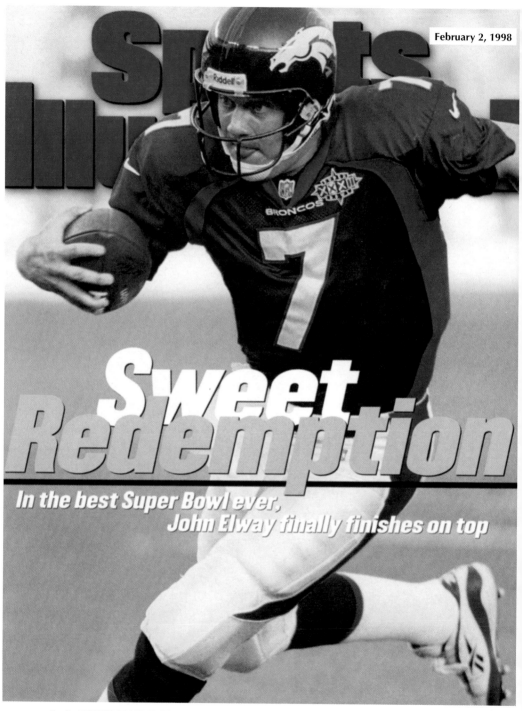

Sweet
Redemption

In the best Super Bowl ever,
John Elway finally finishes on top

Credit: *WALTER IOOSS, JR./SPORTS ILLUSTRATED.* February 2, 1998.

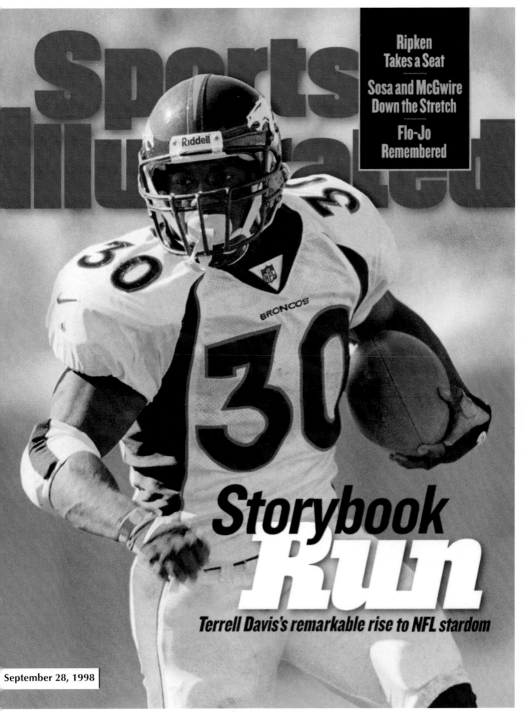

Sports Illustrated

Ripken
Takes a Seat

Sosa and McGwire
Down the Stretch

Flo-Jo
Remembered

BRONCOS

Storybook
Run

Terrell Davis's remarkable rise to NFL stardom

September 28, 1998

Credit: MICKEY PFLEGER/SPORTS ILLUSTRATED. September 28, 1998

Sports Illustrated

Who's No. 1? Tennessee Deserves It

Debunking the Myths
Surrounding El Duque's
Escape from Cuba

BRONCOS

7

**Can
Denver
Win
'Em All?**

Believe It!

PLUS

**John Elway's New Weapon:
Wideout Ed McCaffrey**

November 30, 1998

Credit: PETER READ MILLER /SPORTS ILLUSTRATED. November 30, 1998.

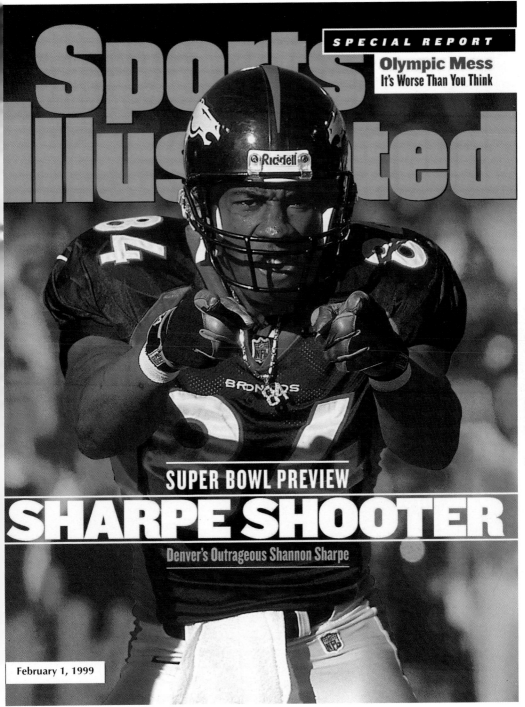

NBA PREVIEW
Scouting Reports
FINALS FORECAST
Pacers vs. Lakers

Sports Illustrated

Super Bowl

How **John Elway** took control

How **Mike Shanahan** rebuilt the Broncos

How three **Blitzes** killed the Falcons

February 8, 1999

Credit: *BOB ROSATO/SPORTS ILLUSTRATED.* February 8, 1999.

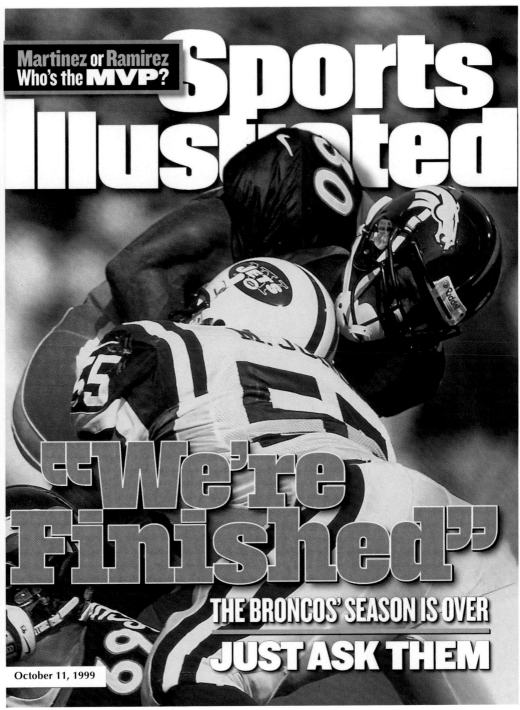

Sports Illustrated

"We're Finished"

THE BRONCOS' SEASON IS OVER

JUST ASK THEM

October 11, 1999

Credit: *PETER READ MILLER /SPORTS ILLUSTRATED.* October 11, 1999.

GEORGE PLIMPTON 1927-2003

Sports Illustrated

SPECIAL REPORT

The American ATHLETE AGE 10
Time of Their Lives or Too Much Too Soon?

Man on the Run

Jake Plummer Leads the Unbeaten Broncos Against the Unbeaten Chiefs

BASEBALL PLAYOFFS
CUBS? RED SOX? MARLINS?
The Best Bullpens Will Survive

By downing Detroit, Plummer and Denver advanced to 4-0

October 6, 2003

Credit: *PETER READ MILLER/SPORTS ILLUSTRATED. October 6, 2003.*

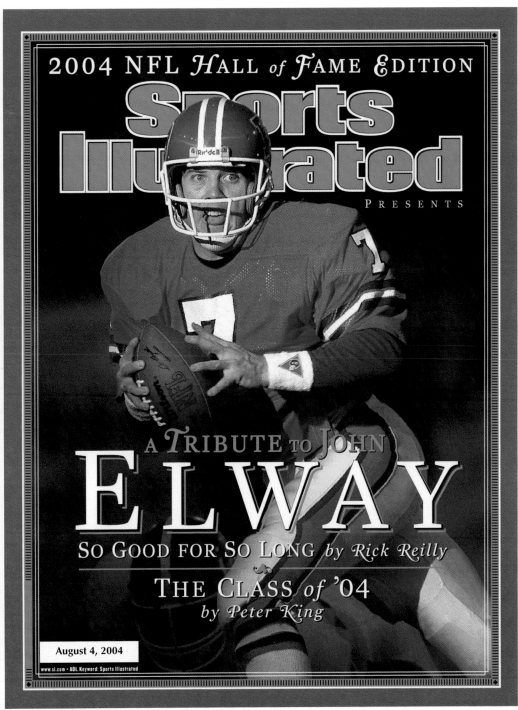

Credit: *PETER READ MILLER /SPORTS ILLUSTRATED.* August 4, 2004.

July 8, 1991

Sports Illustrated

'I LIED'

Former NFL star Lyle Alzado now admits to massive use of steroids and human growth hormone – and believes they caused his inoperable brain cancer

Credit: PETER READ MILLER/SPORTS ILLUSTRATED. July 8, 1991.

Sacramento doesn't have an NFL team because then Oakland would want one too.

DENVER BRONCOS DENVER BRONCOS DENVER BRONCOS DENVER BRONCOS DENVER BRONCOS

John Elway, Deion Sanders and Billy Cannon, Jr. were signed by George Steinbrenner for the Yankees and given $100,000+ bonuses. All three quit baseball for the NFL. In the 1979 Major League Baseball draft, the Kansas City Royals drafted Dan Marino in the 4th round and John Elway in the 18th round.... Also, in the same year, the Royals hired a Missourian for their Group Sales Department. He left five years later for a job in the radio business. Say hello to Rush Limbaugh.

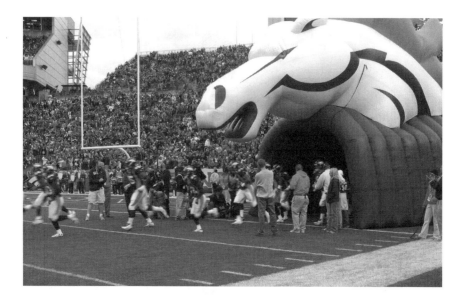

When watching the Cincinnati Bengals, do you root for the defense... or the prosecution?

DENVER BRONCOS DENVER BRONCOS DENVER BRONCOS DENVER BRONCOS DENVER BRONCOS

The Broncos went an entire calendar year (December '97 to December '98) without losing a game...18 games, an NFL record.

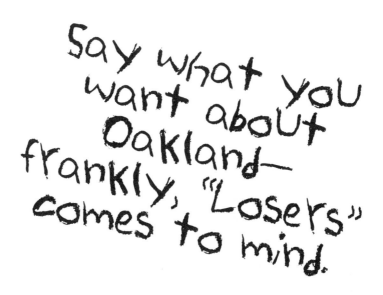

Say what you want about Oakland— frankly, "Losers" comes to mind.

DENVER BRONCOS DENVER BRONCOS DENVER BRONCOS DENVER BRONCOS DENVER BRONCOS

Former NFL commissioner Paul Tagliabue once held the career rebounding record at Georgetown. That mark was broken by Patrick Ewing in 1985.

In those very early games, Denver had not had professional football, so everybody was just gaga and just about anything they did would have been fine. The striped socks really became a bigger thing later on than they did at the time. I don't remember anybody complaining about it when they started. One of my favorite players, and certainly one of the most colorful Broncos who ever played, was a linebacker we got from the New York Jets, Wahoo McDaniel. Wahoo later went on to be a professional wrestler. His showmanship skills were really better suited to professional wrestling than they were to football. He wasn't exactly a big star or an all-star or anything, but whenever he would make a big-time tackle or sack the quarterback or make a good play—which certainly wasn't on every play 'cause old Wahoo wasn't exactly a real star—he would do an Indian dance and whoop and holler around. He was very colorful. We always looked forward to Wahoo making a big play because he made such a big deal about it. I think there would be several players who could be called the most 'underrated.' Floyd Little was sure one. Rich Jackson, a defensive end, would be another one. Rich's career was cut short by a knee injury. If Rich had lived in this era with modern surgical techniques, they'd have fixed him up, and he'd have been back out on the field. In those days, they didn't have the advanced techniques they do today.

———DAN GREEN, 59, a fan since birth

Floyd Little's last game against Miami at Mile High was very memorable. He scored a touchdown on one of the last plays of the game. Floyd was my idol. He was "Mr. Denver." It's a crime he's not in the Hall of Fame. He was as good as it gets, and he was on a terrible team. Back in those days, there were a lot of great running backs. Gale Sayers had just retired. **O. J. SIMPSON** was playing. I was eight or nine when we first got season tickets. We inherited them from a neighbor of ours who had passed away. He willed them to my dad. Floyd Little sat directly in front of me at one

O. J. SIMPSON's cousin is Ernie Banks. Their grandfathers were twin brothers.

of the first games I went to after he retired. That was one of the biggest thrills of my life. I talked to him the entire game. He was incredibly friendly and very in touch with the crowd. The games were different then. The fans were hard-core fans. The Broncos didn't win much then. Fans were really dedicated. Fans now are pretty used to having a good team every year. The players had a different affinity for the fans then. We supported them even when the teams were bad. They didn't make near the money the players do now. They played more for the love of the sport than they do now. Not that the players now don't love the sport, but it was different then. The players were everyday guys. They didn't make enough money to have football as their full-time jobs. They did it as a sideline and had to have another job to pay the rent.

———JOEL TAYLOR, 43, Colorado

I went to the '98 Super Bowl game with the Broncos organization. We were the underdogs and San Diego was full of Packers fans. It was an exciting moment. We had a contest at the store going on. If the Broncos won the Super Bowl, the winner of the drawing would get a free $20,000 ring with a $20,000 purchase at the store. The guy next to me at the game was nervous because he had $4,000 bet on the game. In the fourth quarter, we talked about how much I had "bet" on the game—a million dollars via the insurance policy for the contest in our store....Mike Shanahan and I did commercials together. I did them with Wade Phillips, too. The first commercials with Mike took us forever to get through. We didn't know each other, so we didn't have a flow to the conversation in the commercial. He's a funny guy. I could see in his eyes when he was going to say something that wasn't in the script....We designed the Broncos' Super Bowl ring. We submitted several designs. Pat Bowlen, the owner of the Broncos, had a specific idea in mind. Jostens submitted, too. They used a combination of both the submissions. We built about 25 of the rings and Jostens built the rest. We built two for John Elway. It was a very fun process. We built and continue to build a lot of Broncos jewelry for the fans, too. Elway is a client of the store. When he would come into the store, we'd try to arrange for as much privacy as possible so he could shop. When people did ask him for autographs, he always took the time to do so and talk to the fans—even when he was in a hurry. After a Broncos' loss, I get a ton of "hate mail," especially on voice mail. "I'll never come into your store again, because you support those crappy Broncos…." We seem to be the closest target for some fans to vent their anger on when the Broncos lose. Sales are great after a Broncos win. We've made a number of Broncos pins for fans. Some are very extravagant—diamonds all over them. One fan from Germany contracted a Broncos' lapel pin—a very expensive piece— for his wife.

——RALPH KLOMP, 61, owner of Trice Jewelers,
the Official Jewelers of the Broncos

John Elway was a great guy, a great asset to the team. He could play baseball, which was nice for us. He got here around opening day in June and left about the first week of August. He stayed in a fraternity house on Maple Street with about 14 other guys. He didn't have a car. I guess that's a little unusual for a guy with a bonus, but nobody ever thought about it. He lived with everybody else, so many of them at that time didn't have cars. None of them were making that much money. He was just like everybody else. He integrated very well with his teammates. They called him El-Rod. Our fans were very excited, and we had more press than we'd ever had. He brought so much to the team athletically, but because of him, *Sports Illustrated* was here, and the network television news crews were here. His father, Jack, was coach at San Jose State at that time. He came up with his wife and John's girlfriend, who later became his wife. Jack went and met with George Steinbrenner to talk about John playing baseball. Steinbrenner even came to watch him play. It was always nice to have him in town. Steinbrenner created excitement for everybody. The fans would always recognize him and go over and talk to him. He never failed to give everybody a little attention. Jack Elway gave me a check for $50 for the baseball club to use. We used it for a pizza party. There's no doubt that John could have made the big leagues. No question. He was fast, coachable, could hit and had a great arm. I'll never forget one rifle throw he made from right field to third base to nab a runner. Ken Berry was our manager. Ken always told me he was very coachable. In my opinion, he would have made the Major

Leagues, but he wouldn't have been a star like he was in the NFL. He had good power, hit over .300 for us and led the club in RBIs. He left early that summer to go on a **HEISMAN TROPHY** candidates' tour sponsored by ABC. He also had to get back to Stanford to prepare for the football season. When he left, the players had a party for him. I figured he'd pick football. He'd throw a football around the ballpark. He'd go into right field and throw it from right field to left field. And once you saw him throw a football, it was pretty clear. There wasn't anyone who didn't say, "Oh, my gosh," when he threw a football.

—SAM NADER, owner of Oneonta (N.Y.) Yankees when Elway played there in 1982 or 1981

I know this guy, Oates, who played semi-pro in New York. He got to know Joe Namath real well. He was a teacher of meditation, and taught Namath to meditate when he was playing in New York. His father is a famous sportswriter for the *L.A. Times*, and he later wrote a book on how Namath threw—he threw a little differently. Namath would spin his hips. He put the ball by his ear and spin his hips violently and that would automatically cock the ball. I didn't understand it at the time, but one day I was on the sideline when Joe Namath was playing. I saw him take a hit that picked him off his feet, but he still threw a bullet 40 yards downfield and completed it. The only reason he could do that is because of the way he used his hips—he would generate a lot of torque. I remembered that play real vividly. I understood how it could happen after Oates explained to me how he used his hips to generate torque when he threw. I remember when Marlin Briscoe, the first black who ever played quarterback in pro football, played for the Broncos. He wasn't really a passer. He was a wide receiver and, in desperation, they moved him to quarterback. He was a scat back. I remember the excitement he generated when he played, because he could scramble, and nobody could touch him, because he was so shifty. Back then, the scores were astronomical. You needed a

What **HEISMAN TROPHY** winner has made the most money? The 1959 winner, Billy Cannon of LSU, was arrested for counterfeiting in the early '80s and spent almost three years in jail. Technically, he is the only Heisman Trophy winner to ever "make" money.

calculator. That was exciting. I think the Broncos scored 35 points in the fourth quarter to tie one game.

——STU ZISMAN, a Broncos fan for life

I've met governors of different states as Barrel Man. I've met a bunch of players. I became friends with guys like Billy Thompson and Tommy Jackson. There are so many of them that I've met and enjoyed talking to. I run into older players once in awhile, too. It's harder now with free agency to really meet and get to know the players. Glenn "Lumpy" Hyde is one of the older players I'll never forget. He was always enthusiastic, no matter what. He was high on the game. He was a special teams player in the '70s—a good guy on and off the field. He was a lot of fun.

——TIM MCKERNAN, Denver

When Otis Armstrong came and Little was on the bench, it broke my heart. I couldn't understand why this young kid would be there to take Little's job. I can remember the crowd chanting Little's name when Armstrong went down with an injury. I think Little rushed for 100 yards that game. My cousin and I cried when Floyd Little retired. He was our hero. We were young and thought that football players played forever. Then I realized that they get old, too, and have to retire. The Broncos have been everything in my world, and still are. They inspired me to play football, and I played at the University of Northern Colorado on a football scholarship. I worked at IBM after that. It all goes back to the first day of watching the Denver Broncos. Everything in my life hinged from that first Broncos game. I was there throwing snowballs at the Kansas City Chiefs one game, too, as they made their way into the locker room. The players threw snowballs back at us. We cheered the Broncos and booed the opponents. That's just how football was. I can't imagine it any other way. We'd boo at Joe Namath and his white shoes. Marlin Briscoe's book was called *First Black Quarterback*. I could identify with him, being a little black kid. He was magic. Marlin the Magician. He'd run around and make things happen. I remember him bringing the team back against Miami. He ran well, and could pass, too. Most quarterbacks didn't run well. That was the game I got in trouble at home over. I had to wait for him to come out and sign autographs. He'd shake our hands and rub us on the head. He just seemed so young, not much older than my oldest sister. I was so brokenhearted when he went to Buffalo. He won a Super Bowl in Miami as a wide receiver. No one believed me when I'd tell them he used to be the quarterback for the Broncos. He was more well-known as a wide receiver. I've been in so many discussions about the fact that he truly was the first black quarterback. He was from Omaha, Nebraska. He would always hang out and talk to us after the game. He'd throw the football with us even. He was in Denver for only one season though — 1968.

———**KEN CRAWFORD**, 50, Regis High School assistant football coach

When the Broncos won their first Super Bowl, my emotions got away from me. When I saw Elway get emotional, I think we all got emotional. We'll never forget it. You could tell that to the Broncos fans, the Super Bowl win meant everything to them. Their whole life, their whole being, it was a huge rush to them. Their work was much better, their life much better. The world wasn't so black to them. It was just everybody talking to everybody. Everybody was happy. I didn't realize the emotions that would come out with winning the Super Bowl. Nothing seemed to really bother the fans after we won. When we won the next year, too, it was really special. Nothing is like the first time, though. It was great, but not like the first. Elway left after the second win, at just the right time. Fans keep thinking—when are we going to get another Elway? His pictures are all over the stadium. It's above Gate 7. He did a lot for the Broncos. This was the home of John Elway. It still is. The Broncos are one of the premier teams in the NFL because of the way they treat people. It's what they do, and how they play. The players are very kind and always want to help. A lot of them work with charities in the community. I believe strongly in our organization for what they've done for the city, me, and my family. When I lost my wife, the whole organization was there for me. That was very special. It's only recently that I can even talk about it. Everybody came to the funeral, which was a big surprise. That just says how much we think about one another.

———**RICHARD BLACKBURN**, INVESCO Field guest relations

Cookie Gilchrist was traded from Buffalo to Denver, and he was friends with the gal who owned the shoe store right across the hall from me. She brought Cookie over and introduced him to me. He wanted me to get him a fur coat. My normal policy was 50 percent down up front because if you're going to make something custom-made for somebody, if they don't pay you, or if they don't come back, you don't have a secondary market for it. That's especially true for guys that big. Cookie didn't give me any money down, and I went ahead and made it. He came in to pick it up, and didn't want to pay me. He came back in later and wanted to order a top coat. He asked about the top coat a few weeks later and I said "Cookie, I haven't started it yet." He said "Why haven't you started it yet?" I said "Because I need a deposit on it. That's the way I work." He backed me up into a corner, in my store, and started to give me the 'Do you know who I am?' kind of thing. I said, "Cookie, you can punch my lights out—it's not going to change anything. If you do that, I'm going to have every penny you've ever made." That's basically what I was able to spit out of my mouth. He backed up. I never made the coat and he never came back into the store again. But, there were some nice guys, too. Billy Thompson was one of my all-time favorites. I became friendly with Billy Thompson and there's no nicer human being on the planet than Billy. He's done very well. He stayed in the Denver area and is a super guy. I made clothing for Tom Jackson, and he's a very nice guy, too. Some of the others have egos so big they think, "hey, you know who I am. You should be giving me this stuff because I'm going to bring people to you." That never worked with me.

——RICHARD AGREN

During John Elway's rookie year, my mom and I went to the Burger King that used to be off Arapahoe and Quebec for a take-out dinner. As we were waiting for our food, John Elway and Dave Studdard walked in. I was a young girl at the time, so they looked gigantic to me. Being a huge football/Broncos family, I turned to my Mom and said, "That's John Elway!" We just stood there in awe. They walked up the counter and John proceeded to order, "A chopper with weez" instead of a "Whopper with cheese." It was hilarious and his young baby face turned bright red. It's something I'll never forget.

——ANNA GONZALES, Littleton, Colorado

Broncos football is a source of pride and power for me and for the whole city. Monday morning after a win—regardless of the record for that season—they talk about it on the radio stations and the whole city feels better. It's a source of good energy. It's like, "Wow! This is ours. This is cool." We've been so maligned by people who live east of the **MISSISSIPPI** River—fly-over country stuff, they think we are. Look at the national broadcasters: There's always the sense that we are the Podunk, red-neck types. There was a guy who was some sort of a photographer paparazzi guy who used to run his pictures through a one-hour photo machine here. I got a picture of Terrell Davis, John Elway and Pat Bowlen that he took in the locker room. He took the picture, but he didn't have a release, so it was probably a bootleg. He told us we could make a copy.

——**MIKE FABIAN**, Colorado native

My mother was one big Broncos fan. When 2 p.m. came on Sunday, there had to be total silence in the house and no visitors. Momma would holler and moan at the television depending on what Denver was doing at the time. It was really funny the way this little, reserved, church-going lady would transform into Super fan, but never a swear word left her lips. Even the pastor of her church was taken aback by how serious Momma and many of his congregation took the Broncos games. One Sunday at her church, Momma and the congregation were surprised to find Rick Upchurch and his wife sitting next to my brother. Rick had recently retired from the Broncos and had moved to Pueblo. Momma was so excited that she was actually going to meet one of her favorite Broncos players that she was speechless. Over the next few years, my family and the Upchurch family became good friends, breaking bread together and visiting. Momma was so happy when they came around. She always had a hard time believing that she was friends with them, but she treated them like her own. She was genuinely on a high when they came to visit. Three years ago, Momma got liver cancer and went to live with my youngest brother. As her health declined, Momma could not get out as much, but it did not stop her. Rick and his wife would visit her and they would sit and talk, which made her night better. Two years ago for Christmas, Mrs. Upchurch presented Momma with a beautiful quilt she had made. Momma would tuck herself into her chair with it and take it to bed with her. She was so happy that the Upchurches

> **The speed limit on the University of MISSISSIPPI campus is 18 MPH in honor of Archie Manning's uniform number.**

took the time to make her the quilt. She was so proud of that quilt that she told everyone who made it for her and said, "God Bless the Upchurches for thinking of me in such a nice way." On July 8, 2006, Momma passed away. She asked that two things be done: One was to have her Bible in her hands, and the other was to tuck that quilt around her like she did at home. It was her pride and joy, and knowing Momma, she has it tucked around her every Sunday afternoon cheering on her Broncos and telling everyone in Heaven who made it for her.

——<u>EDWARD TRIVETT</u>, Pueblo

I'd go watch the Broncos in training camp when they were in Greeley. One year on the same day, two memorable things happened. The practice was over and the players were heading to the locker room. Fans on the side were asking for autographs. Most of the players just walked by, not even looking at the fans. One player came over and signed my young son's Broncos cap and signed for others, too. He also talked to the kids while signing, not just standing there and signing. After we talked to him and he walked off, we looked at the autograph, and looked at each other and said, "Who is Rod Smith?" It was his first year off the practice squad. We remember that moment every time we see Rod catch a pass. John Elway always had a golf cart at the practice to get around. After the practice, John got in his cart and took off across the field. He pretty much ignored the people on the side. As he was driving across the field, several kids—including my son—started across the field after him. When he noticed them, he stopped, got out of his cart and signed autographs for the kids for several minutes. Then he got back in the cart and took off. While most of the big names on the team sometimes didn't have time for fans, John Elway most of the time found time for the kids. I always thought he was a class act. During the NFL strike a couple of years into Elway's Broncos career, he didn't play during the strike, but he really didn't support the strike, either. He wouldn't say anything bad about the team's owners, saying he had been treated well, and he stayed out of it. Then came the replacement players and boy, was that awkward. One day Karl Mecklenburg was signing autographs while picketing, trying to drum up support. He gave an autograph to a young boy and the kid was excited about going to one of the games, even if it only had the replacement players. The kid didn't relate to the strike and was just excited about going to a Broncos game. When Karl heard him, he took the autograph back and tore it up. I got to see the last game John Elway played, which was the Pro Bowl in February '99. We were going to Hawaii, and just before we left on the trip, we were able to get tickets on the 40-yard line, 15 rows up from the field. Elway went in the game for his first series and threw a touchdown pass. Immediately, he took himself out and stood on the sideline talking and joking with his teammates. You could tell he was enjoying his last game. My son, now 15, reminisced about the golf cart incident and was glad to see Elway's last game. Priceless! Those incidents leave lasting impressions—good or bad. I will always remember these things about John, Rod, and Karl whenever I think about them.

———**FRANK LOVAN**, lives near Fort Collins, Colorado

John Elway was my favorite player. I feel blessed to have had the opportunity to broadcast most of his games. He's one of the great people to play the game. Charlie Johnson, too. I knew Charlie when he was a rookie in St. Louis. Floyd Little was an established star when I got to Denver. He was an outstanding person and player. We remain very good friends to this day. I was really good friends with Lyle Alzado, too. He was a rookie when I first got to the Broncos' broadcast booth. He used to call me "Rook." He once lost an eight-round fight with Muhammed Ali.

———**LARRY ZIMMER**, Broncos broadcaster

I remember when Randy Gradishar played. He went non-stop. He was always playing. Karl Mecklenburg was a class act. I see him once in a while now, and he is always cordial. You couldn't help but love Lyle Alzado. When he went to the Raiders, it was like a bad divorce. I don't think we'll ever realize how fortunate we were to have a player of John Elway's caliber on the team. You knew all along that he was a Hall of Famer. I'd love to see the Broncos have some events with the old-timers—a chance for the fans today to meet the players of yesterday, listen to their stories and hear about what they do now. I don't think they could get a venue big enough for all the people who would want to hear them. Today's teams don't have the characters like teams of the past had. There are some exceptions. The current team has character, but doesn't have characters. People keep talking about the new stadium not having the character of Mile High. That is a bunch of crap. It's not about the stadium. It's about the players and the fans. It's about the characters who made the plays. New stadiums are too new. No memories have been formed, yet. The biggest memory for many of today's fans is "The Drive," which took place in Cleveland!

———STAN SCHWARZ, operates an electronics company

Karl Mecklenburg was a 12th round draft choice, and all that sort of thing, and my brother-in-law and I spent years going to watch him. We began to see a guy who tooled himself by flat out hard work. For example, I don't know how many times you've seen a linebacker hang out after practice taking receptions from the passing gun, the machine that would shoot the ball to receivers. What he was working to do was to be able to catch balls closer and closer to the gun. Everyone else had left the practice field, but he had some ball boy out there loading up the machine, and he would slowly, but surely, work his way toward it. He was out there schooling himself to catch the interception. I thought that was really cool. He is a hard worker. He knew how to position himself. The thing I remember most about him was one play—a hit he put on Marcus Allen. For those of us who were there, it was the loudest hit I can remember, and I've been a season ticket holder going on 16 years. I don't know if it was a swing pass or a sweep, but Mecklenburg hit Allen at about the line of scrimmage. It was a truly pad thunking, deep throated, THUNK! When you heard it, you felt the shivers go up and down your own spine. Marcus Allen went rolling over backwards like somebody just took the steam roller out and crunched him. It was beautiful. Now fast forward to Mecklenburg's retirement. I go to get his autograph. I ask him to make it out to Marcus Allen. He knew exactly what I was thinking and gave me a high-five!

———JEB BARRY, computer technician

My Broncos memory is on a shelf in my computer room. Years ago, when John Elway was still playing football and still throwing those rocket passes to our Broncos receivers, he came to Farmington, New Mexico. My husband (then boyfriend) was the coach for the Farmington High School girls' basketball team. Farmington's golf course was hosting a charity event and John was the main draw for the tourney. John Hall, the assistant coach of the high school team, took two girls' basketballs to the golf tourney, on the chance that John Elway might autograph them so that we could give them away at one of our fundraisers. John Elway was gracious enough to sign the balls, and my husband and John Hall gave one away at one of our fund raisers. I was so excited to even see a basketball with John Elway's signature. At the time, that was enough for me. I assumed my husband would keep the other one and give it away the next year, but he surprised me and gave it to me for my birthday. I've treasured that basketball for over 20 years. I think I have a special piece of history—along with one other person out there—because I can't imagine that John Elway signed many other women's basketballs.

———**ANN DOWTY**, Amarillo, Texas

Winter 1996, a month before the Jacksonville disaster; I am running into old McNichols Arena for the Avs-Red Wings game, the one that really started that whole mess. Anyway, I was arriving late, as usual, and running through the parking lot when a large oversized Chevy SUV came around a corner in the VIP parking area and quickly four-wheeled its way up a snow bank, a really good sized snow bank at that. Frankly, I was a little shocked and annoyed considering I parked in Lakewood, or at least the walk seemed that way, and the parking was ridiculous. As I stood there and waited to see who rolled out of the driver's seat, I was suddenly stunned into star gazing. My beloved No. 7 fell right out of the door, literally slid down the snow bank, stuck his empty beer bottle into the snow bank, straightened the evening's attire and off he went. The best part about the story was the parking attendants who were ready to give the driver the business, stopped mid-stride when they realized it was John Elway and just stood in awe, like me. Elway exchanged pleasantries with the men, waved at me and a couple of other late runners, and ran into the building.

———**MATTHEW BICKNELL**, Littleton, Colorado

My favorite player growing up was Dennis Smith. He hit HARD. I can remember Dennis Smith hitting players on sweep plays. He hit like a bullet, like a ton of bricks and often created a fumble. He stood out above everyone else to me, and it was when I first got into football. I'm not a memorabilia person. I don't own a jersey. I don't figure I have to spend $100 on a shirt to prove I'm a fan. Games are a great time to hang out with my friends. For a long time, that was really when we got together as friends. Game days were my favorite time of the week—not just because of the game, but because of the friends. I really enjoyed it when everyone came to my place for the game. I didn't have to call anyone, they just showed up. It didn't matter if I was up yet or not, or if I answered the door. They just came in and got the TV fired up and got started.

——JAMES CANTOR, 33

My favorite player is Otis Armstrong. He was one of my heroes as a kid when I was playing pee-wee football. I named my dog after Otis Armstrong. He—the dog—likes to hang out at the bar with me. Al Wilson is a favorite, too. And of course everybody loves Elway. The guys from the Mississippi Mud Walk were great, too. My nicknames include "9-toed Bob," "Chocolate Bob" and "Bronco Bob." I lost a toe a few years back, because of knee surgery gone bad. The operation was in the off-season, so I didn't have to miss a game. They wouldn't let me on the stadium's handicap elevator, even though I showed them my toe.

——BOB NICHOLS, 38, owner of The Lariat Saloon, Grand Lake, Colorado

The margin of error in Dennis Green's play-calling is plus or minus 100%

Chapter 8

Broncopalooza

Time Flies When
You're Havin' Rum

WHEN RED SAW ORANGE

RED MILLER

Red Miller was head coach of the Denver Broncos for four seasons, from 1977-80. In his first season, the Broncos qualified for the playoffs for the first time and advanced to the Super Bowl. He had a four-year record of 40-22 in Denver. Following his stint with the Broncos, Miller coached the Denver Gold of the United States Football League until the organization and league folded. He then worked in Denver as a stockbroker. A self-taught jazz pianist and a member of a barbershop quartet as a youth, Miller enjoys attending barbershop quartet competitions.

I was one of 10 kids. My dad was a coal miner in Illinois. We lived in Macomb. We had no money. We had an outdoor well, an outhouse, kerosene lamps, one cook stove. Life was tough. I slept with three other brothers—two at one end of the bed, two of us at the other, with our feet in the middle. No radio, no phone. My dad was pulled out of the first grade to work in the mines. He never learned to read or write. People take that stuff for granted now. When you grow up that way, it gives you some steel.

In 1959 we won 18 games in a row at Western Illinois University, with Lou Saban as the head coach, me and two assistants. That got Lou the chance to apply for a pro job. The Boston Patriots called Lou and offered him the job. He took Joe Collier and me to Boston with him. I spent two years there. Lou then transferred to the Buffalo Bills. We went with him. The Bills got quarterback Jack Kemp off the waiver wire from the Chargers. That led us to being a great offensive team. Then Jack Faulkner of the Broncos called. We'd become friends from coaching clinics. He wanted a good offensive coach. He offered me a three-year, no-cut contract as an assistant coach. You didn't get those kinds of contracts often.

My third year with the Broncos, 1965, I thought I was becoming a good coach and wanted to jump to the NFL. The Broncos were still in the AFL. Charlie Winner from the **ST. LOUIS CARDINALS** called me. I was there five years. In 1968 all five of my offensive linemen went to the Pro Bowl. The last year, the Bidwell brothers, the owners, decided to split up. They flipped a coin to see who got the football team and who got the dog tracks in Chicago. Stormy liked me, but Billy won the toss and fired the whole staff.

Gerry Phipps called me from Denver, and I took the head coaching job in Denver in 1977. I knew we had a shot that year. I'd been in the league a long time. It's a tough road. You have to get everyone on your side working together.

Denver had been good in 1976, but we had knocked the snot out of them in Boston that year. They had a good defensive base. Joe Collier was out here by then. He was my coordinator. One thing I had to do was to beat Oakland. The Broncos had lost to them 12 consecutive games. That had to stop. We went through the preseason unbeaten and won four games to start the season. Game Five was at Oakland. I knew we had to beat them there. We went out there and beat them. It was a turning point for the season. The team then knew they were good enough to win it all. The Raiders had won the Super Bowl the year prior. We went 12-2 that year, with the NFL's toughest schedule. We had home-field advantage with our record.

The Orange Crush thing came about through the Broncos public relations staff. It happened midway through the season. The Orange Crush bottler came to them mid-season, and they came to an agreement on the use of the name.

The fans in 1977 hadn't had a pro franchise that ever won anything before. It was unbelievable how the fervor grew as we kept winning games. In the past, they'd get excited and then we'd lose. This season, we just kept winning. There was orange everywhere. You could drive

> **In the late 1970s, a ST. LOUIS FOOTBALL CARDINALS fan bought an ad in the** *St. Louis Post-Dispatch* **offering to sell the "Official Cardinals' Playbook" with "all five plays illustrated, including the squib punt."**

down Colfax and there wouldn't be anyone on the street during the games. The **NEBRASKA**, Wyoming and Montana fans got into it, too. The Broncos were a regional team. The Mountain States loved them. At every practice we had to walk through the fans to get to our practice field. People painted their houses and cars orange. I got so many orange gifts from fans—an orange toilet seat, an orange TV. They had one car that read, "Red Miller for President." I was just happy to be a head coach in the NFL. I went to the Super Bowl in my first year as a head coach! As the final game was winding down, the fans began chanting, "We love you Broncos!" They kept it up for 10 minutes.

Super Bowl XXII…strangely, it was just another ball game to me. We went in with a depleted offensive line. Tom Glassick, who weighed about 255 normally, weighed just 223 for the Super Bowl. We took him to the Mayo Clinic after the game and found out he was allergic to grass! We got him cured, though.

Many of the players still live in Denver or the surrounding area. Once a year, Pat Bowlen brings the alumni back if you want to come. He's the only NFL owner who still does that. He's a great owner. He's one of the few. Cal Kunz had bought the team on a $100,000 letter of credit. It's worth hundreds of millions now. Phipps bought the team to keep it in Denver. He was a good owner, too.

I often thought, boy, I've come a long way, especially when I would walk on the field. I worked 15 years in the stockbroker business after coaching, 10 years with Dean Witter, five years with Paine Webber. It was a people business. I did well and now I can do what I want to do. My wife worked 30-some years at IBM and is retired now.

There were two games that were pivotal in 1977—Kansas City in the regular season and Oakland in the playoffs. We had a great team. We were playing in Kansas City, and I think this was the greatest defensive stand in Broncos history. They had to punt. We were up by six

> **Academic All-American teams have been picked every year since 1952. NEBRASKA leads all colleges by a wide margin in number of players selected.**

points. They lined up to punt with about a minute left in the game. They had the "fumblerooski" on. A player broke clean. Louie Wright came all the way across the field and stopped them on the 1-yard line. Then we held them four straight plays to win the game.

We beat Baltimore, and played at home against Oakland for the right to go to the Super Bowl. Morton had taken a bad hit against Baltimore. On Monday, he was black and blue from his ankle to his hip on his left leg. We put him in the hospital, and I closed practices. I didn't want Oakland to know he might not play. We took the game plan to him at the hospital. I asked him if he wanted to play. He warmed up and decided he could play if I would tie his shoes. It was a torture to watch him warm-up. He said he'd start, and if he couldn't play, he'd tell me. He played every down. He's at the University of California-Berkley now. He does fundraising for them.

I've been all over the U.S. The two cities that stood out for me were San Diego and Denver, so I stayed here.

Warren Sapp can't be on the $25,000 Pyramid 'cause he doesn't have a clue.

THE POISE THAT REFRESHES

LARRY ZIMMER

Larry Zimmer was part of the Broncos' broadcast team for 26 years. He was the color analyst for Bob Martin from 1971-89, then took over the play-by-play job. He worked with Dave Logan through 1996.

In the early '60s, the fans weren't too interested in the Broncos. I'm not sure when they really started to get interested, but by the mid-'60s they were very interested. It's my understanding that the bond issue to fund keeping the team in Denver really solidified the fan base. In '68 the NFL-AFL merger was announced and that helped, too. When I started broadcasting in '71, there was a solid fan base. The games were sold out. Lou Saban had a lot to due with that—bringing a real professional organization to the city.

The one thing that really changed things around was the first Monday Night Football game. It was Orange Monday and it helped create the rivalry with the Oakland Raiders. The Broncos were the talk of the town in '73, but they had never had a winning season. Coach John Ralston had a great draft and brought in Charlie Johnson at quarterback. He was a veteran quarterback and the fans really felt they had a guy who could take them to the playoffs and give them wins. And Charlie produced. Floyd Little had a big year that season, too. They had never been on Monday Night Football and Howard Cosell had always ignored the Broncos on his halftime highlights. It was a really big deal that the Monday Night crew was coming to Denver. The mayor had a big lunch for **FRANK GIFFORD**, Don Meredith and

> **Frank and Kathie Lee Gifford have the same birthday, except they're twenty-three years apart age-wise. They were married in 1986. FRANK GIFFORD was a grandfather at the time. Cody and Cassidy are Uncle and Aunt to Frank Gifford's grandchildren. When told that Kathie Lee was pregnant, Don Meredith said, "I'll hunt the guy down, Frank, and I'll kill him."**

Howard Cosell. They arrived in limos and fans were lining the block to see them. It was a holiday atmosphere that Monday at Mile High Stadium.

Charlie Goldberg was the Broncos' No. 1 fan and was the creator of Orange Monday. He was a downtown businessman and political leader and his pastime was the Broncos. Charlie used to get mail addressed to "Charlie Bronco." He had owned a wrecking company and worked hard to obtain his wealth. He lived well into his 90s and never missed a Broncos home game. He founded the Broncos Quarterback Club. He helped build the Mile High Stadium Club. His goal was to turn Mile High Stadium into a sea of orange. He came up with the slogan "Big Orange, How Sweet It Is." He had the idea that Orange Monday should mean everyone wore orange. Charlie went to Mayor McNichols to get the city's backing on Orange Monday. McNichols was an Irish-Catholic, and orange isn't an Irish-Catholic friendly color, so the mayor turned it down. Charlie said, "I'm Jewish. What does any of that have to do with it?" and Orange Monday was then declared by the Mayor's office.

That first Monday Night game was a great game. The Raiders had won the Super Bowl the year before. The Broncos tied the game in the last minute of play. It was like a victory for the Broncos, even though it ended in a tie. The Broncos went on to have their first winning season, and Broncomania began then.

The fans really felt like they made a difference in the games at Mile High. I'm not sure it's that way now, the South Stands especially. The South Stands were a "way of life." Those weren't great seats, and if you were seated low, it was hard to see. It was a badge of pride to have seats there. We used to play with them on the air and reference the South Stands. It always got them off their seats and cheering. If I talked to them, they would respond. The South Stands were special, sort of a fraternity. When they divided those seats up it really changed the group. Mile High was very close to the field, not much room on the sidelines. It was almost like having walls on the sides of the field. The proximity of the fans to the players had a big impact on the game. The new stadium doesn't have that same "snake pit" feeling. When you were on the field, it felt like the fans were right on top of you.

When the Broncos came home from an away game in '77, there were so many fans at the airport that they had to close Concourse A. Fans lined up, and the team walked through the gauntlet of fans. They had to have police controlling the crowd. Then it started to happen every time the Broncos won a game on the road. The mayor was even concerned, because of the impact on the city budget with having extra police on hand. The fans were so much into that '77 season, even when all seemed lost. They won the first six games, then lost to the Raiders at home. Then they won six more games, went into Kansas City and stopped the Chiefs four straight times on a goal-line stand. That team had divine guidance and it lit the fans up. The **STEELERS** were in Denver on Christmas Eve and it was a great game that the Broncos won at Mile High Stadium. They beat the Raiders on New Year's Day, as well, in another great game for the fans. The Broncos were AFC champions that year. The fans went nuts. If there were a seismograph going, there would have been a recorded earthquake from the fans going nuts at the end of that game. The fans stayed around for a long time after the game. They took the goalposts down and took it up to the top of the South Stands. They paraded around the stadium. They just continued to cheer "Broncos! Broncos! Broncos!" They kept going for so long that the team came back out onto the field and took a bow. I had never seen that in a sporting event before. The fans didn't want to leave. They wanted to savor the moment, and the players enjoyed that as well. That atmosphere was reflective of the season. That game is the greatest game I ever broadcast with the Broncos.

There was a definite affinity between the fans and players then that doesn't exist today due to free agency. Those early players made Denver their home and still live in the area. The fans identified with them. They were part of the charities and the communities. The fans saw them as neighbors. Pro football has lost that identification now. Fans could really identify with players back then. People identified with the players when they made the great plays, too, like they were making the play themselves.

> **In 1941, Buff Donelli was the head football coach for the Pittsburgh STEELERS and Duquesne University in Pittsburgh.**

Dan Reeves was one of the nicest, most genuine coaches I've ever worked with. You always knew where you stood with Dan. He was a very honest coach. So much has been made of the feud between Elway and Reeves, but Elway acknowledged that they were both good for each other. The combination of the two help us win a lot of football games. Elway mentioned Reeves in his Hall of Fame acceptance speech, as well. It was touching for everyone involved. The media tried to make it out like Elway and Reeves hated each other, but there was a great deal of respect between the two men. Reeves got more out of the talent that he had than any coach I've seen in the NFL. Dan Reeves had excellent success and was a great football coach.

The Raiders should eat
Randy Moss' contract...
it's low carb.

THESE SEVEN REASONS ARE THE 10 SIGNS THAT SHE'S HOOKED ON THE BRONCOS

DONNA STANG

Donna Stang, 66, is a retired school teacher. Originally from South Dakota, she has lived in Colorado for the last 35 years.

My son got a dog when he was 12-years-old in 1984, the year John Elway was drafted. We had this tiny puppy, and my son sat out back trying to figure out what to name him. We were avid Broncos fans, so we looked at each other and said, "What about Elway?" So, he named the dog Elway. What's unique about this is that we had Elway for 16 years. We had to put him to sleep due to health issues two weeks after John Elway announced his retirement. I've met John Elway on a couple of occasions, most recently at his restaurant. I sat down and talked with him for 10 or 15 minutes and told him the story about our dog, Elway....

We have a big Broncomobile. It has the Broncos logo on it. It's painted orange and blue with white stripes on it. We use it when we tailgate. Back in December 1998 someone from *Sports Illustrated* came to our tailgate party and asked if anyone had a No. 7 on. I had my Elway sweatshirt on and was the only one at my party. They told me to go to Gate 6 for pictures. I stood in line for three hours on a very cold day. *SI* was doing a pictorial for the magazine. The next month, a friend in Arizona called me from his dentist's office to tell me my picture was in *SI*. They had chosen 24 fans out of everyone to go with John's picture....

I have an orange Broncos hat, a cowboy hat I bought in 1971. In 1977 I sprayed it orange and started getting autographs. I now have 218 signatures on it. We go to an away game each year and always stay at the hotel with the players. I remember riding up the elevator with Randy Gradishar so I could get his autograph. I saw him outside the elevator, and he was headed to his room, so he told me to ride up the elevator with him, and he signed my hat. I've sat on the couches at the hotels with a number of players. I talked with them and they would sign my hat. It was such a thrill to get to visit with them....

I truly bleed orange and blue. When I was teaching, I taught PE. During calisthenics, we'd do Broncos cheers and jog to music the Broncos played at the games. All my kids and students knew I was a huge, huge Broncos fan. The year the Super Bowl was in San Diego, we did a contest with our classes. We had a huge map in the gym and as the kids jogged, we'd record how many laps the kids would jog. It was 17 laps around the gym to make a mile. We'd track that on the map to see if they would make it from the school in Colorado to San Diego. The day that I left for the Super Bowl, the kids had reached San Diego on the map! The principal announced it to the whole school. We had a pep rally at the school after the Broncos won. I took four days off school to go to the game. Two of the days were supposed to be "professional" days, but our principal told me I could take them. Someone took a picture of me at the Broncomobile looking for tickets, and that was on the front page of our local paper. One of the school administrators saw it and they docked me two days pay. It was worth it to be able to go to the game.

IF YOU'RE LUCKY ENOUGH TO BE A BRONCOS FAN, YOU'RE LUCKY ENOUGH

SARA LOCKHART

Sara Lockhart, 23, is a Denver Broncos cheerleader and a full-time student, studying marketing at the University of Colorado at Denver.

You have to try out every year. My first year, I was only 18 and was really scared. We had to do a whole day of dance try-outs. There were three cuts the first day. We then went back for an interview with 10 judges. You'd have to answer a football question and a general question. I was very nervous about the football question. Then you do a dance audition again. You find out that day if you made the squad or not. I had been so nervous I could barely talk. It's scary and intimidating. I was in shock when I found out I made the team. That shock doesn't go away until after your rookie year.

Our outfits are kind of revealing. One of the girls had the silicone bra inserts that enhance your breast size, and we were doing a routine in the end zone, and one slipped out. Someone had to go out and recover it. We laughed about it forever in the locker room. We've had hair extensions fall out on the field, too. There's nothing worse than that.

We went as a squad to Iraq and Afghanistan. Those were two of the best experiences of my life. Those mean more than any of the games. I know that the trip changed a lot of our lives. It's something most people don't get to do. It wasn't necessarily scary. We always felt safe. It was a reality check when we had to put on flak jackets and helmets. We were in Afghanistan two summers ago in Kandahar. We went to the building called "the Taliban's last stand." They now fly an

American flag on this building. The building is almost destroyed and our troops operate from there. After our show in Kandahar, they presented the flag from that building to us. We told them we'd fly that flag at the first Broncos home game. It was incredible. Seeing that flag at INVESCO Field, knowing where it had been, was amazing. It is such a significant symbol to what they're doing. It felt good to brighten their days over there. We received hundreds and hundreds of emails from the soldiers and their families. We helped them to forget where they were for the two hours of our show. For the squad to go over there and take them a piece of home is special. It didn't matter what NFL team they liked, they were appreciative of us being there. I know we boosted their morale, and I appreciate them even more now than before the trip. The sacrifices they make are tremendous. We flew in Black Hawk helicopters to the remote bases. The troops had minimal amenities. No running water or restrooms. A few had air conditioning. Many of them lived in mud huts. Our troops are doing incredible things over there. It was an eye opener. We were one of two NFL cheerleader teams to go to Iraq. One of the biggest requests to Armed Forces Entertainment is to have cheerleaders go over. The first time we tried to go, we weren't approved. We have 34 cheerleaders, and we all fought for the spots to go over to see the troops. We had 25 sign-up to go, and could take only 11....

There was a little boy at a charity event for Make-A-Wish Foundation. One of his last wishes was to have some Broncos cheerleaders come see him. His name was Jimmy. He was sick, but was so full of life. The Broncos meant so much to him. His mom sent us a note and said that our visit meant the world to him. He passed away a couple of days later. It makes you think about how little we are in the scheme of things. It's neat to be able to put on a uniform and have such an impact on someone. He made more of an impact on me than any fan ever has.

MAN AND FOOTBALL— IT'S A BEAUTIFUL THING

JIM SACCOMANO

Jim Saccomano is the Vice President of Public Relations for the Denver Broncos. He has worked with the team for 29 years.

The fan involvement in Denver has always been super, super heavy. The league changed how we report attendance a number of years ago, but we continue to announce the no-shows at the games. The fans boo the no-shows! They always have. They get involved with the **P.A. ANNOUNCER**. You can't make them be involved, they just are. You can't make somebody love you—you can't order them to. You have to earn their respect and love, and the fans love the Broncos. The level of support is humbling.

The South Stands really became a cultural thing at Mile High. They were right above the locker rooms and were bench seats—bleachers. Fans would yell, throw snowballs, and the people were proud to be "South Standers." They felt like they were the best fans. It's kind of like the Bleacher Bums at **WRIGLEY FIELD** in Chicago. People

> The public address announcer for the Houston Astros (Colt '45s) in 1962 was Dan Rather. John Forsythe, the actor, was the **P.A. ANNOUNCER** for the Brooklyn Dodgers in 1937 and 1938.

> More NFL games have been played in the Meadowlands than any other stadium. Until 2003, **WRIGLEY FIELD** held the record even though Wrigley had not hosted an NFL game since 1971. When Mile High was razed in 2001, only Wrigley had hosted more NFL games.

pounding their feet on the steel made a colossal noise. It's still exciting at the new stadium.

In a game versus the 49ers, maybe a Monday Night game, there is a legend of a snowball coming out of the South Stands, hitting the field goal kicker, making him miss the field goal at the end of the game. Legend goes on to say he was in a coma, etc. There are even shirts out there that read, "I threw the Denver snowball." The truth is that it was the end of the half, the snowball came out of the East Stands, and it landed at least 15 yards from the kicker. He did miss the field goal, though. It wasn't a decisive moment in the game, but the legend grew to make it something it wasn't.

The first Super Bowl win was bigger than just John Elway getting the ring. It was for the whole city. It gave us some respect. How often have you heard the announcer on TV say a program will be on at "8 Eastern, 7 Central and 5 Pacific?" What happened to "6 Mountain?" It's a respect thing that they still don't get. We're part of the forgotten time zone. The Super Bowl win was surreal for the whole organization and the whole city. We have season ticket holders in every state. It's amazing how many people come here from other states to every game. They come from Arkansas, Illinois, etc. It's astonishing. The support is unreal; it's fantastic.

Some fans have been married at the stadium, and others have had their ashes spread there. It really shows the support. My wife is my favorite fan. She is absolute and resolute. She never gives up, even if the Broncos are down. She never leaves early. Her support is unflinching. She has always been there, even when she was pregnant or sick. She has only missed one home game since '72. She was out of town at a convention.

DOWN AT THE CORNER
OF WHAT AND IF

RICH GOINS, A.K.A. "G-MAN"

Rich Goins is a 46 year-old "radio moron." He has been on the radio for 16 years and currently works at KRFX-FM as the Sports Director on the Lewis and Floorwax Show.

In November '90 Lewis and Floorwax had just started on "The Fox." Jack Evans from the station was creating a series of billboards to promote the show. The concept was that there was a giant fox head on the billboard holding a sheet over other stations' billboards. In September and October, the Broncos had started losing games—games that I felt they should be winning. I was ripping them on the air a bit. It was suggested that I do my sports each morning from the billboard to gain some attention. I did it a couple of days in a row, and then the producer suggested I live up there until the Broncos won a game. The thought was that they would win that weekend against the Bears at Mile High Stadium. I went up there on a Thursday. I took a cooler with food, drinks and my radio so I could listen to the show. I had a broadcast unit, too. They picked me up with a crane, and I told everyone I'd be down on Sunday. There was a blurb in the *Rocky Mountain News* that I was living up there, but that was it.

They lost! The next game was versus Detroit the following Thursday on Thanksgiving. I figured there was no way the Broncos would lose, but they did! By then I had been up there more than a week, and the next game was 11 days away. It was getting cold. On Thanksgiving, I would typically go back to Michigan to spend it with family. Instead, I called my parents to tell them what I was doing….And Mom thought my life wasn't going to work out?

After the loss to the Lions, someone told Bob Costas about me living on the billboard. NBC sent out a camera crew and said Bob Costas wanted to interview me! I was interviewed right after the loss to Detroit. Costas called me a "sniveling wimp" and said I needed to stay up there until they won. My parents saw the interview while they were eating Thanksgiving dinner!

The radio station got me a tarp. I was sleeping on the billboard with a belt to keep me up there. The Broncos lost their next game, too! I had been up on the billboard for two weeks. The Broncos continued to lose. The more they lost, the bigger deal this stunt became. There was more attention and more people wanting to be a part of it. The radio station was even selling sponsorships. Listeners were tuning in to the show to see how I was doing.

After the loss to the Raiders, the station built me a "dog house" to keep me out of the weather. It included a TV and a heater, so there was a little more comfort for the next three weeks. I would come down off the billboard to an RV for just 15 minutes a day to shower and such. I was doing interviews up there, too.

Every night someone from the station was assigned to be there with me. One night the guy who was supposed to be there drank too much, passed out in the RV and didn't come keep me company. It got down to 10 below one night and the generator quit. I woke up at 2 a.m. I was sweating in the sleeping bag, but my head was freezing. There was a ton of snow. I called Jack Evans to find out what was up. I nearly froze to death. I caught pneumonia while I was up there and a doctor made a "house call" to the billboard to give me antibiotics.

The whole thing wasn't big at all until Costas interviewed me. Then I had TV and radio stations from all over the world wanting to interview me. I had stations from Australia, Europe and South America calling. People were telling me I was an idiot and that the Broncos wouldn't win again.

John Madden and Pat Summerall broadcast the Bears game for CBS. Madden came out about four hours before kickoff. I came down off the billboard for a couple of minutes to talk to them. It became a party before each game at the billboard. There were always 700 to

1,000 people, big screen TVs, beer and everything. We were about a mile from the stadium.

Three or four weeks into this, an SUV pulled up. The window rolled down, and it was John Elway. He was laughing hysterically. I told him he better get me down from there. He just waved and took off.

Broncos fans were sending food, beer, liquor, jackets, boots and gloves almost daily. Someone even sent me a workout bike and some weights so I could stay in shape. Qwest sent me a cell phone. Comcast came over and hooked up cable for me. Needless to say, it got easier as time went on. Some people even came up and cooked me dinner. My broadcast partner brought me Thanksgiving dinner.

I read a lot of magazines, watched TV and talked on the phone to pass time. People came by almost constantly to talk to me. Since the billboard faced west, I'd go to the other side of the billboard in the mornings to be in the sun.

One night, after I went back up from the RV, I discovered that a hot girl had climbed up on my billboard. She was in the "dog house" waiting for me. She said, "Your friend Bob sent me to spend the night with you." I didn't know anyone named Bob! It was difficult telling her to go home, but I sent her back down.

The guy who lived next door to the billboard had a dog that I'd drop food down to. I figured that Doberman would kill me if I ever fell off!

The Broncos finished 5-11 that year. The Broncos lost the last game of the year to the Seahawks. Had they not won against the Chargers, I'd have been on the billboard through the off-season!

I was on that billboard for 33 days, 17 hours, 16 minutes and 21 seconds. It was five games total. I went up November 15 and came down December 16. Luckily, the Broncos beat the Chargers, 20-10, at home. I told Costas I wasn't coming down unless I came down on his radio show. I came down on his "Coast to Coast" show a couple of hours after the game. By that time, there were 5,000 people waiting for me. The police had to block off the street, because of the number of people. Coming down to the party, I felt like a rock star! Fans were crediting me for the win.

The station had a limo waiting for me. The station took me out to dinner and Dan Reeves was there. He came over to our private room and thanked me for the support; behind the scenes, it drove him nuts, though. He bought me a bottle of wine and said it was my choice. Someone from the station picked a $300 bottle of wine and Reeves was not happy when he got the bill!

I stayed at a hotel downtown that night and had to get up at 4 a.m. the next morning to be on the "Today Show" with Bryant Gumbel. The station then gave me two weeks off. I think I slept the whole time. I was still sick. I had a month's growth of facial hair.

After I came down, the Broncos invited me to their Christmas party. All the Broncos players, wives, families and staff were there. They brought me up on stage to talk. Even today, Elway and I talk about the billboard when I see him. He knew they were bad that year.

One of the political cartoonists from the *Rocky Mountain News* did a cartoon of me on the billboard. It showed me up there 20 years later with chalk marks showing all the losses. He gave me the original that I have now framed. I also kept the safety belt that the billboard company made me wear while I was up there. I had to wear it all the time due to OSHA rules. It was tethered to a wire on the billboard.

I did it again in '97, but on top of a hotel during the playoffs. I didn't get near as much publicity, though. People had had enough of me by then, I think. I was up there 40 days. It was the middle of the season and everyone had written off the Broncos. They had lost to the 49ers in a Monday Night game. Everyone had climbed off the Broncos' bandwagon. They put a shed on top of the Sheraton Hotel next to the stadium. I went up there the first week of December and I lived in that shed until the Broncos won the Super Bowl. They won a bunch of playoff games on the road that year. I said I'd jump off into the hotel pool if they lost. I had a heater, couch and cable TV. I made sure I had the comforts of home so I wouldn't get sick this time. A bunch of Broncos and Rockies players came by. People would come up on the roof and party every night.

I have a ton of fun working with Lewis and Floorwax. They've backed every stunt that I've ever done. I've been with them 16 years.

People in Denver still introduce me as "the guy who lived on the billboard for 33 days." It's my moniker for life. It's the greatest thing that ever happened to me. I was an out-of-work sportscaster when it happened and it made my career. I was a huge fan of the team and that is much of what motivated me to go up there. The Broncos lost more consecutive games that year than any other Dan Reeves-coached team.

I'd do this again in a heartbeat…but the billboard is gone.

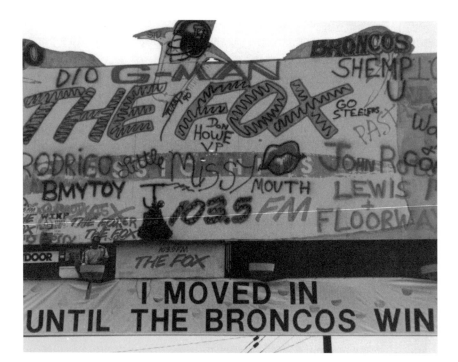

QUICK HITS AND INTERESTING BITS

In '96, the Broncos were 13-3. I'll tell you, to this day, I thank God and the NFL that the Broncos played Jacksonville on a Saturday. It was a big party. Everything was going the Broncos' way. They lost to Jacksonville badly. That one hurt. It was devastating. Felonious Monk was our cat. I came home devastated from the loss. The cat had a puncture in his stomach from another cat. I had him for 20 years. I took him to the vet and left him overnight for surgery. I went back to get him Sunday morning. Sitting at the stoplight at University and Belleview, I saw Coach Shanahan. I rolled down my window and said, "Look, the sun came up today!" I could tell he was still hurting. By the way, the cat came out OK—better than the Broncos fans did....I was on the team plane coming home from the playoff game at Pittsburgh. It was an unbelievable feeling to know the Broncos were going to the Super Bowl. I was on the first bus going to that game—9:15 a.m. for a 12:30 p.m. game. Steelers fans lined the streets. The intensity was unreal. You could tell they really loved their team. At the Super Bowl, I listened to the interviews as they happened. The reporters were really disrespectful to the team. It upset me. The team was prepared, though. They were confident. I interviewed the late Will McDonough the night before the game. He said the Packers would win by two touchdowns. My wife, Linda, and I watched the game from the stands. She and I had been married about nine months then. I teared up when the Broncos won the game. I can't remember ever tearing up for a game before. The highs and lows all came to tears after the game. Everyone in the section was that way. I went to the locker room after the game and onto the field. There were hugs, high-fives, the whole bit.

——TOM MANOOGIAN, Newsradio 850 KOA

One game, one of the Broncos linemen sang the National Anthem, and part way through, his microphone quit. It was amazing. The fans started singing along. Everybody picked up on it and carried the song through, and then the fly-over. Mondays when we lost used to be a bummer day. People would spend much of the day at the water cooler calling for the coach's firing and were really down. I've learned over the years that it really is just a game and there are more important things in life to worry about. I don't have the same level of frustration as I used to. Anymore, Mondays aren't near as bad. Winning a couple of Super Bowls and having winning seasons helps with that, too.

——**FRANK GARRED**, attended his first Broncos game in 1962

I just don't think the crowd is into the games like they were at Mile High. They have priced out a lot of the fans with the pricing for seats at the new stadium. It especially took out the fans from the South Stands. It seems like the seats are a little farther from the action, too. I can't really remember one game in the new stadium that rivals the intensity of the fans in Mile High. The metal flooring at Mile High and the noise from stomping on it was incredible! I don't think the new stadium holds a candle to Mile High when it comes to getting fans involved. It's a nice stadium, but not the same. I miss the old stadium, but I know that with the economics of the NFL, we had to move into the new stadium. The year we won the Super Bowl was almost a let down. After having been to the Super Bowl four times before and losing, and after all the bad seasons, I was pumped. An hour after the game, I felt let down. For some reason, after 37 years, I thought it would be an even greater feeling than it was. It was great, but after that, we started at zero again next year. It's like the Christmas morning let down when you run out of presents. You build things up that are so unsustainable—they're not reality. Then it happens and you are like, "Now what?"

——**MARK JACKSON,** 52, stock investor, Denver

When I was 23-years-old, I was an intern for the Broncos. It was 1999 and I had been there about three weeks. There was an event on a Sunday when the Lombardi Trophy was going to be on display, and on Friday they asked me—the intern—to take the Lombardi Trophy home with me and take it to the event on Sunday. I was tasked with babysitting the Lombardi Trophy. I took it home, petrified all the way that someone would hit the car. I didn't live in a great part of

town and was certain that was the weekend my house would get broken into and everything stolen. I was so paranoid. I slept with the trophy in my bed. I didn't sleep a wink all weekend, fearful something would happen to the trophy. I never let it out of my sight. I told a few friends, who told a few friends, so everyone was coming over to take pictures. They were touching it and picking it up. My parents found out I had the trophy. My parents are divorced, and they both decided they were going to throw parties and show their friends the trophy. So my mom named her party the "Lombardi Party." My dad had already had a party planned with his golfing buddies. One of the buddies was leaving the country club, and they were going to give him a plaque. So my dad decided they would give him the Lombardi Trophy as a gag. There were lots of men smoking cigars and drinking beer. My dad gave a speech. They had the trophy covered up and everyone was gathered around, and they reveal the trophy. So many people had been touching it, picking it up that I was terrified something was going to happen to it. Nothing bad happened to the trophy. Imagine the pressure, though. I was a 23-year-old intern. I was hired full-time a few months later and stayed with the Broncos for six seasons. I now have tons of great memories and terrific pictures from that weekend!

——LYNN ROSEN, 31, Denver

I've gotten pretty philosophical about Denver and the Broncos. You form a community identity oftentimes through your sports teams. The main thing you talk about when you meet strangers is the weather, but when you get a sports team, you talk about your franchise. It was a shared, common identity that brought people from all different backgrounds together. It has a very powerful influence on uniting people.

———STU ZISMAN

When I was about 16, I used to listen to "Broncos Talk" on the way home from games. Sandy Clough was the host, and he was notorious for roughing up the callers. And a lot of them had it coming. When I'd get home, I'd call in and just try to push his buttons. One year, I called every week to tell him that Ron Holmes was having a Pro Bowl season. Holmes was a decent defensive lineman, but I'd compare him to Reggie White and Bruce Smith and Chris Doleman and all of the best guys in the league. Well, Clough would just go off. It was hysterical because I'd do it week after week. Another year, I'd call every week and tell him that Michael Young was an all-pro receiver. I'd compare him to Steve Watson. And then I'd tell Sandy that he once said Watson wasn't going to be any good. This really got him fired up. He'd call me all sorts of names and eventually hang up on me. The fact that he had no idea it was a high school sophomore pushing his buttons was just too funny. Every time I hear him on the radio to this day, I think about those calls.

———JEFF MERILATT, 36, Westminster

Like many Broncos fans, I've been a fan for decades and have watched them win and lose over the years. I've lived in many different cities and states, but remember being a fan in Albuquerque as a young girl. I decided my favorite color was orange because of the Orange Crush defense. Over the years, I moved, went to college and moved some more. But I continued to be a Broncos fan. I was teaching at risk kids in the San Francisco Bay Area. These kids had spunk and creativity and were natural leaders, but not very good students. Of course being in the Bay Area, I was surrounded by 49ers and Raiders fans. I can respect the 49ers due to their history and all, but as a fan of the Broncos, I couldn't deal well with the Raiders. So the year that we played Green Bay in the Super Bowl, I was making

I've gotten pretty philosophical about Denver and the Broncos. You form a community identity often times through your sports teams. The main thing you talk about when you meet strangers is the weather, but when you get a sports team, you talk about your franchise. It was a shared, common identity that brought people from all different backgrounds together. It has a very powerful influence on uniting people.

———STU ZISMAN

When I was about 16, I used to listen to "Broncos Talk" on the way home from games. Sandy Clough was the host, and he was notorious for roughing up the callers. And a lot of them had it coming. When I'd get home, I'd call in and just try to push his buttons. One year, I called every week to tell him that Ron Holmes was having a Pro Bowl season. Holmes was a decent defensive lineman, but I'd compare him to Reggie White and Bruce Smith and Chris Doleman and all of the best guys in the league. Well, Clough would just go off. It was hysterical because I'd do it week after week. Another year, I'd call every week and tell him that Michael Young was an all-pro receiver. I'd compare him to Steve Watson. And then I'd tell Sandy that he once said Watson wasn't going to be any good. This really got him fired up. He'd call me all sorts of names and eventually hang up on me. The fact that he had no idea it was a high school sophomore pushing his buttons was just too funny. Every time I hear him on the radio to this day, I think about those calls.

———JEFF MERILATT, 36, Westminster

Like many Broncos fans, I've been a fan for decades and have watched them win and lose over the years. I've lived in many different cities and states, but remember being a fan in Albuquerque as a young girl. I decided my favorite color was orange because of the Orange Crush defense. Over the years, I moved, went to college and

As a result of a public contest in 1960, **BOSTON PATRIOTS** was selected as the team name. Many years later, when considering a name change, the owner decided on the Bay State Patriots. That name was never adopted over concern about Bay State being abbreviated in headlines. Management decided on the New England Patriots.

day. Jets flew over, fireworks—you knew it was something truly special. I was working with the police and paramedics at that time. Everyone was happy and proud and sad. A happy sad. Emotions ran high that day.

———RICHARD L. BLACKBURN, Broncos' guest relations, Denver

I remember my middle and high school years in Seaford, Delaware, eagerly anticipating the next Bronco's Super Bowl, only to have those hopes dashed with yet another loss. After getting married in 1996, my new wife and I sat down to watch my underdog Broncos in another Super Bowl. Our 18-month-old daughter, Mackenzie, had been doing the Mile High Salute for the previous two weeks leading up to the game. My wife, Tiffany, had seen what the loss to Jacksonville the previous year had done to me mentally, and I'm sure she wasn't looking forward to another off-season of heartbroken sighs. Luckily, with seconds ticking down to our first Super Bowl victory, I was finally able to release all of the pent up emotions…by bursting into tears as I sat on the floor, in front of the TV, hugging a pillow. My wife stared in disbelief, as her new husband sobbed like a baby. Looking back at her, all I could say was, "Just leave me alone…this is one of the greatest days of my life." I certainly couldn't tell her it was THE greatest. I don't like sleeping on the couch. The next year was just icing on the cake. When we finally had a son in 2002, I proudly named him Denver. I can't wait to celebrate another Super Bowl victory, this time, with both of my daughters, Mackenzie and Breck, and my son Denver.

———WILL ELLIS, Wilmington, Delaware

SHE SAYS SHE'S A NUN,
YET SHE DOESN'T HAVE A GUITAR

SISTER MARIE DE LOURDES FALK

Sister Marie de Lourdes Falk, 78, is a Fort Collins native who was a teacher for 37 years. She is a volunteer at St. Joseph's Hospital in the Radiation Oncology waiting room. She and her colleagues try to comfort family members and patients while they are there.

I first got hooked on the Broncos in 1977. That year, when they went to the Super Bowl with Craig Morton, I was just in love with Craig. I've been a fan from then on. I'm nicknamed The Broncos Queen. I've been working at the hospital for about 10 years, and the Broncos Queen thing started right away. In 1977, I went to the parade after the Super Bowl. We elbowed our way to the front of the crowd, wearing our habits. I like to go to the Welcome Home events. I've gone to some of the rallies, too. In the beginning, we'd just watch from the back of the crowd. One of my friends was the press secretary for Mayor Webb. I told him I was in the back. He told me to let him know next time and he'd do better for me. He got me a seat in one of the folding chairs right across from the family members. We were so close we could see the expressions on their faces....

When we first moved into the hospital, 13 of us moved in. There was a sign on our bulletin board that said the hospital was going to have a dinner honoring Pat Bowlen. I had just moved here, so I wasn't sure if I wanted to go or not. I didn't go. I had a hamburger and went to bed. About 10 p.m. the door opened on our floor and it was just electric. They came and pounded on my door. They made fun of me because Pat Bowlen and other Broncos personnel were there. John

Elway was even there. I, The Broncos Queen, didn't go. Now every time we have sisters to come and visit, they always bring up the dinner that I missed. It hurts like you can't believe....

Once, I went to a black-tie dinner for Dan Reeves, when he was leaving. The sisters and I decided we would go. We couldn't go to the dinner. We were sitting up in the bleachers watching them eat at the black-tie party. We still go to hear the speakers. When we went into the parking lot, we were talking with the parking attendant. We told him we wanted to get closer and see John Elway. He told us where he parked his car. We went up and parked our car right next to him. We sat there in the parking lot and waited until he got in his car, then we talked to him. We told him we had waited for him. He came over to the car and talked to us. He was a sweetheart....

Once on my birthday, the man who was the head of Environmental Services came out to sing Happy Birthday to me. He told me to turn around and he put a T-shirt on me. On the T-shirt was a great big picture of me with John Elway. My little nephew was playing baseball against a team with Jack Elway on it, John's son. I put my T-shirt on and went to the game. I figured John would come rushing over to see me. I looked and looked and he wasn't at the game. It's my "date" T-shirt, and he wasn't there....

We always use the Broncos to cheer up the patients—Friday through Monday. We talk Broncos in here a lot. The patients all know I'm a real fan. I talk about them all the time. I watch every play of every game. When the schedule comes out, I mark them on my calendar and schedule everything around the games. I'm heartbroken when I can't see a game. It doesn't happen very often, though. I rarely miss a game. I used to love to go to the games. I'm 78-years-old now, so I love to sit in my recliner with my popcorn, in the warm house and watch it on TV....

I can remember hearing so much about the South Stands, and how wild they were. Once, the tickets I was given were in the South Stands. They were wild. It was great and funny. I've never gotten so many hugs and high-fives. I've had a lot of fun at many games, but that one is the tops. It was just fun to be in the South Stands. I've never met so many strangers in my life. Every time something good happened, everyone was hugging. There were so many good looking guys there hugging me, and I'm a nun!…

As a nun, I pray for the Broncos, but not a lot. I'm there for them, but I don't often pray for them. I'm not a fair-weather fan. I don't leave or stop watching, regardless of the score. I'm not a fair-weather girl. I don't know why I love the Broncos so much. I love the game. I love to hold a program in my lap and look up info on the players I don't know. There is just something about the competitiveness of the game. I really love watching it. It's exciting.

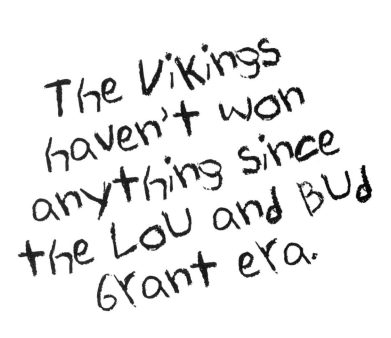

THE GREATEST FOOTBALL PLAYER IN THE HISTORY OF THE STATE OF COLORADO

STEVE SABOL

NFL Films was established in 1964, when Ed Sabol, Steve's father, convinced then-NFL Commissioner Pete Rozelle that the league needed a motion picture company to record its history. NFL Films has mushroomed well beyond the role of mere historian. The entity has won 73 Emmys for outstanding cinematography and sound, and it represents the quintessential standard for sports filmmaking. From theme programs, such as "NFL Films Presents," to team high-light films, to emotional behind-the-scenes detailing the nuts and bolts of HBO's "__INSIDE THE NFL__," NFL Films, as an independently operated arm of the league, captures the essence of football like no other visual entity. No story of Steve Sabol could be complete without a story or two of NFL Films' dealings with George Halas or Sabol's exploits on the gridiron at Colorado College four decades ago.

Once I started working with the NFL, Lyle Alzado became a really good friend. We were doing a profile on him and this was a big rough kid from the Bronx. We found out his mother was a florist, so that off-season we went back to the Bronx with him and did a whole piece on this guy in the flower shop. He was arranging the flowers and everything. Then we went back to training camp and we were shooting Lyle on the blocking sled and he broke it. I've never seen that done before. He hit it so hard, he snapped the pad off. Another time, we had him miked for a game against the Chargers. He was one of those guys who played with this restrained—well, maybe it wasn't

> __INSIDE THE NFL__ on HBO is the longest running series of any kind of cable television.

restrained—but an insanity and a passion coupled with his incredible strength. It seemed like Lyle never got recognized for what he was until he was with the Raiders.

And Floyd Little…he and Bill Brown of the Vikings were the two most bow-legged players I've ever seen. Floyd Little is a guy, to me, who is one of the forgotten great running backs. He and a guy by the name of Dickie Post, who played for the Chargers, are two of the most elusive, great running backs in the game that are totally forgotten. The Broncos of that era had the greatest pass rushing end that I've seen, every bit the equal of Gino Marchetti and Deacon Jones, and that was Tombstone Jackson, Rich Jackson. An unbelievable pass rusher! Paul Zimmerman every year brings his name up to be voted into the Hall of Fame. There were so many great players that played in Denver in the early years, but because the team wasn't that good, they never got any recognition.

I remember doing a piece—I think it was when Elway started as quarterback—showing that he was the 24th quarterback to start a regular season game for the Broncos. We started looking back and it was Frank Tripucka, George Herring, George Shaw, Mickey Slaughter. I remember we said quarterbacking the Broncos has been one of the most insecure jobs in the history of the NFL and that kamikaze pilots have longer tenures than Denver quarterbacks. Steve Tensi, Craig Morton, Jacky Lee, Tobin Rote. There was a Max Choboian and Scotty Glacken, Marlin Briscoe, Pete Liske, Al Pastrana. That's a list that makes a great trivia question: name the Broncos quarterbacks.

With regards to George Halas, who died back in '93, he had a love-hate relationship with NFL Films. Halas used to sell seats on the visitors' bench at Wrigley Field. After Minnesota Vikings Coach Norm VanBrocklin complained to the league office, then NFL-Commissioner Rozelle asked me to shoot footage of the bench as he proceeded to investigate. But I told Rozelle, "I've already got that." So I sent Rozelle the footage and sure enough, there were those guys on the bench. Rozelle confronted Halas and found out that Halas actually sold seats on the bench. They fined Halas and when Halas found out the footage came from us, he tried to have us banned from the sidelines. He also detested the close-ups we took of people like

Dick Butkus and Gale Sayers. He said, "I don't want any face shots 'cause the players will see that and want more money." It helped when we made an extra effort to include clean-cut Bears fans in the highlight films. Because back in '67, Halas became enraged when one of our films showed a fan lunging for a ball in the stands with a pistol tucked in his belt. Halas kept saying, "Those are not Bears fans. We don't have people like that come to our games. We have good fans." But Bears fans in the '60s made the Indy 500 infield look like a parliament. They were wild. But Halas didn't want that. So the next year, I went to Washington and got a close-up of Redskins fans with their camel-hair coats, pretty sweaters, and scarves. Every year I'd splice those shots in the Bears films, so until the day he died, he'd say, "See, those are Bears fans." He never knew. That was one of our running jokes at NFL Films. We always had an assignment for a guy to go to Washington to shoot "Bears fans."

I was raised in a suburb of Philadelphia called Villanova, Pennsylvania. I had great grades in prep school, but I had a lousy SAT score, so I ended up going to school in Colorado Springs at Colorado College. I wanted to play football out there, so one of the first things I did was change my hometown from Villanova to Coaltown Township, Pennsylvania. It was a nonexistent town, but had the ring of solid football to it. Everybody knows that western Pennsylvania is where the football studs come from. I'd never seen a coal mine, but if coaches thought I had been rubbing shoulders with guys like Mike Ditka and Leon Hart, they'd have to start thinking. I carried it off all freshman year and nobody caught on. Guys would come up and ask me why I hadn't gotten a big scholarship from Notre Dame or Ohio State or someplace, and I'd just say, "Aw, I was just third string."

I didn't play much my freshman year, so I knew I'd have to do something to impress the coaches. So when I came back for my sophomore year, I told everyone that I was from Possum Trot, Mississippi, 'cause you can't ignore anyone from a place called Possum Trot. Then I knew I had to change my name. I had an honorable name, but it didn't have the ring of greatness. I wanted something real lethal like "Sudden Death." That fit my initials, too—Steven Douglas Sabol became Steve "Sudden Death" Sabol. Then in the program for the very first game, we had "Sudden Death" Sabol listed by that name. Also, I bought an ad in the program that said, "Coach Jerry Carle wishes 'Sudden Death' Sabol a successful season." Everybody thought the coach put the ad in there, but I paid for the ad myself. Coach Carle was a regular Bear Bryant. He never smiled. The last thing he'd do would be wish me a successful season, but a lot of people took it seriously. I thought it was all pretty funny. But the coach didn't have any scholarships to give, so he couldn't run off any players like me.

Unfortunately, I weighed only 170 pounds, so the nickname "Sudden Death" just didn't seem to go with my build. Nevertheless, in the final program of the season, I ran an ad that said, "Coach Jerry Carle congratulates 'Sudden Death' Sabol on a fantastic season."

So before my junior year, I added 40 pounds. I really bulked up. Then I started sending out press agent stuff to both the local and the Denver papers. One ad told everyone, "The Possum Trot Chamber of Commerce extends its wishes for a successful season to its favorite son, 'Sudden Death' Sabol." Another advertisement included a picture of me in a football uniform at about the age of 10 in Philadelphia where I played on a Midget League team called the Little Quakers. Then came a hundred T-shirts made up with the drawing of a possum and the inscription "I'm a Little Possum Trotter." I gave half of them away and sold the rest for one dollar.

So with my own money, I'd paid for newspaper advertisements, colored postcards, brochures, T-shirts, lapel buttons and pencils on which were written such legends as "The Prince of Pigskin Pageantry now at the Pinnacle of his Power" and "One of the Most Mysterious, Awesome Living Beings of all Times." I sent out news releases reporting incredible accomplishments of "Sudden Death" Sabol on the football field with sidebars describing his colorful campus life. And as testament to my ability, the sports editors swallowed all this stuff hook, line and sinker.

Now football practice itself was tedious. It was a period of intense boredom punctuated by moments of acute fear. So I began writing the game program itself. And I did a column for the school newspaper entitled, "Here's a Lot from Possum Trot." I also was the team cheerleader, and I began plastering the walls of the locker room with posters and slogans and slipping fight songs onto the record player.

Then I shipped off a press release to the hometown paper of our rival team—Concordia College. They were unbeaten at the time. The headline read, "Sudden Death says Colorado College will Crush Concordia College." Their game plan was simple. They wanted to break my neck. But I loved it. It made the game more personal. This one big end was particularly anxious to break something. He seemed very capable of it, too. So at halftime, I go up to the referee. I'm putting on my "choir boy look" and say, "Mr. Referee, sir, that end—well I hate to say it, but he's playing sort of dirty and I wish you'd watch him."

So on the first play, I asked the quarterback to call my number on an end sweep. Sure enough, this big oaf really clobbers me. I whisper in his ear, "You're nothing but chicken s---." Naturally, he takes a swing and there's the referee standing right there, throwing down his flag, and yelling, "You're out of the game." We beat Concordia, 13-0.

I had a good year. I was good enough for first-team all-conference and we won four games, which is about twice what we normally won. The news was going all over the country about Steve "Sudden Death" Sabol. It was carried on the AP wires, and I got a letter from a disk jockey from, of all places, Possum Trot. There really is such a place, but it's in Tennessee, not Mississippi. That was fine by me, because I always had a sneaking hunch I wanted to come from Tennessee anyway.

So I go back for my senior year, but I fought hepatitis all summer, so I had to drop out. I went back to Philadelphia and started lifting weights to get back in shape. In those days, most athletes didn't lift weights. Darned if I didn't work so hard at it, I was actually named Mr. Philadelphia. Well, I couldn't let that honor pass me by, so I had 8-by-10 photographs made showing me all aripple and holding a spear. Underneath the picture was my name and these modest words: "Acclaimed as the Greatest New Adventure Hero of the Year." That was an inspiration I got from my huge comic book collection where I have all-time favorites such as Captain America and Batman. The pictures were immediately dispatched to editors, press agents and fans. I had the mailing addresses of influential people well catalogued from my dad's business.

That was a good start on the year, but I was worried the people back in Colorado had forgotten all about me. So I went to a printer and I had stationery made with "Universal International" and wrote all these letters. "You have been placed on Steve Sabol's mailing list and thus will be able to follow his movie career." Then came the information that Steve Sabol had been cast as a supporting actor in Universal's forthcoming film Black Horse Troop, which is a name I got from a march by John Philip Sousa. The movie would star William Holden, Steve McQueen, Eva Marie Saint and Steve Sabol. The letter was stamped "Approved for immediate release by order of Central Casting." I'd had a stamp made up with that title on it. But I didn't send the letter to the newsmen back in Colorado Springs. They were starting to get a little suspicious. So instead, I sent them to friends in the Colorado Springs area who were most likely to leak the news in the right places. It worked. Local columnists fell all over themselves informing the readers that "Sudden Death" Sabol was Hollywood's newest star. I must have had a hundred calls from people wanting to know if it was true that Steve McQueen was really a jerk. But I told them, "No, he's really a great guy."

So the next summer before returning for my final year at Colorado College, I did a grand tour of Europe, and in Madrid I got inspired again. El Cordoba was the biggest bullfighter in the world at that time. There were picture postcards of him all over Spain. I said, "Now that's class." So when I got back home, I shelled out some more money, actually my dad's money. I got a couple of crates of colored postcards of myself in a football uniform. At the back of the postcard is, "Steve 'Sudden Death' Sabol, All-Time All-Rocky Mountain Football Great." At the bottom it said, "The Prince of Pigskin Pageantry." So in the fall, I went back to Colorado College. I had a new maroon convertible. I had a five-bedroom apartment, even though I lived alone. I can think better when I'm alone. I had a picture of me signing with the Cleveland Browns for $375,000. But the topper was when Coach Carle got upset because outside Washburn Stadium I put up a sign that read, "Washburn Stadium, altitude 7,989 feet," which was exactly 2,089 feet higher than it actually was, but I wanted to psyche out opposing players when they came there. So I had a plaque remade for the visiting team's dressing room that read, "This field is named in honor of Morris Washburn who perished when his lungs exploded from a lack of oxygen during a soccer match with the University of Denver in 1901."

HE GOT A NEW SET OF GOLF CLUBS FOR HIS WIFE...HE FEELS THAT IT WAS A GREAT TRADE.

JIM GATLIN

Marriages are made in Heaven, but so are thunder and lightning. That's an old maxim that Chicago native and longtime Lakewood resident Jim Gatlin found out firsthand in 1988. He ran an ad in the Rocky Mountain News *offering to swap his wife, Sharon, for a Broncos Super Bowl ticket.*

Shortly after I moved to Denver and started up my own company in 1977, I was working on a Sunday afternoon. Some of the other people who were also there working said that they were leaving to go watch the Broncos. I said, "No way. We've got work to do." They just laughed at me and left. I didn't even know what the Broncos were at the time. It didn't take me long to join everyone else every Sunday in watching the Broncos. I became a huge fan. So did my wife. She began wearing her orange Broncos clothes every Friday in advance of Sunday's game. If you're in Denver, you just do it.

Two weeks before the Super Bowl in 1988, I was working in Fort Collins for the day. A snowstorm blew in and it took me about three hours to get back to Denver. I called my wife from the office and asked her to go to the store and pick up some milk. She told me she wasn't going out in the storm and that I should get my own milk. I told my secretary, "I'm going to run an ad in the paper. I'm tired of this stuff, and I'm going to get back at her." So I called the *Rocky Mountain News* and bought a classified ad. It read, "Will trade my non-shopping and non-cooking wife with attitude problem for ONE Super Bowl ticket. No Indian givers. Call Jim at xxx-xxxx. HURRY!" I didn't tell my wife right away. I just wanted to get even with her for not going to the store. I'd done funny things before.

I got to work early that morning, because I had a flight to Chicago later that day to attend a friend's wedding. At 7 a.m., I got a call from San Diego. The caller said, "Is it true you ran that ad?" Before I could answer, another phone call came in, and then another. The phone never stopped ringing. There must have been a thousand calls before I left for the airport. When I landed in Chicago, there were all kinds of newspeople waiting for me. One of the Chicago TV stations took me to their studios and hooked me up with Channel 7 in Denver via satellite. One of the Denver TV stations contacted my wife at her workplace. I still hadn't told her about the ad. When she found out what I had done, that made her mad, really mad. It was horrible. We both did a lot of interviews. She said that some guy offered to give her race horses if she would leave me. I simply asked, "Where's my Super Bowl ticket?" She got even real quick. When I returned from Chicago, there were 200 people at the airport gate wearing "I hate Jim Gatlin" T-shirts. Then she shoved a pie in my face! The media was there and they kept interviewing us. By then, she was playing along. She enjoyed the attention. And I apologized, which I continue to do every week. Channel 7 assigned a crew to stay with us. Every day they taped what we were doing, every move.

I eventually got a pair of tickets, from a friend in the hotel business in Florida. They didn't cost me anything. I took my son, and when we left for the airport, Channel 7 was still there, following us. I wore a T-shirt that read, "Sharon, trust me," and my son was wearing one that read, "Mom, Dad made me go, trust me." In Miami, we attended Baron Hilton's private party, and I made a fool of myself. I ran into Al Davis and told him that he looked kind of grubby and asked him if he had been up all night. He said, "Who let this a—hole in here?" Then someone introduced me to Bob Hope. I was trying to make conversation, so I said, "You'd think someone like Baron Hilton could afford better wine than this. This tastes like oil." Bob Hope said, "I guess you're not used to Dom Perignon." Later, I ran into a photographer from *Sports Illustrated*. He wanted to take some pictures of me, so he got all these gorgeous women at the party and put me in the middle of them. But he told me to turn around. I was still wearing my "Sharon, trust me" T-shirt. That's the photo that ran in *SI*. At the game, we sat in the front row. I was a celebrity among the Broncos fans.

A month later, I thought everything had died down and gone away. Then the National Organization of Women (NOW) offered to pay for our divorce, pay off our house and relocate Sharon to Bismarck, North Dakota, in some kind of protection program. I told them that was OK with me, then asked if I would ever be able to see my wife again. They said that I couldn't have any contact with her for two years. I said that was still OK. They called Sharon and told her what I said. She called me and told me the joke's over. Knock it off. She let it go after that.

Later that year, we were featured in a full-page story in *Star* magazine for having "the wackiest marriage in America." They had pictures of me in a doghouse. Then I got a letter saying that I had been nominated for an Athena Award for top newspaper advertising. My competition was Nike, Ford and Miller Beer. And I won. They said that it was great advertising that so few words could generate so much attention around the world.

I hired an agent and made my demands clear for appearing on national TV shows…first-class air fare, a room above the 13th floor in a luxury hotel, $40 per day for meals, $45 per day for cab fare, and a Rolls-Royce limo for our unlimited use…five-day minimum per show. Despite those demands, we got several appearances—in Seattle, Los Angeles, San Diego. It seemed like everywhere we went, everyone knew who we were. I got on the plane bound for Seattle and on my seat was a sign that read, "Reserved for a male chauvinist pig." We bumped into Oprah Winfrey at one of our fancy hotels and she wanted us on her show. I told her that we couldn't work it into our schedule and passed.

Sharon and I have been married 36 years, so she must have a good sense of humor. But I've been suffering ever since I ran that ad. Don't forget: Hell has no fury like a woman scorned!

TO BE CONTINUED!

We hope you have enjoyed the first *For Broncos Fans Only*. You can be in the next edition if you have a neat story. You can email it to printedpage@cox.net (please put BRONCOS in the subject line), or call the author directly at (602) 738-5889.

For information on ordering more copies of *For Broncos Fans Only*, as well as any of the author's other best-selling books, call (602) 738-5889.

Note: There were no actual Oakland Raiders fans harmed during the making of this book.